THE CORVINA
HISTORY OF
HUNGARY

THE CORVINA
HISTORY OF
HUNGARY

FROM EARLIEST TIMES
UNTIL THE PRESENT DAY

WRITTEN BY
KÁLMÁN BENDA, PÉTER HANÁK, LÁSZLÓ MAKKAI,
ZSUZSA L. NAGY, EMIL NIEDERHAUSER,
GYÖRGY SPIRA, KÁROLY VÖRÖS

EDITED BY PÉTER HANÁK

Translated by Zsuzsa Béres
Translation revised by Chris Sullivan
Maps by Lajos Palovics

© Péter Hanák, 1991

ISBN 963 13 3367 1

Published by Corvina Books, Budapest (Vörösmarty tér 1. Hungary 1051)

This book is a revised and updated edition of *One Thousand Years. A Concise History of Hungary*, published by Corvina in 1988

Contents

5

Maps

...I am he who has gazed a hundred thousand years
On that which he now sees for the first time.
One moment, and fulfilled all time appears
In a hundred thousand forbears' eyes and mine.

I see what they could not because they must
Drag hoes, kill and embrace, for this enrolled,
And they, who have descended into dust
See what I do not, if the truth be told.

We know each other as sorrow and delight.
I, in the past, they in the present live.
They hold the pencil in the poem I write.
I feel them and evoke what they now give...

Attila József: *By the Danube.*
Translated by Vernon Watkins

The history of the Hungarian people, who migrated to their present homeland more than a thousand years ago, has become inextricably linked with the Carpathian Basin and with the river Danube which runs through it. Prince Árpád, the leader of the conquering Magyars, chose Csepel Island—in the middle of the river—as the centre of his rule, and subsequently Hungarian kings established residences at high points along the waterway—at Esztergom, Visegrád, and, eventually, Buda.

The fact that the Hungarians have survived so many trials and tribulations over the centuries constitutes an historical achievement in itself, as well as a factor influencing history. The Hungarians arrived in East-Central Europe not as marauders, but as a people driven by nomads to find a new homeland. It was not their intention to destroy ancient cultures or prospering states—in fact, nothing of the kind existed in the Carpathian Basin in the ninth century. They wished to settle and to integrate other cultures, as well as to win acceptance for their own. They did not wish to appropriate the Danubian region for themselves and to inhabit it exclusively. They wanted to mix with the existing Slav, Gepid, and Avar population, and did so with the passage of time. Prince Géza, King Stephen, and their successors built up the country from very diverse ethnic elements, creating in the process a common home which for centuries offered protection against the Mongol hordes, the Turkish army, and other invaders.

For the Hungarians the Danube has meant much more than a river abundant in water and fish—a river in which sturgeon came as far up as Pest to spawn even in the middle of the last century. It has been more than an important waterway along which barges loaded with merchandise could be taken as far as the Danube Delta. In addition to carrying goods, cattle, weapons, people, and ideas, the river came to acquire symbolic importance. It became a link between East and West, between Danubian states and peoples from the Black Forest to the Black Sea. The notion of the Danube as an important commercial and transportation route also received political content as a factor holding peoples together. It is no accident that since the middle of the nineteenth century ambitious but abortive plans for a confederation embracing Poles, Hungarians, Romanians, South Slavs, and Germans have all been associated with the Danube.

For more than a thousand years the history of the Hungarian people has taken place in an area delineated to the west and east but simultaneously open to influences from both directions. During its history, Hungary has been a bridge between East and West, as well as an island and ferry-country plying between the two. Hungary was once a proud empire full of ambitious plans, and later a truncated and suppressed little country. At the same time Hungarians have been both oppressors and oppressed. For nearly eleven centuries Slovaks, Turks, Hungarians, Romanians, and Germans have swirled together, as in the tortured mind of the great poet Attila József. The different ethnic elements have inspired and supported each other in creating material wealth and fostering spiritual advance. From time to time though, they have wronged each other and each other's cultures.

After all these years, and after a near past leading into a cul-de-sac, we owe the Danubian region and the whole of mankind a happier future.

The contributors to this volume have all attempted to present the greatness of Hungarian history. But as well as showing its high points they also admit the errors which have been committed, thereby helping to turn the suffering of the past into peace for present and future generations.

Péter Hanák

HUNGARY
IN THE MIDDLE AGES

Migration and the Founding
of the Hungarian State

The history of the Carpathian Basin
up to the end of Roman rule

The Carpathian Basin has been populated for thousands of years. In the course of its history it has witnessed the settlement, migrations and struggles of successive peoples. Relics of these historic times are still found today. Some of the buildings which were erected in pre-Magyar days still stand: over many thousands of years the collective efforts of the peoples living in this area have transformed its forests and steppes into a land fit for human habitation.

One of the oldest human finds in Europe was unearthed at Vértesszőlős, in Hungary, about a quarter of a century ago. Between 400,000 and 500,000 years previously, hunters had settled close to the hot-water springs, and the animal and human footprints made on the alkaline mud became covered and consequently preserved. After a long interval, about 100,000 years ago a new type of human being, so-called Neanderthal Man, hunted for mammoths and bears in the area which now comprises Hungary. The first human beings of today's species arrived in the region from the southeast some time around 50,000 B.C. Their knapped flint tools are perfect, and a whistle with three holes which has been discovered suggests that they played music. The fact that they buried their dead with some ceremony (they decorated the corpses with red paint symbolizing blood, and therefore life) would indicate their belief in an afterworld. At Lovas, near Lake Balaton, the source of the pigments they used has also been excavated. These people hunted for large animals, especially reindeer, but a gradual increase in temperature and the development of greater humidity forced the animal species which liked dry cold weather to move northwards. Of the animals formerly hunted, aurochs, bison, deer, wild boars and brown bears remained in the area.

About 10,000 years ago, the climate of the Carpathian Basin was much the same as today. Deciduous forests and lowland steppes alternated with each other, and in the south there occurred brushwood, chestnut trees, vines and figtrees. Changes in the natural environment compelled the inhabitants of the Carpathian Basin to switch to animal husbandry and the cultivation of crops at around 5000 B.C. Wheat, barley, sheep, and goats had been brought to the area by peoples migrating from the Balkans, while cattle and pigs were domesticated from indigenous wild species. By 4000 B.C. Neolithic culture had spread through the Danube Basin to the more northerly and westerly parts of Europe. This involved livestock breeding, land cultivation, weaving and spinning, as well as the production of pots and the building of houses.

The newcomers from the southeast who brought these innovations with them partly assimilated with the existing local population and partly moved on. From time to time their descendants were forced back, while further waves of people repeatedly arrived from the southeast. The Carpathian Basin was in this way a great melting-pot of peoples, into which there poured a succession of newcomers from the west, east, and south. These peoples either brought new cultural assets with them or destroyed the ones they found. They also created flourishing cultures in the region, cultures which lasted for various periods.

The Neolithic era in the Carpathian Basin lasted three thousand years and was followed, at around 2000 B.C., by the Copper Age, which continued for just a few centuries. The new technology was introduced by people arriving on four-wheel carts and originating from the Balkans. Their carts were drawn by oxen and the settlers made good use of the abundant copper supplies which they found locally. They made not only tools but also weapons from the metal they extracted. It was also from the southeast that another wave of peoples arrived. They brought with them the technique of casting bronze, and the local bronze culture which flourished in the area also attracted various additional settlers from the east. These ethnic groups in turn introduced the domesticated horse into the Carpathian Basin.

During the Bronze Age, a military aristocracy living in earthwork forts, well-armed, and sporting gold ornamentation, ruled the masses. At around 1000 B.C., the Illyrians and Thracians from the west and the Scythians from the east introduced the use of iron. The local bronze culture, which thrived on abundant raw material and perfection of craftsmanship, was not entirely superseded though, and it was only in the middle of the first century B.C. that iron became a commonly used metal in the Carpathian Basin. The peoples responsible for this were, in the west, the Celts and, in the east, the Dacians.

In the years after Christ, the Carpathian Basin became linked with the cultures of Greece and Rome, and these connections lasted some 400 years. This development was a result of the Roman conquest of Transdanubia and Transylvania, which became the provinces of Pannonia and Dacia respectively. The coming of Roman power marked the beginning of the use of written records at local level, as well as the introduction of monumental stone architecture and an urban lifestyle, the appearance of vineyards on Pannonian hillsides, and the beginnings of Christianity. Traces of this Roman presence can be found in the remains of amphitheatres, water-mains, temples, basilicas, chapels and sarcophagi, as well as in the objects discovered around them. Roman settlements existed at Aquincum (now Óbuda), Sophianae (now Pécs), Scarabantia (now Sopron), Savaria (now Szombathely) and Gorsium (now Tác). Further indications are the ancient form of the pruning knives used in Transdanubian viticulture and the cult, which eventually spread throughout Europe, of the early Christian martyrs of Pannonia. One should also not forget St Martin, who was born in Savaria, later lived in Gaul, and eventually became the patron saint of France. For a few centuries, therefore, the Carpathian Basin was a civilized region. Only later did it sink back into barbarism in the wake of the Great Migrations.

Huns, Teutons, Avars, and Slavs
in the Carpathian Basin

The Hungarian chroniclers of the Middle Ages regarded the Huns and the Hungarians (Magyars) as one and the same people. According to these chroniclers, Árpád based his claim to the Carpathian Basin and its inhabitants on the fact that the region had formerly belonged to his ancestor, Attila. Also according to the chronicles, the Szeklers were the last group of Huns to remain in the area and joined with the conquering Magyars. Although the question is rather more complex, the idea of Hun-Magyar kinship cannot be entirely discarded, as it was at one time by Hungarian historians.

The Huns spoke a Turkic language and came from North-Central Asia. They are famous in world history not only for their wide-ranging military campaigns, but also for their invention of the stirrup, which made horse riding safe and which later became the technical basis of mediaeval European chivalry. The Huns crossed the Volga in 375 and the Magyars, who lived in the valley of the Lower Volga, became their subjects. The Huns conquered the Ostrogoths, who lived on the northern shore of the Black Sea, and, in the course of the fifth century, the Romans evacuated Pannonia. The great Hun king Attila then moved to the *Tiszántúl*, which had formerly been inhabited by the Sarmats. The Romans had abandoned Dacia long before and the Germanic Visigoths had settled there after 271. The Visigoths, who had fled to the Balkans in the face of a Hunnish attack, were replaced by the Gepids, another Germanic people.

The three major geographical regions of the Carpathian Basin—Transdanubia, the Great Plain and Transylvania—first became a single political unit under Hunnish sway. At the same time the Carpathian Basin also became the base for the large-scale military operations led by Attila. These took the Hunnish king (often called "The Scourge of God") right into the Western Roman empire, first to Rome and later to Gaul where, at Catalaunum, a dozen peoples fought a great battle. After Attila's sudden death in 453, the conquered Germanic peoples rose in arms against their Hunnish masters. Those Huns who survived withdrew to the area between the Don and the Volga rivers. From them emerged the Khazars who, together with other peoples, ruled over the Onogur (i.e. "Ten Peoples") tribal alliance which also incorporated the Magyars. The rulers of both the Magyars and the Danubian Bulgars afterwards left the Onogur grouping. Since they regarded Attila to be their ancestor, it may be supposed that both peoples received their rulers from the Hunnish royal family at the time when the Magyars and the Danubian Bulgars still lived together.

For over a century the Carpathian Basin was occupied by Germanic peoples. For the time being, Transdanubia was occupied by the Ostrogoths, while the Gepids continued to inhabit the eastern area. The Lombards now pushed into the territory occupied by the Ostrogoths, who migrated to Italy. The Lombards then became entangled in a bloody war with the Gepids and were only able to defeat them with the assistance of another conquering people from Central Asia, the Avars. After this the Lombards themselves set out for Italy. In 568 Bayan, the bellicose Avar king, became ruler of the Carpathian Basin. He settled the Slavic tribes he had brought with him in the surrounding mountain areas, and the Gepids, now divested of their leaders, assimilated with these Slavic elements.

In addition to archaeological finds, the memory of the Slav settlers is preserved only by the ethnic name *tót*. This derives from the word *teut*, meaning "people", the name they themselves used. (Incidentally, *tót* was used by the Magyars to describe every native speaker of Slavic languages in the Carpathian Basin.)

For two and a half centuries the Avars maintained Transdanubia, the Great Plain and Transylvania as a single political entity. Although their hegemony was seriously jeopardized by an insurrection among the Slavs, they derived new strength from a group of Bulgaro-Turks who came to the area around 670. A growing number of Hungarian archaeologists now believe that these new settlers may have been Magyars, or rather Szeklers. Although archaeological finds support this theory, there is as yet no evidence to suggest that these arrivals spoke a Finno-Ugric language—i.e. that they were indeed Magyars.

Where then did the Magyars, a people speaking such a language, come from?

From the Urals to the Danube: Hungarian prehistory

Linguists agreed long ago that the ancestors of the Magyar people belonged to the most easterly, Ugrian branch of the Finno-Ugrian peoples. However, the precise geographical location of the Finno-Ugrian homeland continues to be the subject of debate. For many years it was considered to have been situated between the Middle Volga and the Ural Mountains north of the river Kama. This was where the common ancestors of the Finno-Ugrian language speakers were supposed to have lived until 2000 B.C. More recently, however, both linguistic and archaeological arguments have given rise to the view that the Finno-Ugrians hunted and fished on both sides of the Central Urals. The Finno-Ugrian hunters, it is now believed, followed the reindeer and moose from the western regions—wet and rich in grass during summer but covered with thick snow in winter—to the drier eastern slopes. They used sledges drawn by dogs, as well as skis, and in the wake of their prey they returned for summer hunting. The Finno-Ugrians traversed the Ural Mountains, where some rocks were covered during the third millennium B.C. with drawings depicting scenes from the chase, and they also used boats on the estuaries of the Tobol and Kama rivers. Around 4000 B.C. these people still employed knapped flint implements but by this time also had earthenware dishes decorated with drawings of waterbirds. The Finno-Ugrians regarded the wild duck as a sacred animal. This was because, according to an ancient myth preserved from the *Kalevala*, the world came into being from the egg of such a creature.

Around 2000 B.C. population growth forced the western, Finnish, branch of the ancient Finno-Ugrian people to move to the Volga and later to the Baltic Sea. On the other hand, the Ugrian branch, which, in addition to the ancestors of the Magyars, also included the ancestors of the Ostyaks and Voguls, spread from the southeastern slopes of the Ural Mountains to the valleys of the big rivers in the area. Here the settlers switched from hunting and fishing to farming and, above all, to animal husbandry. The words for "horse", "saddle", "halter", and "whip" are the same in all Ugric languages. In Hungarian, the Persian words *tehén* (cow), *tej* (milk), *nemez* (felt) and *szekér* (cart) all originate from the Persian peoples living in the Aral region, and it was these peoples who acquainted the ancestors of the Magyars with Copper Age and Bronze Age civilization. Shortly afterwards, the Ugrian peoples created their own Bronze Age culture which generated works of art depicting their new way of life and subsequently enriching the world of their beliefs. An important symbol in this art was the horse. Indeed, the horse was frequently depicted as a sacred animal, but nevertheless one which was sacrificed as well.

Having become equestrian nomads, the Ugrians left the mountain regions and moved to the steppes. As a result of an increase in temperature between 1500 and 1000 B.C., these expanded northwards by as much as 200–300 kilometres and thinned out the forests. To escape the drought which was caused, the Voguls and the Ostyaks followed the forests northwards. When, after 800 B.C., the climate turned cold and wet, they were encircled by the returning taiga and the reindeer replaced the horse in their homeland along the river Ob. The Magyars remained on the steppes, which, after a period of increasing dryness, became green again at around the same time. These people became nomadic herdsmen and indicative of the influences on them is that, in addition to the Hungarian word *kard* (sword), certain things were borrowed from the Scythians. These included their famous bow, a religious cult based on the stag, and the frequent delineation of that animal. Whilst the symbol of the horse did not disappear, that of the tame wild duck did and was replaced as a symbol by the *turul,* a predatory eagle. During this time iron came into regular use and it was now that a people calling themselves "Magyars" broke away from the other Ugrians. This last event probably took place when the Magyars moved across the Urals to the area of present-day Bashkiria some time after 500 B.C. Here they became the neighbours of other alien peoples—Persians, Alans, and the Turkic Bulgars. According to more recent linguistic suppositions, it was to distinguish the Magyars from these peoples that the actual word "Magyar" was created. This was done by putting together the Finno-Ugric *mon* (speak) and *er* (man). Other peoples also called themselves "speakers" and referred to foreigners as *néma* (mute). A case in point is the Hungarian word *német* (German), which is of Slavic origin.

Although the "speakers", i.e. the Magyars, seemed conscious of some kind of ethnic identity, neighbouring peoples did not remain "mute" for long. Words which the Hungarians took from their languages reveal that under the influence of the neighbouring tribes, the Magyars underwent a decisive socio-economic transformation. Some of the Bulgars, and especially the Onogur group which settled near the Magyars after 700, learned the use of the plough from the Alans of the Caucasus. This knowledge they handed on to the Magyars, as is shown by the Hungarian words *eke* (plough), *sarló* (sickle), *búza* (wheat), *árpa* (barley), as well as by *ökör* (ox), *tinó* (steer), *borjú* (calf), etc. which the Magyars acquired from them. Although the Magyars probably did not entirely give up hoeing as an aid to cultivation, the use of the ox-drawn plough opened the way to a far more advanced agriculture, as well as to the possibility of more lasting settlement. Although the Magyars continued to drink *kumis* (fermented mare's milk), they now, as a result of Bulgarian influence, also drank wine which they made from their own grapes. In addition to mutton, they also

THE MIGRATIONS OF THE MAGYAR PEOPLE AND THE CONQUEST

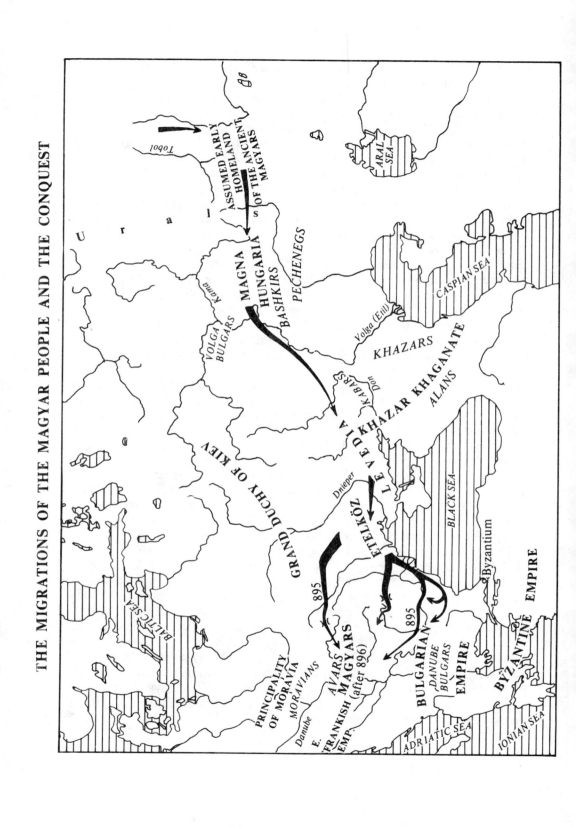

ate the meat of the settlers' favourite animals—both *disznó* (pig) and *tyúk* (hen) are taken from Bulgarian. In summer the Magyars lived in tents, but in winter they lived in cottages in their permanent settlements along the big rivers. From the Alans the Magyars adopted the curved sabre and from the Bulgars armour and the stirrup. In this way, there came into being a permanently armed group of warriors which rallied around a chieftain and which fought with arrows and sabres. These warriors no longer lived from the work of their own hands, but from war booty and the work of slaves captured in foreign parts. In keeping with the Bulgarian model, the clans were organized into military formations known as tribes. As the names *Ungarn, hongrois, vengier*, etc. suggest, the Magyar tribes probably belonged temporarily to the Onogur tribal alliance which lived in the Don area after 500 and which was subordinated to the Khazar khaganate. After throwing off Khazar rule, some of the Magyar tribes moved, at around 800, to Levedia, in the Don region. A few generations later, and under pressure from the Pechenegs, they moved on to the *Etelköz*, the area between the Dnieper and the Lower Danube. Before the Mongol invasion of Hungary in 1241, Julianus, a Hungarian Dominican friar, visited Bashkiria. In this area he found Magyars who had stayed behind, but these people eventually assimilated with their neighbours.

The Conquest and the raids

Both the chronicles and historiography have regarded Árpád as the man who led the conquest of the Carpathian Basin single-handed in 895–96, despite the fact that contemporary Byzantine and German authors speak of the involvement of two Magyar princes, Árpád and Kurszán. Furthermore, from Muslim and Byzantine sources we know that—as in the case of the Avars and Khazars—power over the Magyars was shared between three persons—the *kende*, the commander of the warriors; the *gyula;* and the *harka*. According to the Magyar chronicles, Kurszán was the *kende* and Tétény the *harka*. (The chronicler Anonymus says the *harka* was Tuhutum.) Accordingly, Árpád must have been the *gyula,* the chief military commander, and also explains why tradition has regarded him as the principal figure in the Conquest.

In 895, when the Pechenegs crossed the river Don and took the Magyars by surprise, most of the Magyar army was away fighting the Bulgars. With the bulk of the Magyar forces strung out along the Lower Danube and the river Tisza, the Magyars at home were without adequate protection. Árpád and his son Levente were abroad with this army, and the Pecheneg attack forced the remaining population to take refuge in the Transylvanian mountains. Árpád's father, Álmos, died a voluntary death because he was unable to protect his people's territory. *Etelköz* (land between rivers), as this was called, proved to be the Magyars' last home prior to their conquest of Hungary. In the course of the next few years the Magyars allied themselves with the three Kabar (perhaps Szekler) tribes which had joined them. Reinforced by the fighters who had returned from the Bulgarian campaign, the Magyars now prepared to strike. They drove the Bulgars out of the Great Plain and Transylvania, evicted the Franks from Transdanubia, and freed the western part of Upper Hungary from Moravian control. But in 904 Kurszán, the chief ruler, fell victim to Bavarian intrigue: he was invited to a peace banquet where he and his retinue were murdered. Magyar pagan tradition regarded such deaths as divine punishment, and accordingly Kurszán's family was stripped of its hold on the chief rulership. Kurszán's place was now taken by Árpád. To avenge Kurszán's death, the Magyar army defeated the Bavarians, whose prince fell in battle. The Conquest was now practically complete; the Carpathian Basin was under Magyar domination.

Shortly after the Conquest, the Magyars launched a series of plundering raids westwards. In their wars against each other, the Italian and German princes often called in the Magyars as allies and paid them for their services. Torn apart by internal strife, the Carolingian empire was initially unable to defend itself when confronted with the special cavalry tactics of the Hungarians. Like other equestrian nomads, the Magyars carried out lightning attacks followed by a feigned withdrawal, deceiving the enemy and reducing his alertness. The Magyars would then turn and shower the foe with arrows. In the hand-to-hand combat which followed, the Magyar horsemen would finish off their opponents. "From the arrows of the Magyars, Lord, deliver us," prayed the inhabitants of Italian, German and French monasteries. This was all to no avail, however, until the German king, Henry the Fowler, took charge of the situation. In 933, the German cavalry, strengthened and reorganized, defeated the Magyars for the first time at Merseburg.

The Magyar tribal chiefs, just like contemporary Bohemian, Polish and Russian princes, maintained their military forces from foreign money and from war booty. Their land was cultivated by foreign slaves, and these they refused to give up. As a final great effort, Bulcsú, the *harka* of the tribal alliance, led a series of campaigns against the Western countries. To ensure that there would be no threat from the south, Bulcsú went to Byzantium in 948 and was converted to Christianity there. In 955, however, the Magyars suffered a grave defeat at Augsburg when Otto I, the German king and the subsequent founder of the Holy Roman empire, annihilated most of the Magyar army, capturing and executing Bulcsú and Prince Lél (Lehel). This catastrophe put an end to the raids in the West. Soon the south also became closed to the Magyars. In 970, the Pechenegs murdered the Russian prince, Svyatoslav, who, accompanied by his army, was on his way home after failing to take Byzantium. The Magyars had been his allies and now, like the neighbouring Slav peoples, they had to accommodate themselves to one of their powerful neighbours—the Holy Roman empire or the Byzantine empire. Either way the Magyars would have to join the community of Christian peoples.

This process was, however, hindered by the socio-political composition of the Magyar people and, to a lesser extent, by their pagan beliefs. Magyar society was based on blood kinship and the clan. Each clan was under the leadership of a clan chief (*fő*) who owed his authority not only to wealth accumulated during the raids, but also to his vast number of slaves working the chief's own land, which was arbitrarily expropriated from the common land of the clan. Also important were the warriors, or *jobbágys*, who owed him obedience and the fact that he officiated in the cult of the clan's ancestors. The clan chief's martial glory was proclaimed by the bards, who in turn were closely associated with the sorcerer, or *táltos*, who evoked the spirit of the ancestors to help the clan. Comprising five to six clans, the tribe, another military organization, supported the rule of the wealthy over the poor. Each tribe was headed by a chieftain, who led it during plundering raids. Major campaigns and delegations abroad were led jointly by the chief ruler, or member of his family, and by the *gyula* or the *harka*.

In time, however, the tribal chieftains, especially the *gyula*s and the *harka*s, attempted to act independently of the chief ruler. The *gyula*s were the most successful in this and in Transylvania they created an almost independent province for themselves. Bulcsú had shown his wish to secede by receiving baptism at Byzantium in 948, thereby setting himself apart from the House of Árpád, which looked to Western Christianity. Although Bulcsú would probably have aligned himself with the West by creating an independent Transdanubia, the defeat at Augsburg made this impossible. The disaster not only prevented him from founding a dynasty, but cost him his position as *harka* as well. Only the strengthening of the chief ruler's power could save the Magyar tribal alliance from disintegration, and the Magyar people from assimilation into the neighbouring peoples. Ultimately the Augsburg débâcle facilitated such corroboration.

The foundation of the state

The Magyar conquest of the Carpathian Basin, and the subsequent emergence of the Bohemian, Polish and Russian states, closed Eastern Europe as a source of slaves for the warriors of the Carolingian empire. In Western Europe serfdom emerged when slaves were allowed to own land and when the freemen were subjugated. Magyar society was in similar need of transformation, and Árpád's descendants, following Western models, organized their slaves and the indigenous Slàvs into manors (*udvarhely*s), on which freemen were also forced to serve. To guard the manorial *jobbágy*s, warriors from the seven Magyar tribes were also settled. The memory of these tribes has been preserved in place-names found in various parts of the country (Nyék, Megyer, Kürt-Gyarmat, Tarján, Jenő, Kér and Keszi).

Taksony (955–972), the grandson of Árpád, learned the lessons of the Augsburg defeat and sought contact with Western Christianity. In 961, he asked the Pope in Rome to send a bishop. Bishop Zacheus was despatched but was prevented from reaching Hungary by the German king, Otto I, who wished to thwart the establishment of a Hungarian bishopric owing direct allegiance to the Holy See.

Prince Géza (972–997) continued the domestic policy of his predecessors and also pursued a far-sighted foreign policy. In 973, shortly after he came to power, Géza was invited by Otto II to Quedlinburg. Otto, who was now Holy Roman emperor, also invited the Danish, Bohemian and Polish princes and it was his plan to extract an oath of allegiance from all four rulers. Prince Géza, however, sent envoys who were not authorized to take such an oath, although they did convey Géza's goodwill by asking the emperor to send missionaries to Hungary. These missionaries were headed by Bruno, who was consecrated "Bishop of the Magyars". Géza also admitted a few German knights into his princely escort. It was their task to prepare the prince's armed forces for battle against possible Western enemies and against any domestic foe. The prince received baptism and encouraged his entourage to follow suit. What he regarded as even more important, however, was the breaking of tribal opposition. This he promoted by speeding up the resettlement of warriors leaving the tribal framework and entering his service. The tribal chieftains and clan chiefs therefore lost the military basis of their power. However, Géza did not feel strong enough to break the authority of the *gyula*s in Transylvania, the principal centre of resistance to him. He therefore sought a compromise with them for the time being.

Vajk, the son of Prince Géza by his wife Sarolt (herself the daughter of the Transylvanian *gyula*), was christened Stephen and, after a Christian upbringing, the young man took over from his father in 997. He established the institutional framework for social and political transformation and organized the Hungarian state. Stephen confiscated the hill forts belonging to the clan chiefs, together with two-thirds of the clan territory and people. From these lands emerged the counties. Their inhabitants became the "castle-people" and "castle-serfs" responsible for the economic and military upkeep of the castles. Some proprietors of the remaining clan land joined the retinue of the prince. From these there emerged an élite, the *ispán*s (appointed royal officials who headed the counties) and the soldiers who served in the prince's regular army. The former princely estates were enlarged by means of new acquisitions and became independent economic units. Blood kinship thereby ceased to be the fundamental relationship in society. Everyone became a subject of the ruler, who now organized his country on a purely regional basis.

Social and political transformation had to be accompanied by ideological change. With the help of missionaries, and by force where necessary, Stephen led the entire population of the country into the Christian fold. Christianity did not recognize differences of social origin and was a universal religion organized territorially. The Church filled the vacuum left by disintegrating tribal and clan relations, and Stephen issued orders that every ten villages build a church and support its priest. The counties roughly corresponded to the decanal districts. There were ten bishoprics, two of which (Esztergom and Kalocsa) were made archbishoprics. Christian culture was spread by Italian, German and Czech monks. Monasteries were founded and subsequently supervised by the Benedictine house at Szentmártonhegy (Pannonhalma). Bishop Gellért of Csanád, who died a martyr, was the first ecclesiastical writer in Hungary, although Stephen himself was the first Hungarian to write a literary work, in the form of admonitions to his son. The keeping of Latin records began at local level in the monasteries.

Stephen carried out his great work with the assistance of both Hungarians and foreigners. Naturally, he encountered powerful internal opposition. In bloody battles he defeated his relations Koppány of Somogy and the *gyula* of Transylvania, although pockets of resistance remained even after this. Continuing opposition did not, however, alter the fact that the feudal Hungarian state had come into existence, and this state was formally recognized when the Pope sent a crown to its creator. With his coronation in 1000, Stephen became king of Hungary. However, uncertainty soon loomed when the legendary Prince Imre was killed in a hunting accident. Vászoly, the next in line to the throne, was a pagan and a supporter of the old order. To prevent him from asserting his rights, the king had Vászoly blinded and molten lead poured into his ears. Vászoly's sons fled the country and Stephen named Peter Orseolo—the son of his sister by the doge of Venice—as his heir.

Medieval Hungary

The early vicissitudes of the Hungarian state

A critical period for Hungary ensued after the death of King (St) Stephen I in 1038. The independence, indeed the very existence, of the young Hungarian state became seriously jeopardized.

There were several reasons for the crises which occurred during the period of early feudalism. Discontent among the subjugated freemen and rivalry between temporal and ecclesiastical lords gave rise to rebellion and conspiracy. The new order placed great burdens on the poor and tedious restrictions on the rich. From without, two neighbouring powers threatened the country. These were the Holy Roman empire, which had already made the Czechs and the Poles its vassals, and the Byzantine empire which had by this time swallowed up the Bulgarian state. Both had designs on Hungary.

Although the talented Árpád dynasty had great determination, its members often channeled vast energies into family feuds. The princes of the House of Árpád fought primarily over the principle governing the succession. One faction held that the oldest male member of the dynasty should succeed to the throne when the reigning king died, the other that the king's eldest son should be heir. When they were forced to compromise, they divided the country between them. Consequently, large parts of Hungary came under the rule of the princes, who governed them almost independently of the king. Yet the will to preserve state and people conquered selfishness and dissension. The eleventh- and twelfth-century kings of the House of Árpád strove consistently to ensure firm royal authority and the country's independence. To this end, they utilized both external and internal forces—the same forces that exploited the personal ambitions of these rulers for their own benefit.

The rule of St Stephen's successor Peter Orseolo (1038–41 and 1044–46) was threatened by rebellion among Hungarian feudal lords who were jealous of the foreigner. Peter Orseolo turned for assistance to the Holy Roman emperor, then at the height of his power, but the price of this was recognition of German suzerainty. Concerned for the country's independence, the feudal lords turned to princes András and Levente, the exiled sons of the executed Vászoly, and asked them to re-establish order. The princes encountered a pagan rebellion of elemental force, which even claimed the life of Bishop Gellért. After Peter Orseolo was overthrown, András was crowned king of Hungary in 1046. Andrew I (1046–60) did not wish to put the clock back, and instead suppressed the pagan rebels and restored St Stephen's state. In his efforts he could count on support from Byzantium, ever-jealous of German expansionism. Andrew's younger brother, Béla, repelled a German attack by scoring a victory over the invaders.

Andrew I established family links with his powerful German neighbour, and his brother, Prince Béla, used these to procure the throne for himself. After Béla I's sudden death in 1063, Salamon became king. The new monarch, the son of Andrew I and brother-in-law of Holy Roman Emperor Henry IV, reigned until 1074. Béla's sons, Géza and Ladislas, were granted duchies, but as a result of German and Byzantine intrigues, the king and the princes came into conflict with each other. Géza (1074–77) emerged victorious from this family feud and at his coronation wore a crown presented to him by the Byzantine emperor. The first great period of crises in Christian Hungary ended with the succession to the throne of King (St) Ladislas I in 1077. The international situation favoured the new ruler. It was at this time that the Investiture Controversy broke out between the Papacy and the Holy Roman empire. Ladislas sided with the Pope in order to free himself from German pressure, but rejected the Pope's ambition to make Hungary his vassal, as had already happened with neighbouring Croatia. Byzantium was now preoccupied with attacks from the Seljuk Turks and was therefore unable to prevent Ladislas from beginning the occupation of Croatia and Dalmatia. Threatened by Venice, an ally of Byzantium, the Dalmatian towns welcomed the protection of the Hungarian king.

The Hungarian conquests in the south certainly conflicted with the interests of the Byzantine empire. Byzantium therefore sent her allies the Pechenegs against Hungary but their attack was beaten off. By means of draconian laws, Ladislas restored domestic calm, which had been precarious for a long time. He supported the Church, the guardian of ideological order, not only with lavish gifts, but by the canonization, in 1083, of Stephen, Imre, and Gellért. Ladislas was succeeded on the throne by his nephew, Coloman Beauclerc (1095–1116). Coloman completed the occupation of Croatia and Dalmatia and defeated the Pope's renewed attempts to make Hungary his vassal. Himself an educated man, Coloman opened his court to Hungarians who encouraged literature written in Latin, as well as to numerous drafters of laws and writers of legends and chronicles. It was at this time that Romanesque art in Hungary achieved European standard, primarily in the work of the Pécs architectural school.

By the early twelfth century the German threat to Hungary had been averted and the Pope reconciled to the existence of the Hungarian state. Byzantium also considered it advisable to improve relations with its Hungarian neighbour. As a sign of rapprochement, Piroska, Ladislas's daughter, married the Byzantine emperor. (She was henceforth called Eiréné, to signify peace between the two countries.) After Piroska's death, the Byzantine Church canonized her, thereby paying tribute to her life of self-restraint and charity. Piroska was the first of many Árpád dynasty princesses to lead saintly lives. However, Piroska's son, Emperor Manuel, attempted to use his Magyar origins as a pretext for occupying Hungary. First he supported pretenders to the throne and then took the younger son of Géza II hostage with the promise that he would make him his successor. This younger son, Béla, possessed the duchies of Sirmium, Croatia and Dalmatia, and Manuel's real motive was to acquire them immediately. However, Manuel encountered fierce resistance in Hungary and finally had to relinquish his grand design—the union of Byzantium and Hungary. In 1172 Prince Béla returned to his native land to occupy the vacant throne and was crowned Béla III. After Manuel's death in 1180, Béla recovered the southern provinces taken away from Hungary.

Hungary thus survived its second major political crisis and, after nearly one and a half centuries of struggle, both its Western and Eastern neighbours had learned to fear and respect it. A typical foreign opinion of the Hungarians at this time is to be found in the work of a Byzantine historiographer. He speaks of the "Magyar people, who have good horses, good weapons, and wear iron and armour". They constitute "an uncountable mass, are as measureless as the sands of the seashore; their audacity is insuperable, and their boldness invincible. They are irresistible in battle, independent, free, walk with their heads held high, love liberty, and are their own masters..."

The consolidation of the feudal state

With the accession of Béla III (1172–96), Hungary acquired a very talented ruler. Béla was an outstanding politician and was fortunate enough to operate under favourable international conditions. The Holy Roman empire was very much distracted by its conflict with the Pope, as well as by internal opposition, and had relinquished its claims to suzerainty over Hungary. Byzantium, too, was paralysed by dynastic struggles and its Serbian and Bulgarian subjects had also risen in arms. For a while Béla III acted as the protector of the Byzantine empire, but eventually accepted the independence of the Serbs and the Bulgars. This meant an end to direct links between Byzantium and Hungary. During the two centuries after this time, Venice became Hungary's great rival, and attempted to acquire Dalmatia from the Hungarian king. Venice, the "Queen of the Seas", was now at the height of its influence but, nevertheless, repeated Venetian attacks on Dalmatia were frustrated by the loyalty to Hungary of the Dalmatian towns themselves, which were concerned for their commercial independence. A turning-point came in 1202 when Crusaders, bribed by Venice, occupied Zara and, two years later, Constantinople.

Hungary was strengthened by dynamic economic and social progress along with closer bonds with a generally developing Europe. Later, however, a number of serious problems were to arise as a result of this. Waves of French and German settlers flocked to Hungary from the West and immigrants from France spread viticulture north and east of the Danube. Western settlers (*hospes*) also brought with them the crop rotation system. More efficient agriculture led to the emergence of towns. The "Latin" (i.e. the French and Italian) merchants of the two earliest such settlements, Esztergom and Székesfehérvár, carried on a profitable trade. They exchanged wax, animal skins, and precious metals from Hungarian mines for Western luxury goods. These included cloth from Flanders, French enamelled bronze items, German weapons, and Italian silk. Esztergom and Székesfehérvár also served as the locations of royal residences, and during the reign of Béla III the requirements of the royal court increased significantly. Béla himself had been accustomed to a life of luxury in

HUNGARY IN THE ELEVENTH CENTURY (UP TO 1090)

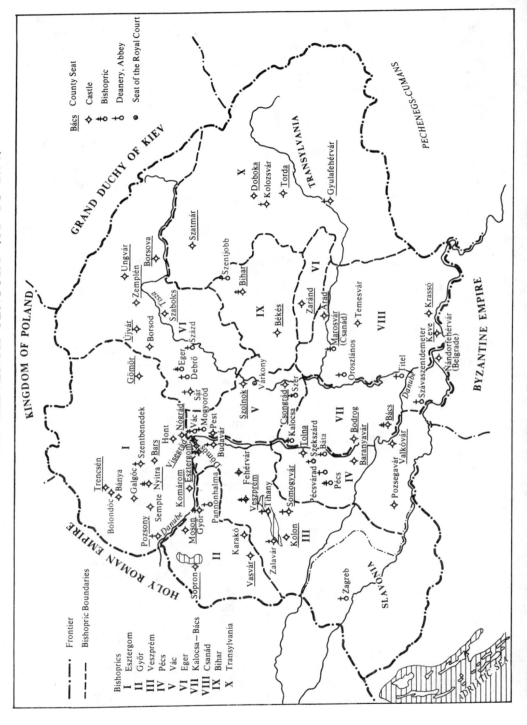

Byzantium, and through his two French wives had also become familiar with Western fashion. Previously, the king and his entourage had been content with the primitive articles made by the rural craftsmen on the royal estates, and the services of the cooks, dog-catchers, and minstrels who were ordered to the palace once a week had in the past satisfied the requirements of the royal party. At this time Hungary did not have a permanent capital. The king travelled from one royal estate to another, using up the revenue of each on the spot, as well as the two-thirds of county revenues that were his due. Now, however, the court purchased better quality goods. These were either imported from abroad or made by craftsmen who had settled in Hungarian towns. A class of professional officials also emerged. Béla III had a permanent residence built at Esztergom. This was a splendid palace where he could even receive Holy Roman Emperor Frederick I Barbarossa in a manner befitting the latter's rank.

Changes in economic conditions and demands were accompanied by changes in the structure of the economy. The use of money began. Although only a quarter of Béla III's annual revenues came from the counties, his income, at 166,000 marks yearly (1 mark equalled approximately 200 grams of silver), was substantial even by European standards. Béla now demanded only one-third of the counties' revenue. The rest of his income derived from foreign settlers, from minting money and from the mines which produced salt and precious metals. With the growth of these sources of revenue, the financial importance of the royal estates and the counties declined. The king could afford to cede these to ambitious feudal lords and the latter gradually adjusted to the expensive lifestyle of the knights of Western Europe. But the feudal lords were not satisfied with the income received as *ispáns*, namely, one-third, and later two-thirds, of the county revenues. They wished to acquire estates of their own, as the feudal aristocracy in the West had done. These aspirations were amply satisfied by Béla III's younger son, Andrew II (1205–35). The new king was himself full of ambition and much attached to pomp, and having entangled himself in a hopeless war with Russia, even ceded Zara to Venice in exchange for the latter's assistance in his Crusade adventure (1217). Andrew bestowed royal and county estates on the feudal lords and attempted to offset the resulting loss of revenue by levying taxes and customs duties.

The money economy received forceful encouragement in this way. However, the process created too great a burden for society and engendered general discontent. Already worried by the territorial acquisitions of the secular magnates, leading churchmen felt that their old commercial privileges in salt and wine were being jeopardized. Discontent ran high among the king's professional soldiers, the so-called *servientes*. These men were oppressed by the aristocracy and the same held true for commoners who had lost all their assets. The *servientes* now organized themselves into a nationwide movement in defence of their interests. A group of nobles led this movement and, in 1222, compelled the king to sign the "Golden Bull". Deriving its name from the gold seal appended to it, this document guaranteed protection for the *servientes* against harassment from the magnates, promised to put an end to financial abuses, and recognized the nobles' right of armed rebellion should the monarch fail to honour its provisions.

The greatest opponent of Andrew II's policy was his own son, who later ruled as

Béla IV (1235–70). Prince Béla was quite different from his father, who was a light-hearted person and who often lapsed into frivolity. Béla was also a devout Christian who took inspiration from St Elizabeth his sister, from St Francis, and from St Dominic. It was as though Béla had a premonition of the danger which was to threaten Hungary in the wake of Mongol expansionism. Even before he succeeded to the throne, Béla tried to fortify the Transylvanian frontier, and after his coronation he made every effort to reconstitute the disintegrating crown lands and counties. However, this was not a viable path to social development. Béla also sought help from abroad. He sent Julianus, a Dominican friar, to Bashkiria to invite the Magyars remaining there to move to Hungary. Afterwards, he also invited the Cuman people, who had already been attacked by the Mongols, to settle in the country. But Béla's measures gave rise to internal tensions which contributed to the devastating defeat of 1241. In that year Béla's army was routed by Batu Khan at Muhi on the river Sajó. The Mongols ravaged the country for more than twelve months and, when they eventually left, the Hungarian state had to be refounded.

Hungarian culture in the Early Middle Ages

The Magyar conquest of the Carpathian Basin marked the end of the Great Migrations in the area. After the consolidation of the Hungarian state, culture began to flourish. The royal household, the castles of the ispáns, the episcopal sees, and the Benedictine monasteries all served as the early centres of Christian civilization.

The material and intellectual achievements of European culture soon found their way to Hungary. As a result, the cultural heritage of the pagan period disappeared almost entirely. Memories of this age survived only in the songs of minstrels and from these the legends of the mythical stag, the turul, the white horse, Lehel's horn, Botond's battle-axe and other things were incorporated into the Magyar chronicles. The minstrels' tunes were preserved for a thousand years in pentatonic folk music and were rediscovered in the twentieth century by Béla Bartók and Zoltán Kodály. From ancient shamanism the Hungarian folktale preserved the myth of the tree of life and the legend of the shamans who fought in the guise of animals.

Hungarian fine art in the early Middle Ages still contained something of the Magyars' pre-Conquest times. The palmette, a popular ornamental motif during the period of the Conquest and then used in wood carving, gold work and textiles, was now applied to stonework. Under Lombard influence also, the palmette continued to develop in the foliated scroll carvings of the Pécs school of architecture. St Ladislas's frescoes in the churches of the Székelyföld (in eastern Transylvania) depict the tree of life and animal fights. A good example of such work is to be found at Erdőfüle.

As time passed, however, the heritage of the pagan era gradually disappeared from Hungarian art and gave way to European ideas. Initially, Christian culture found its way to the country through Czechs and Germans. Priests, friars, and knights from these ethnic groups introduced this; nevertheless, Hungarian literature and art followed Italian and French models. The earliest Hungarian school of architecture was inspired by Lombard art, and the late eleventh-century Pécs and late twelfth-century Esztergom schools were influenced by French architectural achievements. All three had a nationwide impact and raised imitation to the level of national practice. Although the Romanesque style of the time was international, its details mirrored Hungarian reality. Cases in point are the satchels, staffs, and special Hungarian sandals, which had straps going up to the knee. These were standard equipment for Hungarian herdsmen during the twelfth century and are depicted on the commoners' altar in Pécs Cathedral. (In the Early Middle Ages a separate altar was erected in front of the bishop's *cathedra* and was for commoners only.)

Literature was predominantly ecclesiastical. Liturgy, monastery yearbooks, the legends of saints, and secular works were all in the hands of the sole experts in writing at the time, the Benedictine friars. As well as performing other tasks, they recorded the early chronicles, tabulated the laws of St Stephen, St Ladislas, and Coloman Beauclerc and drew up the majority of legal documents. The larger monasteries and the collective chapters founded by St Ladislas were authorized to draft official documents and eventually acquired the functions of notaries.

In spite of all this though, culture did not remain exclusively ecclesiastical in character. The lay aristocracy strengthened its position and became increasingly prosperous, with the result that the secular element in culture expanded. During the twelfth century the ecclesiastical intelligentsia, who visited the universities of Oxford and Paris, introduced the courtly culture of England and France into the country. By this time the material trappings of the Western way of life were already established in Hungary. Stockings and tunics sewn from Flemish cloth, body armour, helmets, the straight sword, and war-horses had already found their way, through foreign merchants and Western enemies, to the Hungarian élite. "Magister P." (commonly referred to as Anonymus) was an important chronicler during the early years of the thirteenth century. Anonymus, who was also Béla III's notary, did not consider introduction of Christianity as the most important result of the Conquest: he regarded the legacy of the pagan Attila and the family histories of the Hungarian feudal lords to be the main subjects of his work, the *Gesta Ungarorum* (The Exploits of the Hungarians).

However, not all courtly culture spread in the Latin language. It was probably Anonymus himself who wrote an account in Hungarian of the Trojan War, the favourite subject of the knights at this time. In any event, it was now that it became fashionable in aristocratic circles to name children after figures in the Trojan legend, and Ecsellő, Perjámos and Iktár—the equivalents in Hungarian of Achilles, Priam and Hector—survive in place-names to this day. Famous representatives of Western courtly culture came to Hungary. The Provençal troubadour Vidal and the eminent German singer Tannhäuser visited King Andrew's court, as did Villard d'Honnecourt, the most distinguished French architect of the age.

The early thirteenth century was, however, also a period of fundamental change. A secular era was again followed by a religious revival, the chief representatives of which were the Dominican friars. It was they who converted the Cumans to Christianity and searched for those Magyars who remained in the East. Also important were St Elizabeth, the House of Árpád princess who corresponded with St Francis, and, above all, Béla IV and his entire family. The mendicant orders now determined the whole character of Hungarian culture and their influence was to last for the next two centuries.

The struggles with the barons, 1242–1308

The catastrophe represented by the Mongol Invasion accelerated the changes already initiated by economic and social development. The population of the Crown lands either fled or were killed, and the same was true of the inhabitants of the disintegrating counties. Béla IV had no choice but to donate the devastated lands to the feudal lords. The king's reasoning was that the magnates would resettle the countryside, partly with liberated serfs attracted by special benefits and partly with immigrants from abroad.

Previously, too, settlers had come to Hungary. These had primarily been Germans (so-called Saxons) who had moved across to Transylvania. The numbers of Saxons in the country remained small until after the Mongol Invasion, when many more arrived. Moravian, Ruthenian, and Romanian peasants came with them and from this time onwards Hungary was a truly multinational country. The economy began to flourish as hitherto-uncultivated areas, primarily the forested mountain regions, were drawn into the mainstream of production. The resettlement of the country also improved the lot of the Hungarian peasantry, and Hungarian bondsmen won the liberty enjoyed by the foreign settlers. By 1300 there had emerged a homogenous peasantry that farmed independently, was free to move, and which owed dues to the landlords in kind. Peasants inherited the appellation *jobbágy* from the freemen who had acted as officials during the early feudal period and who had served in the royal castles.

The magnates who repopulated their estates with settlers new to the country profited most, and the king was compelled by circumstances to give them a free hand to increase their power. These landlords were allowed to recruit private armies from among the ranks of the lesser nobility (the former *servientes*). They built castles for themselves, and these were initially designed on the multistorey keep pattern. By doing this the feudal lords contributed, albeit indirectly, to the defence of the country and allayed fears of a possible new Mongol attack. Isolated from the rest of the nobility, the feudal lords, or barons as they came to be called, increasingly broke with the royal power. To halt this process, Béla IV encouraged a new type of county formed from the royal knights, the *jobbágy*s, and the *servientes*. After 1267 this new kind of county institutionalized the autonomy of the lesser nobility—an autonomy which received military backing from the county's head, the *ispán*.

The king settled foreign, primarily German, "guests" in some of the former royal castles, for example Sopron, Győr and Kolozsvár. These new arrivals became assimilated with the existing castle inhabitants and this mixture gave rise to Hungary's urban, burgher population. The *civis* (citizen) of the previous era now became a burgher, a word of identical meaning but of German, not Latin, origin. Mining towns began to flourish and acquired a special importance. Through them Hungary became one of the major precious metal-producing areas of medieval Europe.

In addition to the lesser nobility and the town population, Béla IV also regarded the Cumans as a support for the royal power, and offered them asylum in Hungary. The Cumans lived as nomads and were organized along tribal lines but, because their men were all soldiers, they constituted an important force. In order to strengthen its bond with the Cumans, the royal house allied itself in marriage to the

Cumans. Stephen, heir to the Hungarian throne, married the Cuman prince's daughter, who was christened Elizabeth.

However, Béla IV's effort to offset the power of the barons proved futile: the wealth and power of the magnates were increasing all the time. Not only did the latter split into warring factions, but they also tried to subject large parts of the country to their rule. Exploitation of tensions within the royal family had long been an effective policy, and as a result of the barons' machinations, Béla IV and his son István became entangled in bloody conflicts with each other and the country was plunged into civil war. It was in vain that Margaret, Béla's saintly and charitable daughter, tried to mediate. Matters were made worse by the international situation. In 1254 the Austrian Babenberg dynasty, which had continually been at war with the House of Árpád kings, died out. Béla was determined to thwart the expansionist ambitions of the Bohemian kings, who were aspiring to hegemony in East-Central Europe. He occupied Styria and placed his son in power. However, a few years later Ottokar II of Bohemia occupied not only Styria but the other provinces of Austria as well. Ottokar now enlisted the help of the Kőszegi family, who were barons and who owned land along Hungary's western frontier. The Bohemian king then mobilized traitors inside Hungary against Béla IV, who by this time had again fallen out with István.

After his father's death, Stephen V (1270–72) himself fell victim to the anarchy which his own rebellion had done so much to precipitate. Ladislas IV, entitled "the Cuman", was brought up by his mother, but the ten-year-old boy monarch was initially the plaything of the warring baronial factions. In 1278 they forcibly took him to the battlefield at Dürnkrut, where Hungarian arms helped lay the foundations of the power and imperial authority of the House of Habsburg.

When Ladislas IV (1272–90) grew up, he turned against the baronial factions and sought support from the Cumans, his mother's people. However, the Cumans still practised paganism and the Church joined the opposition to Ladislas. The king consequently became isolated and was eventually assassinated. Since Ladislas had no heir, he was succeeded by Andrew III, the grandson of Andrew II who lived in Venice. But he too, was unable to overcome the anarchy which paralysed Hungary. The most powerful barons—the Kőszegis, Máté Csák, László Kán and others—tore the country into independent provinces and ruled them as petty kings. They maintained their own courts, entered into alliances with foreign powers, and ignored the legitimate monarch.

Andrew III tried to use the lesser nobility against the barons and established one of the first feudal diets in Europe. Although this body enacted legislation and excluded the barons from its proceedings, it was unable to wield sufficient power to be effective. In fact, for a long period it ceased to function at all.

With the death of Andrew III in 1301, the male line of the House of Árpád died out and a struggle for the throne immediately began between descendants of the House of Árpád through the female line. First King Wenceslas II of Bohemia and later Prince Otto of Bavaria organized factions for themselves but failed to win over a majority of the magnates. Finally, the Pope's candidate, Charles Robert of Anjou, was crowned king of Hungary in 1308, although he, too, needed a long time to stamp out anarchy in the country.

The loss of Hungarian possessions on the Adriatic

The century which followed the extinction of the House of Árpád also witnessed an end to Hungarian expansionism towards the Adriatic. At first it seemed that the succession of Charles Robert, who belonged to the Neapolitan Anjou dynasty and who was a descendant of the House of Árpád through his grandmother, would strengthen links between Hungary and Italy. Charles Robert consolidated his rule with moral backing from the Pope and financial support from the Italian bankers. Moreover, he tried to guarantee his authority in Italy by betrothing his younger son, Andrew, to Johanna, heir to the throne of Naples. However, Hungary's grave internal problems made it impossible for Charles Robert to pursue an active foreign policy. It was only in 1321, after he had defeated the last rebellious barons, that he succeeded in establishing his control over the whole of Hungary. In 1323 Charles Robert transferred his seat from Temesvár to Visegrád, which was by now the site of a magnificent Gothic castle.

It was around this time that Charles Robert put the royal finances in order. It did not even occur to him to reconstitute the decayed royal counties. He entrusted the administering of the new county system to chief *ispáns* appointed by him and to justices elected by the nobility. From the barons and the nobility generally Charles Robert required military service only. The county and baronial armies which fought under their own flags were called *banderia*. The barons marched off to war with their *familiares* (vassals), while those nobles who did not enlist in the army of one of the barons fought under the command of the county *ispán*. The remaining royal estates were organized around castles and made independent of the county administration. Charles Robert based his income on royal revenues, which were raised both directly and indirectly. These were known as *regalia* and derived from customs dues, taxes, and, above all, from the royal monopoly of precious metals. The mining of silver had been carried on for a long time in Hungary and during Charles Robert's reign the mining of gold also greatly increased (at Körmöcbánya and Nagybánya). As a result, minting of the gold florin began in 1325.

Military and economic reforms guaranteed internal order for the country, as well as favourable conditions for commerce. Trade with the West suffered considerably from Vienna's ability to prevent the passage of goods. In 1335 Charles Robert convened a highly important meeting at Visegrád of the kings of Hungary, Bohemia and Poland. There the monarchs concluded a trade agreement and established alternative international routes for merchants. This success indicated that it was primarily with his northern neighbours that Charles Robert was able to achieve good political relations. In the south, however, he was unable to salvage anything from the legacy of the Árpád kings. Dalmatia, Croatia and Slavonia accepted Charles Robert as their king only in name and were under the control of local rulers. In former Cumania, the Romanian voivodes, who had been appointed chief officials under the Árpád kings, governed independently of the Hungarian monarch. Wallachia was the first to secede and Moldavia then followed suit. After this, it was merely a loose and often abrogated oath of allegiance that bound them to the Kingdom of Hungary.

Charles Robert's son became King Louis I in 1342. Louis was to occupy the throne for forty years and came to be called "the Great" on account of his grandiose plans and ambitious military campaigns. The new king not only wished to win back the southern provinces which had broken away, but also planned to extend Hungarian power into the Balkans. In addition, Louis coveted territory even further afield. On the basis of dynastic right, he attempted to acquire the throne of Naples and in 1370 he succeeded in acquiring the kingdom of Poland, a legacy from his uncle. However, Louis's excessive ambition in Italy was unacceptable both to Venice and to the Pope. The Hungarian king fought two campaigns against Naples and, with the help of Genoa, also waged war on Venice. His Italian victories, however, could not bring the result Louis intended. In the south he succeeded in procuring only Dalmatia and Croatia, and his Bulgarian, Serbian, Bosnian and Romanian vassals were soon afterwards conquered by the Turks. Louis himself launched one campaign against these invaders from Asia who, later on, would advance still further into Europe.

Louis I died in 1382 without male issue and was succeeded by his daughter Mary. In 1387 Mary's husband, Sigismund of Luxemburg, came to the throne. Sigismund had to defend his rule against the Anjous of Naples whose candidate, Charles of Durazzo, was actually crowned king of Hungary in 1385 but was murdered a few weeks later. Ladislas, Charles' son, allied with Venice against Sigismund, who was helped to retain Dalmatia by Florence, itself jealous of Venetian power. From Florence Sigismund acquired the services of the excellent military commander and financial expert Filippo Scolari. However, when the Medicis came to power, Florence entered into an alliance with Venice, with the result that Sigismund lost his Italian possessions.

The situation was aggravated by Ottoman expansionism in the Balkans, which was now threatening the frontiers of Hungary. Sigismund of Luxemburg (1387–1437) tried to ensure Hungarian hegemony in the Balkans, but his multinational campaign against the Turks there met with resounding defeat at Nicopolis in 1396. After 1420 Sigismund (now also king of Bohemia and, from 1433, Holy Roman emperor too) was preoccupied with the suppression of the Hussite uprising and ending the struggles of the anti-popes, although he was unable either to solve these problems permanently or to counter the Ottoman threat, to which he paid very little attention. Sigismund did, however, score one important success for Hungary: in 1404 he issued an edict, the *Placetum regium*, in which he laid down that no papal bull or encyclical could be published or read in the country without his prior approval. In 1428 Sigismund was defeated again by the Turks, at Galambóc, although he had been compelled to give up Dalmatia even earlier. Hungary was no longer in a position to pursue an expansionist policy along its southern borders—indeed she now had to make desperate efforts to defend itself.

Early struggles with the Turks

In 1418 the Turks broke into Croatia and, in the following year, entered Transylvania. Wherever the Turks went they burnt, looted, and carried off the population. Their attacks became frequent and, although King Sigismund's military commanders were more or less successful in organizing Hungary's defences, those who lived in the southern frontier regions suffered increasingly from the war. It was no coincidence that it was precisely in these areas that Hussitism, the embodiment of anti-feudal discontent, became widespread. Ruthlessly persecuted by the Inquisition, some Hussites fled to Moldavia where the Bible was being translated into Hungarian. Other joined the peasants of Transylvania who were in revolt against excessive tithes.

In 1437 Hungarian and Romanian peasants headed by Antal Budai Nagy rose in arms against their oppressors and sought justice from King Sigismund. At the time the latter lay seriously ill in Moravia and died shortly afterwards. The peasants scored two victories over the forces of the bishop and nobility, winning over the town of Kolozsvár to their cause. Despite this, they were eventually defeated by the forces of the Kápolna League, an alliance between the Hungarian nobility, Saxon patricians, and the Szekler leaders.

Such internal dissension did nothing to avert the growing Ottoman threat to the country. Only Albert of Habsburg (1437–39) was able to take effective action with regard to this. Albert entrusted the defence of the southern frontiers to János Hunyadi, the son of a Transylvanian landowning family. As a child Hunyadi had been taken to King Sigismund's court (contemporaries regarded him as Sigismund's illegitimate son) where he had been instructed in modern warfare by Italian mercenary commanders. (Hunyadi also learned a great deal from the fighting tactics of the Hussites.) In addition to making use of the Hungarian lesser nobility and the ennobled Romanians, he often instigated popular uprisings as an aid to his military campaigns. Hunyadi's achievements were amply rewarded by the king, who bestowed on him offices and estates. By the year of his death Hunyadi had acquired some two million hectares of land, thus becoming the greatest Hungarian landowner of all time. However, Hunyadi did not spend his vast revenues merely on furthering his own political career: his income went primarily on national defence needs.

In his capacity as voivode of Transylvania, Hunyadi had already fought a successful battle against Mezid Bey, a Turkish commander who was killed during the encounter. In 1443 Hunyadi launched an offensive and, after a string of victories, was forced only by a harsh winter to return from the Balkan Mountains. The new king, Wladyslaw III Jagello of Poland (now also Wladislas I of Hungary, 1440–44), denounced his treaty with the Turks but died in the Battle of Varna, from which Hunyadi himself barely escaped. Wladislas was succeeded by the boy king Ladislas V (Albert of Habsburg's son) and Hunyadi was elected regent. He was to occupy this position from 1446 until 1453, when Ladislas came of age.

As regent, Hunyadi concentrated all his energies on realizing his great plan—the expulsion of the Turks from Europe. In this he counted on the help of the Balkan peoples—the Serbs, Bulgars and Romanians. The latter, however, were so intimidated by the Ottoman invaders that they dared not, indeed could not, resist as strongly as the Hungarians. Accordingly, Hunyadi's great undertaking ended in crushing defeat—at the Battle of Kosovo in 1448.

The struggle against the Turks was not handicapped merely by the enemy's superior numbers and by weakness on the part of the allies. Internecine strife also played its part. In Hungary the early fifteenth century witnessed the intensification of rivalry between the barons and the rest of the nobility. The lesser nobles also demanded representation in the running of the country, thus giving rise to the re-establishment of the feudal Diet. In 1440, the lower house, which was made up of lesser nobles, won the concession that all future laws would require the approval of the Diet before they could be enforced. The various baronial factions—the so-called leagues—now quarrelled among themselves and the resulting disharmony in these groupings undermined the country's unity still further. What usually happened at this time was that one of the baronial factions sided with the king and the other with the rest of the nobility. The lesser nobility tried to counterbalance the wealth of the barons with the power it derived from its numerical strength.

The lesser nobility supported the Hunyadi faction and, because of this, the opposing Cillei–Garai–Brankovics clique had to bide its time. When Ladislas came of age in 1453, Hunyadi's own pre-eminent position changed dramatically: he had to step down as regent and be satisfied with the office of captain-general of Hungary. The new king, Ladislas, was just thirteen years old and was entirely under the influence of his relative, Ulric Cillei. Through Cillei other enemies of the Hunyadi faction also enjoyed access to the young king, and this made matters potentially difficult for Hunyadi himself.

In this tense situation news arrived that Sultan Mohammed II, having occupied Constantinople in 1453, was now launching a campaign against Hungary. In 1456 he laid siege to Nándorfehérvár (now Belgrade). At the head of an army composed of mercenaries, lesser nobles and Crusaders recruited from among the people, Hunyadi raised the siege of this important border fortress. Hunyadi's victory halted the Ottoman advance for nearly a century. In honour of this great victory and to encourage further resistance, Pope Calixtus III ordered Christian churches to toll their bells at noon each day—a practice followed ever since. However, immediately after Hunyadi's victory, plague broke out in the Hungarian camp and the great military commander fell victim to it. After Hunyadi's death the Cillei and the Hunyadi factions launched a desparate struggle against each other and Hunyadi's supporters murdered Ulric Cillei. The king arrested both Hunyadi's sons, had László (the elder son) beheaded, and imprisoned Mátyás (the younger son) in Prague. But in 1457, Ladislas V died unexpectedly and the country was faced with the problem of having to elect a new monarch.

Attempts to create a Danubian empire

The Hunyadis were the most powerful baronial family in Hungary at this time and, in alliance with the lesser nobility, they forced the other magnates to elect Mátyás, the only surviving son of the former regent, as king of Hungary. Mátyás Hunyadi was, however, still a prisoner of George Podiebrad in Prague, and his mother, Erzsébet Szilágyi, had to pay a large ransom for his release. Mátyás's uncle, Mihály Szilágyi, now demanded a price for his assistance—the title of regent and the power that went with it. However, the new king rejected his family's patronizing attitude and relied for advice on János Vitéz, his excellent humanist tutor, whom he made archbishop of Esztergom as well as chancellor. At Vitéz's suggestion, Matthias strengthened the royal power against the barons. He also curtailed the power of the magnates and chose his officials from the ranks of the lesser nobility, the town burghers and, indeed, sometimes from the peasantry.

Matthias did not wish to rely on the private armies of the barons. He therefore hired mercenary forces, which later became the famous "Black Army", and placed them under his personal command. Matthias was obliged to place finances on an entirely new footing. By introducing a new system of taxation and, above all, by stringently monitoring the collection of taxes, Matthias created a sound basis for his reign. As a result, he was able to follow the example of his illustrious father and launch a military campaign against the Turks. In 1464, Matthias took the fortress of Jajce in Bosnia, but, owing to the sudden death of Pope Pius II, the promised help of a Crusader army did not materialize. Matthias could not, therefore, continue the struggle.

From this episode Matthias learned the very important lesson that Hungary's military strength was, in itself, insufficient to halt the Ottoman advance. In addition, he realized that even casual alliances were ineffective as they tended to collapse at the critical moment. A united empire needed to be organized from the peoples of the Danube area which alone would be strong enough to resist the Turks. Matthias therefore made peace with the sultan, a peace which, during his reign, was disrupted only by sporadic Turkish incursions and Hungarian reprisals. In 1479, one such Turkish onslaught was defeated by Matthias's military commanders Pál Kinizsi and István Báthori. This engagement took place between Alkenyér and Szászváros.

Matthias devoted the last twenty years of his life to attempts to establish the Danubian empire he considered so important. The idea of such an empire was nothing new, however. As early as the thirteenth century, King Ottokar II of Bohemia had striven to forge a kingdom out of the Bohemian, Hungarian and Polish lands. Sigismund had been Holy Roman emperor as well as the king of Hungary and Bohemia, while Archduke Albert of Austria had procured the Hungarian and Bohemian thrones. Among Matthias's contemporaries Emperor Frederick III and members of the Polish Jagiellon dynasty pursued policies that strove to bring countries together. Matthias aimed to conquer Bohemia, but Frederick III and the Jagiellons joined forces against him.

In Hungary many felt that Matthias's designs on Bohemia were motivated by personal ambition and that he was neglecting the Turkish threat to the country. Another criticism was that his expansionist schemes in the West would make new enemies for Hungary at a time when the Ottoman danger was already great. Archbishop János Vitéz headed those who were dissatisfied with Matthias's policies, but his conspiracy against the king was discovered. Vitéz was imprisoned and died not long afterwards. Matthias, however, went on to confound his critics. In 1474 the united Polish and Bohemian armies broke into Silesia and besieged Breslau, with Matthias himself inside the town. The siege was soon given up and peace was established by the Treaty of Olmütz, signed in 1478. Under this, both Matthias and Wladyslaw recognized each other as kings of Bohemia and that country was divided between the two rulers. Matthias retained Moravia and Silesia, while Bohemia went to Wladyslaw.

Silesia was a flourishing province during this period. Breslau, its capital, was a centre of trade in East-Central Europe, with Vienna being the other important commercial town in the Danubian region. Matthias knew that these two cities supplied foreign commodities to the Hungarian market and that much Hungarian gold went there in payment, and this was one reason why Matthias wanted to bring them under his control. Matthias now went to war with Frederick III, from whom he captured Vienna in 1485, moving his seat of government to the city.

By this time Matthias was not only known as a great king, but also as a generous patron of the arts and sciences. In 1476 he married Beatrice of Aragon, the daughter of the king of Naples. Matthias's queen introduced Renaissance culture into the Royal Castle at Buda. To the existing Gothic palace were added doors, windows and statues in the Renaissance style. Gardens and fountains were also created which bore the same stamp. A splendid library, the "Bibliotheca Corviniana", was set up which contained beautifully illustrated codices, and the castle's own pottery workshop made colourful utensils and tiles. Buda developed into a densely-populated and affluent town—the worthy seat of an European monarch.

The memory of Matthias, the greatest of Hungarian kings, survived not merely because of his grandiose political designs, his successful war, and his generous patronage of the arts. The common people referred to him as the "just king" long after his death. It was not as though Matthias showed much financial consideration for his subjects: on the contrary, he made them pay heavy taxes. In return for their sacrifices though, Matthias established order and security. "In this country no one can rely absolutely on his power and cannot be completely certain of it. Everyone is entitled to maintain, if need be even against Us, his right ... Here officials and powerful men do not dare to oppress the people with any form of servitude because they know that they themselves serve only for a time. And the source and guardian of this just legal system is not the law, but the king who is not a slave to, or tool of, the law, but who stands above the law and who presides over it." This was how Matthias described his own conception of royal power to Brandolini, the Italian humanist. Matthias's early attempt to centralize power was made in the spirit of righteousness. Legends about this remarkable king, who travelled the country in disguise and brought powerful wrongdoers to book, still live on in folklore.

The Hungarian economy in the Middle Ages

Contemporary Hungarian and foreign sources praised the natural resources of Hungary during the medieval period, and historic Hungary certainly offered numerous economic opportunities. The country was the meeting-place of three major climatic regions of Europe. These were the Atlantic region, characterized by forestry and grain production; the Mediterranean, which ripened grape and figs; and the Continental, which produced grasslands for grazing. The Magyars, as well as the other peoples living in the Carpathian Basin, made good use of this diversity.

The twelfth-century memoirs of Abu Hamid, a Moslem trader, described Hungary as belonging "to those countries in which prosperity and abundance are the greatest". Otto of Freising, a German bishop, was understandably angry with the Hungarians for defeating his fellow countrymen. However, at this time he wrote: "Fate may justifiably be blamed, or rather the divine error wondered at, that gave these human beasts (for they cannot be called human beings) such a beautiful country."

But whatever others thought of the Magyars, the fruits of their labour had to be acknowledged. As early as 1300 a French Dominican travelling in Hungary recalled the fertility of the Hungarian soil. "Formerly the Kingdom of Hungary was not called Hungary, but Moesia and Pannonia. Moesia received her name as a result of her rich harvests and Pannonia received hers because of her abundance of bread. And this is only natural since from a good harverst there follows an abundance of bread." (In Latin, *messio* means "harvest" and *panis* "bread". It was mere coincidence that the pronunciation of these words resembled the "Moesia" and "Pannonia" of Roman times.) The Magyars had cultivated the soil even in their ancient homeland, but in Hungary they learned how to grow oats, rye, wheat, and barley—although for a long time arable farming took second place behind livestock breeding. Ploughed land appeared as small islands in a vast sea of pasture. On the grassy expanses of the Great Plain the Magyars raised horses and cattle, while the mountain-dwelling Slavs and Romanians bred sheep and goats.

At the beginning of the fifteenth century, Bertrandon de Brocquière, a Burgundian knight, made interesting observations on the Hungarian horses of the time. "There are quite a few horse dealers in Pest," he wrote. "Should anyone want to buy two thousand good horses, he could probably do so here. Horses are sold in lots of ten and the price of each lot is two hundred florins. I have seen two or three horses which alone are worth this price. Most are from the Transylvanian mountains which surround Hungary's frontiers. I myself bought an excellent running horse, but generally those available are saddle horses. Abundant and fine pasture facilitates horse breeding in this country. It is, however, a fault of Hungarian horses that they are slightly unruly and difficult to shoe."

For a long time it was generally believed that the large, long-horned, greyish-white cattle in Hungary had been brought to the country during the Conquest. Bone finds have since revealed, though, that up to the end of the fourteenth century only the small Central European reddish-brown variety was bred by the Magyars. The long-horned, grey breed appeared almost without antecedent, and from this (and from the subsequent breeding areas of this grey strain) it is reasonable to conclude that it were brought in by the Cumans. Following the settlement in Hungary of these people during the thirteenth century, the breed spread. The new cattle were bred by the burghers who lived in the market-towns of the Great Plain. During the fourteenth century the Italian chronicler Villani wrote that in Hungary "many oxen and cows are raised which are not used as draught animals. They therefore grow fast and become fat on the lush pastures. They are slaughtered and their skins and fat traded on a large scale. The meat is boiled in big cauldrons and, when it is cooked, it is salted and removed from the bone. The meat is dried in ovens or elsewhere and ground into a fine powder. This is how it is preserved." At first cattle skins and fat were sold abroad but, from the second half of the fourteenth century onwards a growing number of fattened Hungarian cattle were driven on the hoof to Germany and to Venice. During the course of the fifteenth century the number of animals involved in this trade was more than 100,000 annually. Cattle constituted Hungary's most important export commodity in this period.

The wines of Tokaj were equally famous. The Romans were the first to produce wine in the Tokaj area and French settlers helped to expand the vineyards northwards. Large quantities of Tokaj wine were exported to Poland. Sheep breeding was one of the important branches of agriculture. The Hungarian *racka* variety of sheep provided the wool needed for broadcloth. At the same time the *purzsa* breed, the type raised by the Romanian mountain herdsmen, supplied the whole population with ewe cheese, as an important part of the diet.

Hungary was also rich in mineral resources. Even in the twelfth century written records mention silver and gold mines, as well as the salt of Transylvania. Germans were the chief mining experts in Hungary and, prior to the appearance on the market of precious metals from Africa and the Americas, Hungary supplied most of Europe with gold and silver. Even more important here was Hungarian copper, which had a high silver content. As early as the fifteenth century, copper mining was mechanized when the Hungarian Thurzó family introduced the water-wheel into the industry. Later, the Thurzós joined forces with the Fuggers, the banking family, and concluded deals worth millions.

Up to the end of the sixteenth century Hungary was a major raw materials supplier in Europe. Precisely because of this, however, it remained an industrially backward country. This was to have serious economic consequences later on.

The peasant war of 1514 and the Battle of Mohács

The successful realization of King Matthias's far-reaching plans would have required both an obedient civil service and a mercenary army. However, the weakness of urban development in Hungary meant that the king was unable to reward good service with grants of money. Accordingly, military commanders were given estates in payment for their achievements and officials received leading posts in the Church. Despite his intentions, Matthias thus contributed to the strengthening of the large landed estates. At the same time, Palatine István Szapolyai, the head of what was now the wealthiest baronial family, and Tamás Bakócz, Matthias's secretary and bishop of Győr, agreed that a king should be elected who would not curtail the power of the magnates. Consequently, in 1490, the weak Wladislas II succeeded to the throne. Wladislas was also king of Bohemia until 1516 but to prevent him exercising power Matthias's Black Army was disbanded. The barons' private forces once again monopolized military might in the country. These they maintained from public money and forced even the royal court to economize drastically.

Wladislas II turned to the leading churchmen for assistance against the barons. He made Tamás Bakócz his confidant, and appointed him archbishop of Esztergom and chancellor, in effect entrusting the entire government of the country to him. Bakócz was an intelligent, albeit ruthless, prelate who was quite prepared to augment his wealth by any means possible, and the pomp of Bakócz's surroundings rivalled the splendour of the royal court. The nobility rallied behind the Szapolyais in their struggle against Bakócz. In 1505 the Diet declared that, should Wladislas die without an heir, a "national" king should be elected to rule Hungary. The nobility was thinking of János Szapolyai, and the growing popularity of this magnate led the king and Bakócz to seek an alliance with the Habsburgs.

While the "national" and "court" parties were locked in conflict with each other, popular discontent grew. The ordinary people were defenceless against the powerful—especially the burghers of the market-towns who bred cattle and produced wine for export. Growing prosperity had brought greater consciousness to these individuals and they were hard hit by the Diet's resolution that, instead of the former lump-sum payment, they would now have to give a ninth of their cereal and wine production to the landlords. In this way the bitterness of the poor peasants was compounded by the despair of the more affluent. In 1513 Bakócz was defeated in the papal election and Leo X (of Medici) ascended the Throne of Saint Peter. By way of compensation, the new pope commissioned Bakócz to lead a Crusade against the Turks; the resentments of the people were soon to receive forceful expression.

By spring 1514 the Franciscan friars entrusted with the recruitment of Crusaders had collected an army of peasants so vast that it endangered not only spring agricultural work, but also the security of the landowners. The Franciscans, who lived in the market-towns and sympathized with the people, advocated the idea of a peasant kingdom based on equality of wealth. On May 15 the apprehensive barons and nobles forced Bakócz to order the army of Crusaders to disperse.

By this time, however, the first troops had set off from Buda across the Great Plain. Their response to the disbandment order was to turn against the landowners, and they elected György Székely (Dózsa), a soldier of Szekler origin, to be their leader. Dózsa had earned a reputation for bravery in skirmishes with the Turks and wanted to lead the peasant army to Transylvania. There they would unite with the dissatisfied Szeklers and would establish a people's state. However, János Szapolyai, already voivode of Transylvania, used his troops to block the road which led there. Dózsa's army therefore marched south against Temesvár, a town defended by István Báthory, the *ispán* of Temes. Szapolyai hastened to the relief of Temesvár and by July 15 had scattered the peasant army. Dózsa was burnt alive on a red-hot iron throne and his associates were tortured to death. The Diet passed a law which declared the peasants to be perpetually and without exception bound to the land and deprived of their right to own it. Peasants were now serfs tied to their landowner. For centuries to come the peasants were outcasts in their own country, for the development of which their work had been largely responsible.

After the defeat of the peasant insurrection, the conflicts between the barons and the nobles continued. Bakócz and his clique tried to offset the growth of Szapolyai's authority by concluding a succession agreement between the Hungarian Jagiellos and the Austrian Habsburgs. After the death of Wladislas II, Louis, his son, was crowned king of Hungary in 1516. Louis II married Mary of Habsburg, whose brother Ferdinand in turn married Anna Jagello. This constituted a violation of the 1505 law which had stipulated the election of a "national" king. The struggle between the baronial faction and the lesser nobility now became more acute than ever.

After the death of Bakócz in 1521, Palatine István Báthori, the wealthiest person in Hungary after the Szapolyais, became the leader of the court faction. In 1525, however, Báthori was ousted by István Werbőczy, the influential spokesman of the Szapolyai faction and the compiler of the famous *Tripartitum*, a work on Hungarian common law. (The *Tripartitum* recognized the equality of barons and nobles and listed their rights, but it also included the punitive laws against the peasantry.) The voting power of the lesser nobility now overthrew Báthori and made Werbőczy palatine. The first thing the new palatine did was to deprive the Fuggers of their lucrative mining leases. The miners, now without pay, rose in revolt—only to be suppressed and punished by Werbőczy. This antagonism of the Fuggers served to deny the country credit at a time when the Turkish threat was growing.

In 1521 Sultan Suleiman the Great occupied Nándorfehérvár (Belgrade) and in 1526 launched a new campaign against Hungary. Louis II could rally only 25,000 troops against a Turkish army numbering almost 100,000 men. Unable to wait for Szapolyai's 10,000 strong contingent, Louis II was forced to accept battle with the Ottomans at Mohács (August 29, 1526). Under the command of Pál Tomori, archbishop of Kalocsa, the Hungarian army attacked the enemy—only to be routed by the Turkish artillery. During his flight from the battlefield, Louis was drowned in the Csele stream. Half the Hungarian troops present, including numerous barons and prelates, also died in the confusion. The prosperous days of medieval Hungary were over.

Gothic culture in Hungary

In Hungary the Gothic style of architecture became established in the middle of the thirteenth century. The firts major Gothic buildings were commissioned by the royal court, and the earliest Gothic edifices still surviving are St Mary's Church (now the Matthias Church) and the tower of the Church of St Mary Magdalene in Buda. The former was built for the German burghers and the latter for their Hungarian counterparts. King Béla IV, who originally built these churches, also built a convent for his daughter Margaret on what is now the Margaret Island. Of this only a few fragments now remain. Béla IV started the construction in the thirteenth century of one section of Buda Castle but only the foundation walls of this have survived. The most impressive examples of Hungarian Gothic architecture were to be found in that central part of the country which was later devastated during the Ottoman invasion; castles and churches in this region were indiscriminately destroyed.

In the second half of the thirteenth century, the castles of the secular lords still took the form of keeps. The fourteenth century witnessed the emergence of the for-tified castle with towers encompassed by an outer wall. The royal residences were the finest examples of these and could be found at Visegrád, Buda, and Diósgyőr. Secular lords also built castles—for instance, the Laczfis at Tata and János Hunyadi at Vajdahunyad—in the more complex style of late Gothic architecture.

The evolution of Gothic architecture was accompanied by the emergence of new types of residential building for burghers and peasants. The burghers' houses in fourteenth- and fifteenth-century Hungarian towns faced the street with their slop-ing roofs. Under the "palace" of the first storey, which rested on supports, there opened an enormous gateway. This opened into a wide passage with Gothic sediles to the right and to the left, and these awaited the paying guests of the winegrower host. During the same period, the single-room shack of the Early Middle Ages was replaced by the three-room peasant house. The windows of this type of building faced the street and its entrance was from a yard. One went into this yard through a gateway. Inside the entrance to the house itself was the kitchen with an open fire. On one side there opened a door to the guest room which was heated by a stove. This stove would burn coal and would be stoked from outside the room. On the other side was an unheated pantry. This type of peasant dwelling became widespread even amongst the nobility and burghers of the market-towns. However, the houses of these people were of better quality, built of stone and with vaulted ceilings.

The mendicant orders of monks produced the finest examples of Gothic ecclesiastical architecture in Hungary. The examples provided by the monasteries were soon followed, in the second half of the fourteenth century, by the towns. The most important Gothic town parish churches to have survived are located in Kassa, Kolozsvár, and Brassó. In the fifteenth century the basilica-type church became common, especially in the market-towns of eastern Hungary. The most beautiful examples are Szeged's Lower City church and the church in Farkas Street, Kolozsvár.

Whilst Hungarian architecture was dominated by French and German influences, painting and sculpture were powerfully inspired by Italian art. This was only to be expected during the rule of the Anjou kings. In addition to fresco painting (e.g. the St Ladislas series in the *Székelyföld*) which flourished during the fifteenth century, Hungarian miniature painting also revealed Italian influence, especially in the Nekcsei Bible and the *Képes Krónika* (Illustrated Chronicle), the latter a masterpiece by Miklós Meggyesi. At the beginning of the fourteenth century, panel painting also became widespread and examples were often found in churches. Tamás Kolozsvári, whose work was also influenced by Italian art, was the greatest master of this type of painting, and among other things he painted the winged altar-screen at Garamszentbenedek. This can be seen today in Esztergom.

Italian influence is even more obvious in the sculpture of the period, primarily in the works of the Kolozsvári brothers, Márton and György. It was they who sculpted the statues of Hungary's canonized kings which once stood outside Nagyvárad Cathedral. (These were destroyed by the Turks in 1660.) However, their St George statue, made for Prague in 1372, has survived. This is a very early example of a statue standing apart from a building, and its style combines realism with a touch of Renaissance influence. The statues of knights and prophets which were made in the Buda Castle around 1440 showed signs of the "Northern Renaissance", as found in the Dutch and Burgundian art of the time. The same was true of the carvings of Pál Lőcsei, who lived at the beginning of the sixteenth century.

The two centuries of Hungarian Gothic art were dominated by the activity of the mendicant orders, the Dominicans and the Franciscans. These orders were based in the towns and their preachings, in the vernacular, were primarily addressed to the burghers and well-to-do peasants who lived there. To draw attention to what they had to say, they introduced motives from old fables and this was how numerous stories from the East became known to the Hungarian people. They were also the first educators of Hungarian women: the so-called "beginas" who were affiliated to their orders. It was probably for these that the first known poem in the Hungarian language, the *Ómagyar Mária-siralom* (The Lament of the Holy Virgin) was written. In the fourteenth century, these orders wrote and performed most of the legends, hymns, passion plays, and meditations, and in doing so served all sections of Hungarian society. Towards the end of the period, the "beginas" themselves cultivated literature in the vernacular, or at least translated religious texts into Hungarian. (Lea Ráskai and Márta Sövényházi are examples.)

The predominance of ecclesiastical art did not entirely eclipse the work of the secular intelligentsia. A large number of people pursued university studies without intending to embark on a career in the Church. In 1367 Louis the Great founded a university at Pécs, but this did not measure up to foreign standards and the Hungarian clergy continued to attend universities abroad—primarily Vienna, Prague, Cracow, Bologna, and Padua. It was from the clergy that the officials of the royal chancellery were picked. Master Simon Kézai, who lived at the court of Ladislas the Cuman, was the first to expound the idea of Hun-Magyar kinship in the chronicle he composed, thereby supporting his monarch's policy of looking to the pagan Cumans for backing. In the middle of the fourteenth century, János Küküllei wrote an account of the reign of Louis the Great, and although this has not survived in its original version, the Toldi and Tar legends prove that the secular epic also flourished during this period. A well-known, albeit late, example of this kind of writing is *Szabács viadala* (The Struggle at Szabács).

Early Renaissance culture in Hungary

Up to the early sixteenth century Renaissance culture was largely confined to Italy and seldom penetrated north of the Alps. Hungary was therefore especially fortunate in being an early centre of Renaissance art, in spite of its geographical position. While in the Western European countries Gothic art still predominated, in Hungary Renaissance achievement appeared alongside a flourishing Gothic culture. Naturally the royal court was the first centre of this. From 1476 onwards, Beatrice of Aragon—Matthias Hunyadi's second wife—strove to transform Hungarian practices and to bring them into line with Italian ideas. Beatrice regarded existing Hungarian culture as barbaric, and King Matthias, receptive to anything that was new and beautiful, supported her. Matthias himself soon took the initiative in this transformation and set very high standards.

The stone carvings and furniture at Buda and Visegrád castles were soon changed. It was probably at this time that the splendid Gothic fountain built by the Anjous at Visegrád was demolished, being replaced by the new Renaissance basin made of red marble from Piszke and decorated with representations of Hercules as a child. The Gothic statues at Buda which had been made just a few decades earlier were also removed and buried during this period. They were replaced by the works of Italian masters. Not only foreign experts worked at Buda, however. Hungarians also became proficient in the new skills: Italian faience ceramic art was soon copied in Hungary and Matthias was able to set up his own ceramic works in the town. Indeed, as the latest finds have revealed, this type of ceramic art also became established in Pécs.

Hungarian goldsmiths had less to learn from the Renaissance masters. Abounding in gold and silver, Hungary had never lacked fine jewellers. Silver fittings from belts and headdresses have been found even in medieval peasant graves. The application of *cloisonné* enamel made the Hungarian goldsmith's art, which otherwise used international Gothic motifs, especially appealing.

Local traditions also persisted in panel and mural painting. The great painter who used the initials M. S. and who worked during the early sixteenth century was familiar with the works of Albrecht Dürer—his contemporary and a Hungarian by origin. It was not, however, Renaissance inspiration that M. S. took from Dürer, but rather his Gothic forms. The window frames, door frames and statues at Buda and Visegrád are splendid relics of Renaissance stone-carving and sculpture. The same is true of the Bakócz Chapel in Esztergom and the Báthori Madonna. In addition, numerous Gothic churches, burghers' houses, carved altars, and items of furniture have survived from this period. Not only did the Gothic and Renaissance styles exist alongside each other, but there was also a certain amount of intermingling between them. This took place in the fine arts and also in literature.

King Matthias invited foreign humanists to his court—mainly Italians. Among them were Antonio Bonfini, the historian; Galeotto Marzio, who recorded the king's witty sayings; and Naldo Naldi, who looked after and described the magnificently-illustrated codices of the famous Corvina Library. There were many other visitors, for example the most famous German astronomers of the age, Regiomontanus and Peuerbach. A number of Hungarians also represented the new, secular spirit in literature and science. They included János Vitéz, a writer of fine letters, and his nephew Janus Pannonius, bishop of Pécs and one of the most talented of Europe's medieval Latin poets. The latter wrote odes on the exploits of the Hunyadis, elegies lamenting Hungary's backwardness, satirical epigrams and lyrical poems. These last were imbued with gentle emotion and a sensitive love of nature, and were admired even in Italy.

At the same time, however, at the Franciscans' monastery in Buda Pelbárt Temesvári and his disciple Osvát Laskai castigated humanist thinking, which they considered to be faithless and immoral. Not even King Matthias was spared criticism. They demanded of him the devout religiosity of the "Holy Kings", albeit in a new form—that of the pre-Reformation "New Piety" advocated by no lesser figures than Thomas à Kempis and Erasmus. The words of the Franciscan friars had no effect on the king, yet it did elicit a considerable response among the burghers of the towns and in the ranks of the lesser nobility. Indeed, because their preachings were published also in Latin, these Franciscans were even able to disseminate views beyond Hungary's borders.

The printing of books in Hungary also began during Matthias's reign. In 1473 András Hess set up a short-lived printing press in Buda and brought out the *Chronica Hungarorum*. Another printing press also functioned in Hungary at this time but also quickly closed; new ones started only after 1536. The chronicle of János Thuróczy, Matthias's Hungarian historian, was published in Brno in 1488. Thuróczi's work, imbued with national pride and identifying the Magyars with the Huns, compares Matthias to Attila. This work greatly influenced the outlook of the Hungarian nobility and for many decades determined national consciousness. Although a large number of works from the reign of King Matthias perished later, this particular idea was passed on to subsequent generations. It was to provide emotional succour during the misfortunes that were already in store.

HUNGARY AT THE BEGINNING OF MODERN TIMES

The Division of Hungary into Three Parts

The aftermath of Mohács

Contemporaries regarded the Ottoman invasion of Hungary as divine punishment for internal anarchy, party strife, social injustice, and moral and intellectual profligacy. Although each of these had in fact weakened Hungary in its struggle against the Turks, it was also true that the Ottoman Empire was a very formidable adversary. The Turks were incomparably stronger economically and possessed an army which far outnumbered that of the Hungarians. Only assistance from outside could have enabled Hungary to resist the Ottoman onslaught with success.

When the childless Louis II died at the Battle of Mohács in 1526, it was of paramount importance that the new king be able to mobilize adequate foreign help against the Turks. The lesser nobility wished to see János Szapolyai, voivode of Transylvania, as the new monarch. Szapolyai was son-in-law of King Sigismund I of Poland, a state then at the height of its power and a good potential ally. The Diet elected Szapolyai king, with the title John I, but a small group of barons led by Palatine István Báthori opted for the Austrian archduke, Ferdinand of Habsburg. As the Bohemians had also elected Ferdinand king, the tradition of a common ruler for Hungary and Bohemia would therefore be continued. Indeed, there was even hope that through Ferdinand's brother, the powerful Emperor Charles V, the Holy Roman empire would also be drawn into Hungary's struggle against the Turks.

Szapolyai offered to marry Mary, the widow of Louis II and the sister of Ferdinand of Habsburg, but was rejected. Charles V helped Ferdinand against Szapolyai but did nothing against the Turks. Ferdinand now drove Szapolyai out of the country. Szapolyai fled to Poland and, enlisting French and Polish help, won the support of Sultan Suleiman II, the Ottoman ruler. In 1529 the sultan used force to restore Szapolyai's rule and, what is more, even tried to occupy Vienna, Ferdinand's seat. In 1532 a second Turkish advance was halted by the heroic efforts of Miklós Jurisics, the defender of the castle at Kőszeg.

Szapolyai died in 1540 and Ferdinand took the opportunity to besiege Buda. However, Bishop György Martinuzzi, regent of the country, wished to ensure the succession of Szapolyai's infant son, John Sigismund, who was also the bishop's ward. Martinuzzi therefore turned to Suleiman II for help. In 1541 the sultan drove off the Germans besieging Buda, but then occupied the city for himself. John Sigismund—the sultan's adopted son by now—was sent to Transylvania, along with his mother, the Polish princess Isabella Jagello. The Turkish-occupied part of Hungary—the Pécs–Esztergom–Szeged triangle—was now wedged in between Habsburg western Hungary and the eastern Szapolyai kingdom.

Hungary was now divided into three parts. Martinuzzi, who governed the kingdom in the east, regarded Habsburg assistance as vital to Hungary's reunification, although a powerful army would be required to overcome the inevitable Ottoman resistance to this. In 1551 Ferdinand of Habsburg nevertheless sent an army to Transylvania which, according to contemporaries, "was too large to conduct a diplomatic mission, but too small to fight a battle". Martinuzzi asked for reinforcements and, to gain time, entered into negotiations with the Turks as well. Afraid of treason, the commander, Castaldo, had Martinuzzi assassinated but was unable to prevent Ottoman revenge. In 1552 the important border fortresses fell to the Turks one after the other: the towns of Temesvár, Szolnok and Drégely all came under Ottoman control. However, the Turkish advance was checked at Eger, where the garrison, under István Dobó's leadership, put up a heroic defence.

In 1556 the kingdom in eastern Hungary was re-established under the rule of John Sigismund and became an Ottoman protectorate. For a whole decade there followed a struggle to fix the frontiers of the two Hungarian states. István Báthori, the captain of Várad, wanted to end internecine strife by arriving at a compromise agreement. This would have acknowledged the duality of the kingdom, but would, at the same time, have given war-torn Hungary a chance to recover. However, while Báthori was negotiating in Vienna, Suleiman II launched an offensive against that city in 1566. The sultan promised John Sigismund to enlarge the eastern kingdom threefold but in fact occupied additional Hungarian territories for himself. These included the castle of Gyula, formerly in Habsburg possession.

However, Suleiman's campaign against Vienna soon ran into difficulties and at Szigetvár the Turks encountered stiff opposition. The Ottomans' siege of the castle dragged on and, by the time victory was theirs, the elderly sultan was already dead. At the very last moment, Miklós Zrínyi, the commander of Szigetvár, broke out of his ruined and burning castle at the head of his Hungarian and Croatian soldiers. All died in the battle which followed. In the meantime, Maximilian II (1564–76), Ferdinand's successor, had been waiting at Győr with a large mercenary force but refused to heed Zrínyi's desperate calls for assistance and to risk his army, which had been assigned to the defence of Vienna. It was at this time that the Habsburgs' policy towards the Hungarian territories became clear, i.e. that they regarded western Hungary as a buffer zone to protect their hereditary provinces. For the time being at least, they had no plans to expel the Turks from Hungary's central regions.

The heroic feat of Zrínyi and his soldiers was, however, sufficient in itself to stem the Ottoman advance temporarily. Owing to time lost during the lengthy siege and the sultan's death, the Ottoman army withdrew. The new sultan was unable to match his father's effort and in 1568 concluded the Peace of Adrianople with Maximilian. Under this treaty the conquests of Suleiman II remained in Ottoman hands. The front line between the two great powers now stabilized and both sides established an extensive network of border fortresses. Hostilities were reduced to the level of regular skirmishing between the Habsburg and Ottoman forces and this state of affairs persisted for many years.

The rise of Transylvania and the Long War

The era of the Ottoman conquest in Hungary was not only characterized by defeats. It also abounded in victories. As early as the late sixteenth century it seemed that the Turks might well be driven out of the country if the two Hungarian states joined forces against their common foe. Such a bold undertaking held out hope of success for two reasons. Firstly, the Habsburgs were able to mobilize foreign assistance and, secondly, the Hungarian state in the east had also become stronger.

In 1570 John Sigismund (Szapolyai), the ruler of the eastern kingdom, concluded the Treaty of Speyer. In this he relinquished the Hungarian crown to the Habsburgs and became prince of Transylvania. (Transylvania now annexed the territories east of the river Tisza.) His successor, István Báthori (1571–86) defended Transylvania against the Habsburgs and, in competition with Maximilian, also became king of Poland in 1576. However, through his brother, Kristóf, who had been appointed voivode, Báthori retained control over Transylvania, which was now united with Poland for all practical purposes. For the time being, the Poles enjoyed the advantages of this union. Báthori (as King Stephen of Poland) fought his successful battles against Russia's Ivan the Terrible largely with Transylvanian mercenaries. Of these the majority were Szeklers.

In 1562 John Sigismund made serfs of the Szekler commoners and for some thirty years their only opportunity to rise socially was through military service. Generally speaking, the sixteenth century witnessed the deterioration of the peasantry's lot in Hungary. It was then that "perpetual serfdom" was instituted in the east and west. István Báthori's military policy not only alleviated the misery of the serfs, but also laid the foundations of a Transylvanian army which could later challenge the Turks with some chance of success.

In 1591, and after a long period of peace, Hassan, the pasha of Bosnia, laid siege to Sziszek castle. This move marked the beginning of renewed hostilities between the Habsburgs and the Turks. The army of the Habsburg emperor Rudolph, largely made up of German and Hungarian mercenaries, scored a victory against the Ottomans at Sziszek in 1593, and another at Pákozd. Although Rudolph's troops surrendered the fortress of Győr, they had every chance of continuing the struggle successfully. Zsigmond Báthori, the new prince of Transylvania, heeded the advice of his uncle István Bocskai, the captain of Várad, who realized that Transylvania could not appear to be pro-Turkish at a time when Ottoman fortunes might be on the decline and that with the Ottomans expelled from Hungary a principality aligned with the sultan would be in great danger from victorious Habsburg forces. Accordingly, Zsigmond Báthori eradicated the pro-Ottoman faction in Transylvania, restored the liberties of the Szekler commoners, and extracted oaths of allegiance from the voivodes of Wallachia and Moldavia. In this way, he was able to enter into an alliance with Rudolph on equal terms.

In 1595 Bocskai's Szekler forces together with the Romanian and Serbian troops of Mihai, the voivode of Wallachia, conducted an impressive campaign against the Turks. An Ottoman attack through Wallachia was beaten off and the enemy driven back as far as the Danube. Most of the Turkish troops who tried to escape across the bridge at Giurgiu were massacred. At the same time Báthori and captains György

49

Borbély and Mózes Székely occupied Lippa, Jenő, and numerous other castles along the river Maros. The nobility was not, however, prepared to accept the loss of its Szekler workforce. With Zsigmond Báthori's tacit approval, the nobles therefore once again made serfs of the Szekler commoners at the so-called "Bloody Carnival" of 1596. Deprived of his finest soldiers, Báthori could not render much assistance to the Habsburg army, which was now seriously defeated by the Turks at Mezőkeresztes. Eger also fell.

After this the war soon ground to a halt and the Turks ruthlessly devastated the Great Plain. The free Heyducks in turn revenged themselves on the Ottomans, capturing their supplies and burning their principal crossing point, the bridge over the river Drava at Eszék. Although Győr was recaptured from the Turks in 1598, Kanizsa was lost to them in 1600. Gradually both sides became exhausted, while the country itself suffered depopulation and pillaging.

Having lost all hope, Zsigmond Báthori relinquished his title of prince and decided to cede Transylvania to the Habsburgs. Later, however, he changed his mind and handed over the throne to his cousin, Cardinal András Báthori. In 1599, Mihai, the voivode of Wallachia, occupied Transylvania with the help of the cheated Szeklers. Although claiming to act on behalf of the Habsburgs, Mihai was in reality pursuing his own objective—the uniting of Transylvania, Moldavia, and Wallachia. Fleeing from the scene of the lost battle, András Báthori was killed by the Szeklers in the mountains. But Mihai's ascendancy was short-lived. The Transylvanian nobility enlisted the support of Georg Basta, the Habsburgs' famous general, who defeated Mihai and, in 1601, had him murdered.

The Transylvanian nobles were not enamoured with the prospect of Habsburg rule and wished to make peace with the Turks. Mózes Székely, the former hero of the struggles against the Ottomans, even wanted to organize the principality with assistance from the latter. In 1603, however, Székely's army was defeated by Habsburg troops at Brassó and Székely was himself killed. His followers, among them the young Gábor Bethlen, fled to Turkish territory. Basta took bloody revenge on Transylvania: his mercenaries looted and set fire to the villages. The people fled to the mountains to escape death, and famine and plague swept the land. When Basta left Transylvania in the spring of 1604, the principality lay in ruins. It seemed that the two Hungarian states had again been reunited, albeit at great cost.

Humanistic culture and the Reformation in Hungary

Although Hungarian culture entered a period of decline after 1526, there nevertheless remained some scope for development. The influence of humanism and the Renaissance was now coupled to that of the Reformation. As a result of all this, European culture could receive full expression in Hungary.

The century of Ottoman occupation did not produce conditions which favoured the fine arts. What is more, the Reformation was satisfied with fewer churches and in ecclesiastical art rejected higher-quality figuration. However, it was also at this time that the Tuscan-style painting of wooden ceilings and quires began to spread.

This was the Renaissance "floral decoration" which was becoming increasingly popular and which also began to find expression in the work of goldsmiths. Unlike its medieval counterpart, the fine art of this period served secular as well as ecclesiastical purposes. With the exception of the Turkish-occupied areas, where this type of culture stood no chance, the whole country went over to Renaissance taste. This was manifested primarily in door and window frames carved by Italian and Hungarian masters, as well as in a great diversity of sepulchral monuments.

Large construction projects were planned and supervised by Italian engineers. During this period border castles were provided with modern defence structures —low, wedge-shaped "Italian" bastions which served as smaller targets for enemy artillery. The castles designed by Pietro Ferabosco at Pozsony, Komárom, and Győr were outstanding, as were the castles of Érsekújvár, Eger, and Szatmár, which were designed by the two Baldigaras, Ottavio and Giulio. In the Principality of Transylvania, the fortresses of Várad, Szamosújvár, and Fogaras were all rebuilt along Italian lines. The big magnates converted their residences into fortresses with quadrangular or circular corner bastions, suitable for defence purposes. Good examples include the Egervár and Sárvár homes of the Nádasdy family, the Nagybiccse home of the Thurzós, the Martinuzzis' Alvinc residence and the Bethlens' home at Keresd.

Sárvár was also famous for its printing press, established in 1537. There, in 1541, the first book in the Hungarian language was published. This was János Sylvester's translation of the New Testament. Books in the vernacular and the printed word generally were among the principal weapons of the Reformation, and this was true for the Counter-Reformation as well. During the sixteenth century, some 850 publications were put out by the twenty printing presses in Hungary.

The Reformation began to spread in the decade preceding the Battle of Mohács, although not without opposition. In 1523 supporters of the new ideas were condemned to the stake and some were actually burnt. After Mohács, however, central authority in the state weakened and although both King John and King Ferdinand were devout Catholics, the overwhelming majority of the country's population became Protestants. This was possible in Hungary because a very large number of clergy could be presented to livings independently of the king. Every landlord and every autonomous body, including the free towns as well as the market-towns endowed with this right by the local landowner, could appoint a parish priest and be the judge of his suitability.

Initially the German and Hungarian towns employed Protestant clergymen but later the magnates and nobles generally followed their example. This was not only because their maintenance and religious ceremonies were less expensive but because they convinced congregations with their arguments. Another factor was that a fair number of Franciscans—members of the most popular religious order—had supported the Reformation and had converted their adherents as well. Mátyás Dévai Biró, the first Hungarian reformer (the "Hungarian Luther") was originally a Franciscan, as were András Szkhárosi Horvát and Mihály Sztárai, outstanding poets and preachers who took the part of the serfs. Other former Franciscans were István Kopácsi, the founder of Sárospatak College, and probably even István Szegedi Kis, the pioneering and internationally-acclaimed Calvinist theologian. Calvinism first established itself in the market-towns of eastern Hungary and from these early centres gradually spread through the whole of the *Tiszántúl*. The most popular Calvinist leader, Péter Melius Juhász, bishop of Debrecen, conducted heated theological debates in the 1560s with Ferenc Dávid of Kolozsvár. Dávid advocated Unitarian ideas and was the protégé of John Sigismund.

The Calvinists were saved by István Báthori, who oppressed the Unitarians but who simultaneously called in the Jesuits, thereby initiating the Catholic Counter-Reformation. At his court Báthori provided conditions conductive to a second flowering of humanism in Hungary. In addition to the historians Ferenc Forgách and Pál Gyulai, the political philosopher Farkas Kovacsóczi and Bálint Balassi—the greatest Hungarian poet of the century—all lived at Báthori's court for a time.

Bocskai and the Heyducks' war of independence

One of the causes of Hungary's misfortunes in this period was that, owing to an absence of the necessary economic and political preconditions, the country was without a standing mercenary army. King Matthias's "Black Army" had not inspired the establishment of a similarly effective professional force and the lack of a "field army", specially trained for open battle, was certainly a handicap. To create one would have cost a great deal of money and the Hungarian magnates preferred to direct resources to their own private armies, which they stationed in their fortresses. For the Habsburg emperors western Hungary served as a useful buffer zone which shielded Vienna and they, too, therefore concentrated on strengthening their castles. Without a field army it was impossible for Hungary to drive out the Turkish invader, and this had become obvious. The Habsburgs maintained their hold on Transylvania by employing a ruthless reign of terror but the central part of the country was still occupied by the Turks. Initially, in the early years of the seventeenth century, the Habsburg military leadership wished to suppress the Hungarian Heyducks, whom it regarded as a dangerous element, although later it tried to recruit an inexpensive army from them. A few thousand Heyducks were actually provided with firearms, the intention being to send them against the Turks.

(The Heyducks were peasants who had escaped in great numbers from the areas devastated by the Turks or from oppressive conditions on landlords' estates. Either they took service as mercenaries or plundered the countryside for a livelihood. In the wars against the Turks they distinguished themselves by their toughness. The fact that there was no standing mercenary army meant, though, that only some of them could become regular soldiers.)

The purpose of reorganizing the Hungarian field army at this juncture was to create a force for use not only against the Turks, but also Hungarian nobles. Habsburg tyranny in Transylvania and in Royal Hungary engendered opposition which needed to be dealt with. In order to obtain money, the Habsburg dynasty, deeply in debt after the war, initiated inheritance and, later, high treason law suits against big Hungarian landowners. Furthermore, to guarantee the spiritual obedience of a country where Protestants constituted the majority, it forced the Counter-

Reformation on Hungary, which so far had been spared religious strife. In 1604, General Belgiojoso, the captain of Kassa, occupied the town's Lutheran church on behalf of the bishop of Eger and further seizures of churches were also planned. To silence the nobility, a forged Law XXII was appended to the legislation passed in 1604. This prohibited the discussion of religion at the Diet.

By this time discontent was running high in both the lower and the upper strata of Hungarian society. The peasantry, oppressed by both the Turks and the Habsburg forces; the free Heyducks, destined either for extermination or serfdom; the Protestant commoners, burghers and nobles; as well as the big landowners whose property rights were under threat—all regarded the Habsburgs as their principal enemy.

Insurrection was now imminent, and all that was needed was a man to head it. Gábor Bethlen, the young leader of Transylvanian émigrés who had fled into Ottoman territory, chose István Bocskai, the greatest landowner in the *Tiszántúl*. Bocskai had regretted his previous policy of linking the fate of Transylvania to that of the Habsburgs and was now willing to reorganize the Principality of Transylvania with Ottoman help. His activities were, however, discovered and General Belgiojoso set out against him with a large army. Belgiojoso's force included the 5,000 well-armed Heyducks originally intended to constitute the core of a Hungarian field army. Not wishing to kill their own people, these troops joined Bocskai. On October 15, 1604, Bocskai launched a surprise night attack between Álmosd and Diószeg and routed Belgiojoso's German, Walloon and Serbian army—despite the superior strength of the Habsburg general's forces. The panic-stricken Belgiojoso fled to Upper Hungary and Basta's army, which had hastened to Belgiojoso's assistance, was also destroyed in the course of the Heyducks' constant surprise attacks.

Bocskai occupied Transylvania and Royal Hungary but although the Turkish sultan sent him a royal crown, he concluded a peace treaty with the Habsburgs at the request of the Hungarian nobility and satisfied himself with the title of prince of Transylvania. The Treaty of Vienna (1606) guaranteed the right of the Hungarian Diet to enact legislation, confirmed the power of the officials elected by the Diet, and granted freedom of religion to the Protestants. Bocskai settled some 10,000 Heyducks on his own estates, and later Heyduck settlements grew up there. Afterwards the princes of Transylvania and the Hungarian aristocracy established more free Heyduck settlements. The inhabitants of these did not pay tax and did not hold land on feudal terms; their sole duty was to render military service. Bocskai also restored the freedom of the Szeklers and thereby procured a large number of free peasant soldiers for the princes of Transylvania.

However, owing to Bocskai's early death in 1606, neither the final settlement of the Heyducks nor the implementation of the Treaty of Vienna was assured. Emperor Rudolph stubbornly refused to comply with the wishes of the "rebellious" Hungarians, and the Heyducks therefore rose in arms. Intending to elect their own national king, they wished to dethrone the Habsburgs but Archduke Matthias of Habsburg, who had concluded the Treaty of Vienna, and the Hungarian aristocracy persuaded the Heyducks that they should turn against Rudolph instead. With Rudolph forced to abdicate, Matthias was elected king of Hungary as Matthias II. At the Diet of 1608 Matthias put the Treaty of Vienna into effect. Those Heyducks who were not permanently settled joined the young Gábor Báthori and in 1609 helped him to acquire the Transylvanian throne. This was, however, due to him, as Bocskai had intended Bethlen to be his successor.

Despite the political storms of the first decade of the seventeenth century, Hungarian culture was not entirely without outstanding achievement. The greatest poet of the age, János Rimay, lived at Bocskai's court. So did István Szamosközy, the greatest representative of Hungarian humanist historiography; Simon Péchi, the humanist scholar who organized the Sabbatarian sect; and the Calvinist minister at Kassa, Péter Alvinczi, who worded Bocskai's proclamations and who took issue with the Counter-Reformation. It was at this time that the Jesuit Péter Pázmány began his career as a writer. Pázmány subsequently became archbishop of Esztergom and converted the greater part of the Hungarian aristocracy to Catholicism. It was also during this period that Albert Szenczi Molnár, Bocskai's foreign propagandist and the compiler of the first Hungarian grammar and dictionary, worked as a linguist and translator.

Gábor Bethlen's efforts to unify Hungary

Gábor Bethlen was a worthy successor to István Bocskai and strove to continue the latter's work. On Bethlen's banner God's protective arm, holding a sword, stretches out to help the prince. Bethlen certainly needed divine assistance to achieve his highly important goal: the unification of tripartite Hungary under his own rule, and the re-establishment thereby of a national kingdom.

Bethlen became prince of Transylvania in 1613 and intervened in the Thirty Years War six years later, taking the side of the Bohemians who had rebelled against Emperor Ferdinand II's Counter-Reformation. Since 1608 Transylvania had been in alliance not only with the Bohemians, but with the Moravian, Silesian and Austrian nobility as well. On behalf of the Hungarian Estates, Protestant magnates now invited Bethlen to support and lead their war of independence against the Habsburgs. Together with his allies, Bethlen besieged Vienna, although a counter-attack forced him to withdraw temporarily. In 1620 Bethlen again occupied Royal Hungary and on August 25 the Diet of Besztercebánya elected him king of Hungary. Bethlen wisely postponed the coronation ceremony to await the final outcome of the war. Unfortunately on November 8, 1620 the Bohemians suffered a decisive defeat at the Battle of the White Mountain; Frederick, the king of Bohemia, died in exile and Ferdinand II stripped the country of its autonomy. The leaders of the Bohemian uprising were executed and shortly afterwards the Moravian, Silesian and Austrian Estates also capitulated.

These dramatic events naturally caused some panic in Hungary but Bethlen kept this well under control. In Europe Bethlen alone dared to continue the struggle against the Habsburgs, thereby gaining time for the forces of Protestantism to reorganize. Although, by the Treaty of Nikolsburg, Bethlen succeeded only in ensuring autonomy for the Hungarian Estates, together with freedom of religion, he soon had the opportunity to enter into alliance with the Protestant powers of Western Europe. In 1623, in consort with the German Protestants, he launched a new offensive against the Habsburgs. Three years later, in 1626, another campaign followed in support of the English-Dutch-Danish alliance. However, the abandonment of Bethlen's cause by Hungarian magnates frightened by the events in Bohemia frustrated his plans. All Bethlen finally achieved was the annexation to Transylvania of seven counties of Upper Hungary.

Nevertheless Bethlen won international recognition for his state. Two of the most famous imperial generals, Dampierre and Buquoy, died in battle against him and a third, Wallenstein, retreated from him. During Bethlen's lifetime the enemy never once reached Transylvanian soil. Bethlen led his army of Heyducks and Szeklers in person and no one defeated him in the field. The international renown of the Hungarian hussar dates back to Bethlen's time. The prince was a politician with an excellent sense of diplomacy; it was he who initiated and organized the anti-Habsburg European coalitions. For the most part Bethlen acted independently of the Turks—indeed, he often exploited them for his own purposes.

At home, Bethlen was the first Hungarian ruler since Matthias Hunyadi to succeed in establishing centralized rule in accordance with the principles of modern absolutism. In his economic policy he followed the principles of mercantilism, which were then current. Although he could not abolish the institution of perpetual serfdom that had spread throughout Eastern Europe, Bethlen tried to protect the serfs from the excesses of the landowners and made it possible for the sons of serfs to attend school. Two decades before Pázmány he founded a college at Nagyszombat, from where he moved it first to Kassa, then to Kolozsvár, and finally to Gyulafehérvár. After Bethlen's death this famous school settled permanently at Nagyenyed.

Although it was in support of his own Calvinist faith that he founded a college, printing press, and library, by the standards of the time Bethlen was extraordinarily tolerant in matters of religion. He recalled the Jesuits—previously expelled from Transylvania—and gave financial support for a translation of the Bible by the Jesuit György Káldi. Bethlen allowed the Catholics of Transylvania to keep a religious administrator and the Orthodox Romanians were permitted to have their own bishop. Romanian priests were exempted from feudal obligations and Jews in Transylvania no longer had to wear a yellow star. Bethlen even settled a group of Anabaptists, then persecuted everywhere, in Transylvania.

Bethlen's contemporaries recall primarily his splendid court and magnificent construction projects. Accounts written at the time have survived to relate the exceptional beauty of Bethlen's palace at Gyulafehérvár. This matched the Baroque royal palaces of the age not only in decor, but also in the cultural life carried on there. The quality of music was especially high at Bethlen's court and Italian opera, a novelty of the age, also flourished within its walls.

Bethlen's loyal associate and subsequent successor János Kemény mourned the prince with the following words: "He should either not have been born at all, or he should have lived for ever."

The fortunes and misfortunes of the two Rákóczis

Gábor Bethlen secured for Transylvania peaceful affluence at home and international renown abroad. Such was the state of affairs when György Rákóczi I was elected prince of Transylvania in 1630, thus ending a brief power struggle which resulted in the ousting of Bethlen's widow, Catherine of Brandenburg, and afterwards of Bethlen's younger brother, István. Rákóczi owed his succession largely to the Heyducks who, after Bethlen's death, once again found themselves under Habsburg rule. The Heyducks were justly afraid that Palatine Miklós Esterházy, the Habsburg's main representative in Hungary, would curtail the liberties Bocskai had bestowed on them. Accordingly, the Heyducks took up arms against the Habsburg mercenaries sent out to subjugate them.

István Bethlen, the captain of Várad, and Dávid Zólyomi, the captain-general of Transylvania, gave military help to the Heyducks and in 1631 routed Esterházy's army at Rakamaz. The Transylvanian throne was then offered to György Rákóczi, the richest Calvinist magnate of eastern Hungary. The hope clearly was that he would keep the seven counties of Upper Hungary which Bethlen had acquired but which should have been returned to the Habsburgs on his death. Indeed, retaining these counties served Rákóczi's own interests since large family estates, with Sárospatak as their centre, were located not far away.

Rákóczi was, however, a cautious man. With the help of the Heyducks he had himself elected prince of Transylvania, but ceded the seven counties to Royal Hungary. In return for this he secured confirmation of the rights of the Heyducks. Rákóczi thereby retained the support of the Heyducks but was at the same time able to conclude peace with a Habsburg monarch who, deeply preoccupied by the complicated situation produced by the Thirty Years' War in Germany, did not wish to fight on two fronts. Esterházy was embittered by these developments as his most fervent wish had been to annex Transylvania to Royal Hungary. However, Esterházy's hopes were dashed not only as a result of Ferdinand II's displeasure and that of the moderate Archbishop Pázmány. Also important was the peasant uprising which broke out in 1631. This was led by Péter Császár and was caused by looting on the part of mercenary troops recruited for the occupation of Transylvania. Esterházy had to suffer the additional humiliation of seeing the insurrection suppressed not by his own slack mercenary commanders but by Rákóczi's Transylvanian troops.

An even greater threat loomed over Rákóczi in 1636. Gábor Bethlen's younger brother, István, who had since regretted renouncing the throne, was given a promise by the Turks that they would install him as Transylvania's ruler. Rákóczi was unperturbed and called the people to arms. At Nagyszalonta his Heyducks routed the Turkish army. The sultan was forced by a Persian attack and a Janissary rebellion to accept this defeat and to recognize Rákóczi's authority.

Having consolidated his position, Rákóczi could now think of continuing Gábor Bethlen's policy of intervention against the Habsburgs in the Thirty Years' War. The opportunity arose when Protestant Swedish troops advanced so far as almost to threaten Vienna. In 1643 Rákóczi entered into alliance with Sweden and in 1644 launched a campaign to occupy Royal Hungary. He was not, however, a particularly able general and his commanders lacked real talent. Accordingly, imperial mercenaries and Esterházy's Hungarian troops were able to drive him back as far as Kassa. Here the fortunes of war turned; the Transylvanian army not only occupied Royal Hungary, but in 1645 also invaded Moravia. Outside Brno Rákóczi linked up with Lennart Torstenson, the Swedish military commander. But the sultan was jealous of the prince's feats and ordered him home. Rákóczi was therefore obliged to sign the Treaty of Linz with Ferdinand III. This treaty confirmed the re-annexation of the seven counties won by Bethlen and extended freedom to practise Protestantism to the peasants as well.

Although György Rákóczi I lacked Bethlen's conspicuous talents as a politician and military commander, he skilfully and steadfastly followed the course set by his great predecessor. Rákóczi did not keep a splendid court, but economized and increased his family's wealth, although he, too, spent a great deal on schools and printing presses. He could do this primarily because his two principal enemies, the Habsburgs and the Turks, were occupied elsewhere. Rákóczi therefore had a free hand not only in the internal affairs of Transylvania, but also to some extent in foreign policy.

György Rákóczi II succeeded his father as prince of Transylvania in 1648. The younger Rákóczi inherited his father's throne and vast wealth, but not his luck, despite the fact that at this time the leading politicians of Royal Hungary were his friends rather than his enemies. At this very moment the Treaty of Westphalia concluded the Thirty Years' War and the Habsburgs could now turn their attention to Hungary, where their aim was to introduce an absolutist regime on the Austrian model. Also at this time, the reform policies sponsored by the grand viziers of the Köprülü dynasty halted the decline of the Ottoman empire. Now threatened from two quarters, the magnates of Royal Hungary looked to Transylvania for help. The anti-Habsburg faction led by Palatine Pál Pálffy and Miklós Zrínyi, the *bán* (viceroy) of Croatia, intended to make György Rákóczi II king of Hungary, but because of the loyal clergy's influence, after the death of Ferdinand III the Diet elected Leopold I (1657–1705)—Ferenc Wesselényi having become the new palatine two years earlier.

György Rákóczi II did not pay sufficient attention to the change in Transylvania's international position and soon became involved in an ill-considered political game. Rákóczi occupied the two Romanian voivodates (a move which had been the ruin of Gábor Báthori) and in 1657 he set out to procure the crown of Poland, offered him by certain Polish magnates. The Swedes encouraged this venture but Rákóczi had neglected to obtain permission from his patron, the sultan. The Porte now sent the Tatars against Rákóczi and on Polish soil these troops took almost the whole of Rákóczi's army prisoner. Although Rákóczi himself fled home with a few supporters, the sultan stripped him of his title and forced Transylvania to elect a new prince. Requesting help from the Habsburgs, Rákóczi tried to put up armed resistance. Vienna not only failed to respond—despite pressure from even the Zrínyis —but even showed spiteful pleasure in watching the demise of Transylvania, the bastion of Hungarian independence. As early as 1658 Ottoman troops sacked Gyulafehérvár and devastated the surrounding countryside. On May 22, 1660, Rákóczi clashed with the Turks at Szászfenes, outside Kolozsvár, where he was defeated and mortally wounded. In August that year Várad, the principality's most important frontier fortress, fell into Turkish hands. Having lost part of its territory and having suffered economic ruin, Transylvania lost its international standing and ceased to be the defender of Hungarian national independence.

Perpetual serfdom and hereditary aristocracy in the period of the Turkish occupation

The seventeenth century was a period of Hungarian independence struggles, although liberty did not flourish for everybody. At the time when the Hungarian magnates and nobles were defending their privileges and autonomy against Habsburg tyranny, and when the upper classes generally were making a tremendous and popular effort to halt Ottoman expansionism, the peasantry in Hungary was going through the gravest trials of its history. Hungarian town and village dwellers were plundered by the Turks and by Habsburg mercenaries, but still had to contend with their own landlords' exactions. By the seventeenth century a system of "perpetual serfdom" had emerged. Under this the peasants, who previously had been free to move and able to render their services in either produce or money, became bound to their landlords and, through them, to the land. In addition, they were forced to perform labour on the landlord's own farm, the so-called *major* (manor).

This was not a specifically Hungarian development, and not everybody approved of it. Firstly in Poland and later throughout the whole of Eastern Europe, this was how landowners tried to procure grain for export. The demand for grain was increasing in Western Europe and they could use their earnings in this trade to buy Western luxuries. In Hungary, the situation was slightly better than in the neighbouring countries. Owing to transportation difficulties, grain was not taken abroad and it was in land cultivation that labour service was most extensively utilized. Beef-cattle and wine were difficult to produce and needed high-quality work. Since the landowners did not hire wage-labourers, viticulture and cattle breeding were left to the comfortably-off peasants and citizens of the market-towns. This was how Debrecen, Tokaj, and the other market-towns became prosperous. The inhabitants of these settlements did not have to render labour service, but paid their dues in money.

Even those suffering from feudal tyranny had a protector: the Reformation. This advocated not only liberty of conscience, but social justice as well. From the very beginning Protestant preachers, who largely came from a peasant background, denounced the tyranny of the landlords, and the Hungarian Calvinist Puritans—János Tolnai Dali, Pál Medgyesi, János Apáczai Csere and György Martonfalvi Tóth—were influenced by the English Revolution and condemned the entire serf system. Their opinion was summed up at the end of the seventeenth century by Pál Lisznyai Kovács of Debrecen. In his *Magyar Krónika* (Hungarian Chronicle), Lisznyai writes as follows: "Certainly, that which the Hungarians have learned from the neighbouring Poles, namely that one nation should thus afflict other people of the same nation, that a Hungarian should do the same to a Hungarian, that he should afflict a Christian member of that same Christian religion, is against God, is against the Scriptures, and is against the law of every learned and Christian republic in this world. Indeed, to do this is sufficient for God to make you, too, the serf of another nation."

This warning was addressed to the Hungarian magnates and nobles, over whom loomed the very real threat of being made serfs of the Habsburgs. This dynasty was then preparing to reconquer the country from the Turks. The danger to the Hungarian upper classes existed in spite of the fact that they conducted a hard fight, both at home and abroad, for the retention of their privileges. Their struggle during this period also served the defence of Hungarian national autonomy.

The Hungarian nobility was rather large, and accounted for 4–5 per cent of the population of the country. (At this time some four million people lived in the territories of Royal Hungary and Transylvania.) The vast majority of nobles were, however, members of the lower nobility who farmed their own land, had only a few cottars, and who were no better off than a free Heyduck or market-town citizen. Two hundred wealthy families and two thousand comfortably-off ones owned the greater part of the land and possessed most of the political power. In Royal Hungary rich magnates owned *latifundia* comprising hundreds of villages and thousands of serfs. Private armies were not unknown. There were a few pre-Mohács aristocratic families (the Báthoris, Zrínyis, Csákys, Bánffys, Thurzós, Erdődys, Homonnais, etc.) but most aristocrats had risen on the social ladder through service to the Habsburgs (for example, the Nádasdys, the Batthyánys, the Illésházys, the Pálffys, the Esterházys and the Rákóczis). From those nobles who served them, the Habsburgs created a closed order. While in the Middle Ages wealth and office raised certain magnates to the leading stratum, Ferdinand I created a "hereditary aristocracy". In certain families sons enjoyed the hereditary titles of baron, count, and, in exceptional cases, prince. Members of this hereditary aristocracy came to comprise the upper house of the Diet and established their right to high positions in the state.

Since the royal court was constantly abroad, a significant centre of national culture could only emerge at the Gyulafehérvár court of the princes of Transylvania. In Royal Hungary this cultural function was performed by the castles of the magnates. Built in the Renaissance style, these castles housed not only the master and his family, but also young noblemen and noblewomen who wished to learn court manners. Also present were soldiers for the defence of the castle as well as numerous domestic servants. Vast numbers of people from all over the country gathered in the castles to attend christenings, weddings, and funerals and in this way the castles served to mould political and aesthetic views.

In short, Hungary under Ottoman rule was a country of extremes where the "perpetual serf" and the "perpetual aristocrat" were separated by a whole world. Yet it was at around this time that danger from outside began to forge a nation out of those living in the country.

Culture in the "Century of Hungarian Decline"

From János Rimay to Miklós Zrínyi, all Hungarian poets—and even the majority of Hungarian politicians, philosophers and preachers—describe the seventeenth century as the "Century of Hungarian Decline". The failure of military endeavours to expel the Turks, the sharpening of religious conflicts, and the fear of being crushed completely between the Habsburgs and the Turks did nothing to inspire confidence in the future. Also, the depression which affected the entire world economy in the form of inflation and marketing difficulties added to the anxiety. Contemporaries were even more concerned about the fate of the country when they realized exactly how far Hungary lagged behind the developing states of Western Europe. They acknowledged the superiority of material and intellectual culture in Italy, Germany, Holland and England. However, their despair was overcome by the hope that Hungary's ills could be remedied. Through the concentration of resources, through learning, and through work they believed that the decline could be halted and Hungarian culture could again be raised to European levels.

The awakeners of Hungarian national consciousness rediscovered Gábor Bethlen's initiatives. During Bethlen's time, the overwhelming majority of educated Hungarians worked as clergymen: doctors, engineers, artists, and musicians had to be recruited abroad. Bethlen's objective was to create a secular Hungarian intelligentsia. He hoped to do this in two ways. The first was by sending students to foreign universitites where they would learn not only theology, but philosophy, law and architecture as well. The second was by founding a Hungarian college, printing press, and library at Gyulafehérvár. Bethlen invited to his capital the German scholars of the age, including Professor Alsted. The latter was a versatile intellectual who advocated the necessity of practical culture and compiled a Latin-language encyclopaedia to prove it.

Bethlen forebade landowners to prevent the sons of serfs from attending school. In this way knowledge became a means of rising socially. In 1629, Bethlen ennobled those clergymen of serf origin who had qualified for the Church through their erudition. The phrase "to fight with knowledge and arms" in the letter-patent of nobility granted to these clergymen signified that the sons of the recipients would not become serfs if they chose to follow their fathers' profession—or even some secular career.

Gradually Bethlen's guidance began to produce results—primarily in the development of school education. The first Hungarian college was founded in 1629 at Gyulafehérvár and was the predecessor of the famous Calvinist Bethlen College which eventually moved to Nagyenyed. The Gyulafehérvár college produced a whole host of outstanding scholars of the calibre of János Apáczai Csere who, following in the footsteps of his master, Alsted, published the *Magyar Encyclopaedia* (Hungarian Encyclopaedia)—written in Hungarian instead of Latin. This was a synthesis based on contemporary scholarship and came out in Utrecht, Holland, in 1653. Hungarian Catholicism followed suit: in 1635 Péter Pázmány founded a university in Nagyszombat, and this was the ancestor of Budapest's present-day university of arts and sciences. Pázmány's university had a faculty of philosophy and a faculty of law, in addition to a faculty of theology. One of the greatest educators of all time, the Bohemian Jan Amos Comenius, became head of Sárospatak's Calvinist College at the invitation of Zsuzsanna Lórántffy, György Rákóczi's widow. During his four years at Sárospatak, Comenius raised teaching standards to university level. In addition, he also wrote numerous textbooks, among them *Orbis Sensualium Pictus*, in which he described the world of perceptible things. The book was the first to bring visual presentation into teaching and brought the sciences onto a par with the humanities, which had previously enjoyed a privileged status.

Apáczai was the first man in Hungary to spread the teachings of Copernicus and Descartes—the pioneers of modern natural science. He also advocated the ideas of Althusius, the founder of the modern theory of the state and the scholar who advocated the principle of popular sovereignty. Althusius praised the English Revolution which had toppled feudalism, thereby paving the way for the spread of liberal ideas. As for the second part of Bethlen's maxim, which related to fighting with arms, a splendid example was to be found in Miklós Zrínyi who, incidentally, was also a poet.

The works of Apáczai and Zrínyi marked the zenith of mid-seventeenth-century Hungarian culture. Just one generation earlier, religious works such as Péter Pázmány's *Isteni igazságra vezérlő kalauz* (A Guide Towards Divine Justice, 1613) and Albert Szenczi Molnár's psalm translations (1607) had been the most influential Hungarian literary works. Apáczai's encyclopaedia and Zrínyi's epic poems were, however, secular in both subject and purpose. Through them the seed sown by Gábor Bethlen began to bear fruit.

While at the beginning of the century the struggle between the Reformation and the Counter-Reformation tied down the nation's forces, by the 1650s a fight was under way for the very survival of the Hungarian people. Culture also served this struggle. Its representatives were imbued with the determination to hold their ground in spite of all difficulties, and with feelings of patriotism and self-sacrifice. The relatives of Apáczai's Dutch wife tried to dissuade him from returning home from Holland, but to no avail. Although in Hungary he was misunderstood and persecuted, Apáczai persevered, exerting himself so-much that he died of overwork at the age of thirty-four. Zrínyi lashed out sarcastically at the Hungarian nobility, saying that if nobles did not wish to do their duty and defend their country, they should emigrate to Brazil. However, Zrínyi only intended to castigate and to warn. "Our noble liberty is nowhere else than in Pannonia," wrote Zrínyi in 1661 in his famous pamphlet *Az török áfium ellen való orvosság* (Remedy Against the Turkish Opium).

The Reunification of Hungary within the Habsburg Empire

"Arms, arms are required, and heroic determination"

The fall of Várad in 1660 sealed the fate of Transylvania. The fertile Bihar areas which the castle had earlier protected now came under Ottoman occupation, and the same applied to the region stretching northwards to Debrecen. The Porte made Mihály Apafi ruler of a diminished and devastated principality: after a few glorious decades, Transylvania lost its political significance.

The situation was no better in Royal Hungary. The Habsburgs were still absorbed by their policies elsewhere in Europe and, accordingly, steered clear of any actions which might provoke the Turks. Although the imperial army lined up for the defence of Vienna every time an Ottoman campaign was launched, it did not intervene in the sieges of Hungarian fortresses.

In the midst of all the vulnerability, devastation, and hopelessness, Count Miklós Zrínyi, the greatest Hungarian statesman of the period, rose to eminence. His family was of Croatian origin and it was in the course of the constant struggle with the Turks that the first Zrínyis had moved from the Adriatic region to the *Muraköz* and to Transdanubia, where they became magyarized. Miklós Zrínyi himself had seen battle at a very early age and was not only a brave soldier but later an excellent military commander also.

Zrínyi made the expulsion of the Turks from Hungary the aim of his life's work. He realized that the Ottoman empire, once feared by all, was no longer its old self. "Certainly, if there existed a strong and mailed fist, now would be the time to unbalance the Turks," he wrote. However, Zrínyi was also well aware that the Hungarians should conduct this struggle on their own. Hungary would lose its independence if the Habsburgs led the war to expel the Turks.

To shake up an exhausted and apathetic nobility, in 1651 Zrínyi wrote his great epic poem *Szigeti veszedelem* (Peril at Sziget). In this he celebrated his great-grandfather's heroic death, which occurred in 1566. In a number of treatises, Zrínyi expounded his ideas on military organization and on strategy. Meanwhile he proved his bravery and talent as a general in endless frontier clashes.

Zrínyi was not yet thirty when he became *bán* of Croatia. However, the establishment of a national army and the launching of a military campaign required national, not local, authority. Accordingly, at the 1655 Diet Zrínyi made a bid for the office of palatine in which he enjoyed the enthusiastic support of the nobility. However, the Habsburg Ferdinand III did not appoint Zrínyi. It became increasingly clear that Vienna did not support the plans he entertained.

Zrínyi was now convinced that the Habsburgs not only disapproved of the expulsion of the Turks, but were in fact also obstructing it. In 1656 he wrote a meditation on the life of King Matthias, in which he, the son of a family that had been loyal to the Habsburgs for generations, advocated the idea of a national kingdom. György Rákóczi II was the candidate Zrínyi favoured for the Hungarian throne but the fall of Transylvania meant that such a scheme was no longer realistic.

Zrínyi did not give up. He had a fortress (New Zrínyi Castle) built for defence of the *Muraköz* and the southwestern parts of Transdanubia. He did this in defiance of Vienna, which feared that the construction of the new castle would serve as an excuse for the Turks to launch a new attack into Habsburg territory. In 1661 Zrínyi wrote his most influential work, *Az török áfium ellen való orvosság* (Remedy Against the Turkish Opium). The pamphlet was a desperate cry, a warning, and a determined call to arms: "See, I am calling, see, I am shouting, hear me, Hungarians! Here is the danger, here the consuming fire... We, the descendants of the glorious Magyar race, must go to our deaths if need be for our wives, our children, and our country."

In 1663 the Turks launched another major offensive. The Viennese Court was widely expected to appoint Zrínyi overall commander, but this did not happen. It was only after Érsekújvár, the key to the western part of Upper Hungary, had fallen that he was briefly appointed to this position. In hard-fought battles Zrínyi defended the *Csallóköz*, afterwards launching a famous winter campaign during which he advanced along the river Drava as far as Eszék. Here he burned the military bridge built by Sultan Mohammed IV, thus cutting off Turkish supplies for months. Zrínyi wished to use this time to recapture Kanizsa Castle, but Vienna, which wanted peace at all costs, prevented him from doing so.

In 1664 the Court appointed Count Raimondo Montecuccoli to Zrínyi's command with instructions that he should only intervene if the Turkish advance actually threatened the Habsburg capital. Montecuccoli therefore stood idly by as Ottoman troops captured New Zrínyi Castle, which was unable to defend itself without help. When, however, the grand vizier turned his army in the direction of Vienna, Montecuccoli blocked his path at Szentgotthárd. In the battle which followed the Ottoman army was driven into the Rába marshes and its remnants forced to flee. Montecuccoli's victory was total.

However, the Habsburg commander did not pursue the defeated enemy and a few weeks later the Viennese Court concluded the Treaty of Vasvár with the Turks. It was as though the latter had won the Szentgotthárd battle. The treaty acknowledged Ottoman possession of many parts of Hungary, among them Várad, Érsekújvár and New Zrínyi Castle. Nationwide indignation and bitterness compelled Zrínyi to seek contact with Louis XIV of France, an enemy of the Habsburgs. Later the same year, however, the Hungarian commander was dead. While out hunting, Zrínyi was killed by a wild boar.

In this way the statesman, poet, and military commander Miklós Zrínyi met his end. Contemporaries were reluctant to believe that he was the victim of a hunting accident and there were rumours that the Court in Vienna had hired assassins to murder him.

"Zrínyi's blood has inundated Vienna..."

As we have seen, the Treaty of Vasvár in 1664 caused profound shock across the whole of Hungary. It became obvious that Vienna was willing to sacrifice Hungary's interests if by doing so it could stem the Ottoman advance and thereby win a free hand for its policies in Western Europe. Soldiers in the frontier fortresses were given strict instructions not to respond to Turkish provocation and not to retaliate for the forays of the Ottoman garrisons. After the fall of Várad, Kanizsa and Érsekújvár, no part of the country could feel safe from the plundering Ottoman troops.

The country was utterly helpless and defenceless. During the reign of Mihály Apafi, the principality of Transylvania was but a shadow of its former self, and no assistance could be expected from that quarter. Neighbouring Poland was preoccupied with its own troubles. In this desperate situation even the country's leading dignitaries turned against Vienna and discussed how the country could be saved from total destruction. These prominent figures included Baron Ferenc Wesselényi, palatine of Hungary; György Lippay, the archbishop of Esztergom; Count Ferenc Nádasdy, the lord chief justice; Count Péter Zrínyi (Miklós's younger brother and *bán* of Croatia), and Ferenc Rákóczi I, the elected prince of Transylvania. All were Catholic aristocrats loyal to the king. (Ferenc Rákóczi had been driven from his throne on account of his conversion to Catholicism and on account of his father's policy.) They were also the largest landowners of Transdanubia and Upper Hungary.

Consultations between these distinguished men were soon followed by conspiracy. The aristocratic plotters were planning an armed insurrection and expected external help primarily from the anti-Habsburg powers. They sent a representative to the court of Louis XIV, sought links with the Polish court, and established contact even with the Ottoman government, promising to pay an annual tribute in exchange for the sultan's support. However, the conspirators had neither clear ideas nor concrete plans for the organization of an uprising. Also lacking was a strategy for the more distant future. The plotters considered ambitious schemes to capture Emperor Leopold I, but at the same time did practically nothing to win over the lesser nobility or the peasantry.

After several years of hesitation—during which time Wesselényi and Lippay died—the conspirators decided in 1670 to organize an armed uprising. As leader of this insurrection, Rákóczi summoned the counties of Upper Hungary to arms. The call, though, was not successful. It now became clear that this conspiracy of aristocrats had no backing either at home or abroad. Alarmed by this, Péter Zrínyi and his brother-in-law Ferenc Frangepán hurried to Vienna, where they revealed everything and asked for clemency. The imperial army had no difficulty in suppressing the conspiracy. Nowhere was armed resistance encountered.

The Viennese government believed that it had to make an example of the plotters and therefore put the leading figures on trial. This was done in Vienna where they appeared before a jury made up of foreigners. On the basis of alien legislation, the conspirators were sentenced to death and their property confiscated. In 1671 Zrínyi and Frangepán were beheaded in Wiener Neustadt. Nádasdy was beheaded in Vienna, and Mária Széchy (the "Venus of Murány" and widow of the late palatine) was stripped of her property and locked up in a convent. In case the lesser nobility should think that only aristocrats would be punished, Ferenc Bónis, a lesser noble, was also beheaded. Ferenc Rákóczi's life was spared—but only in return for the huge ransom of 400,000 florins. In Rákóczi's case, allowances were also made for the merits of his mother, Zsófia Báthori. She was a devout Catholic who had always given extensive help to the Jesuits.

The aristocratic conspiracy provided a good pretext for Vienna to implement its old plan of finally putting an end to Hungary's autonomy. Employing the argument that the country had now forfeited all its rights, the Court suspended the Hungarian constitution. In 1673, Caspar Ampringen, the Grand Master of the Teutonic Order, was appointed governor of Hungary. Hundreds of nobles were put on trial charged with conspiracy and, although most were eventually released owing to lack of evidence, their property was declared forfeit. Some two-thirds of the native-born soldiers stationed in the Hungarian border fortresses were dismissed without pay and replaced by foreign mercenaries.

The country became the "outpost of the Germans" and the reign of terror instituted by the foreign soldiery defies description. Unprecedented taxes were levied on the peasantry which, in addition, had to provide for the soldiers' keep. The open persecution of Protestants, who were now deemed rebellious, also began. Armed force was used to take away their churches and schools. Calvinist and Lutheran municipal councils were driven out. In 1674 several hundred Protestant preachers were brought before a summary court charged with collaboration with the Turks and with conspiracy against the emperor. Those who refused to be converted to the Catholic faith or to leave the country were sentenced to death. The executions were not, however, carried out. Instead, forty-two of the preachers were driven on foot to the coast and sold as galley-slaves in Naples.

Brutal oppression and persecution obliged huge numbers of people to flee. Nobles, former garrison soldiers, town burghers, and peasants chose to go into hiding in their tens of thousands, escaping eastwards to the Transylvanian border. There they were safer from alien power.

"Forward, *kuruc*, forward!"

The origin of the word *kuruc* goes back to the crusades against the Turks, and derives from the Latin *cruciatus*. During Dózsa's peasant uprising, the name became associated with the anti-feudal peasant wars, and was used in that sense throughout the second half of the seventeenth century... In due course a new nickname was applied to the pro-Habsburg party, the opponents of the *kuruc*. This was *labanc*, deriving perhaps from the German *Landsknecht*. The fugitives gathering along the Transylvanian frontier soon began to form an army. In this they were supported by Mihály Apafi, the prince of Transylvania, who sent Mihály Teleki, the captain of Kővár, to organize them. They attacked the imperial troops on several occasions, but did not accomplish very much.

The situation changed when the nineteen year-old Count Imre Thököly became leader of these refugees. The scion of a large landowning aristocratic family from Upper Hungary, Thököly was fourteen when, in 1671, the imperial forces besieged the castle of Árva, their purpose being to capture Thököly's father, who had participated in the Wesselényi conspiracy. The elderly István Thököly died during the siege, but his son, Imre, managed to escape to Transylvania. From this time onwards, he was driven by the desire to avenge the injuries done to his family and to his nation. Thököly's passionate make-up was coupled with outstanding military and diplomatic talents. He had a way with people and was a born commander.

In 1678, the *kuruc* army went on the offensive and in a few months drove the imperial troops (the *labanc*) out of northeast Hungary. The population received the *kuruc* army as liberators and joined up by the thousand. In addition to the nobles and former frontier castle soldiers, the burghers of the mining towns also joined the uprising. In less than two years, the *kuruc* troops occupied the whole of Upper Hungary.

Elected commander-in-chief of his army in Hajdúszoboszló at the beginning of 1680, Thököly possessed practically unlimited power. His authority rested on the *kuruc* soldiers, among whom he tried to maintain strict discipline. He did not always succeed in this and from the beginning there were many complaints against abuses committed by the troops. Marriage with Ilona Zrínyi, the widow of Ferenc Rákóczi, meant for Thököly a significant increase in strength, since through this alliance Thököly was able to make the Rákóczi estates serve the uprising. Thököly maintained good relations with the Ottomans and, at the zenith of his success in 1682, he was appointed king of Hungary by the sultan. Thököly, however, rejected kingly status, taking only the title "Prince of Upper Hungary". Thököly was, in any event, more inclined to value links with France than links with the Turks. King Louis XIV of France, who opposed the Habsburgs, gladly supported the insurrection.

The Viennese government was finally forced to retreat. In 1681 the Diet, meeting in Sopron, restored the country's constitution (Count Pál Esterházy was elected palatine), and the freedom of the Protestant religion was permitted within certain limits. Vienna sought peace with Thököly as well, promising a complete change in its policy towards Hungary.

Nevertheless, Thököly and his followers did not trust the Habsburgs, doubting —not without reason—the sincerity of their promises. In any case, Vienna's concessions were not considered satisfactory. Thököly thought that only the creation of an independent national state could resolve the problem and therefore continued the struggle. Since he was too weak to do this by himself, and as he could not count on the French, who had come to terms with the emperor, Thököly overestimated Turkish strength, as did almost everyone in contemporary Europe.

In 1683, Grand Vizier Kara Mustapha marched against Vienna at the head of a huge army. Thököly thought that in the event of Ottoman victory, which he felt was almost certain, he would be given the entire territory of the kingdom of Hungary. Thököly would then organize a vassal, albeit national, state along Transylvanian lines. However, Vienna was successfully defended by the Polish king John Sobieski, assisted by the armies of the German empire. The attacking forces fled and the Ottomans suffered a decisive defeat. Recognizing the growing weakness of the sultan, Vienna changed its policy: Emperor Leopold I now decided to expel the Turks from Hungary.

Pope Innocent XI established the Holy League directed against the Turks. This was an alliance of the Habsburg empire, Poland, and Venice. In 1684 *labanc* armies launched their campaign in Hungary and swept away Thököly's power, which rested on Ottoman support. Ahmed, the pasha of Várad, hoped to buy peace by handing Thököly over to the Habsburgs and managed to capture him. Thököly soon regained his freedom, though, but his support and principality in Upper Hungary were gone for good. Seeing that the Ottomans were unreliable allies, the multinational *kuruc* forces went over to the imperial armies, and, realizing that they had a good chance against the Turks, offered their services in the liberation of their homeland. The Court denied Thököly the opportunity to take part in this great venture and, with only a few hundred followers, he therefore remained in the Ottoman camp. Thököly was eventually compelled to leave Hungary along with the Turkish troops. By 1685, *kuruc* power was confined to the castle of Munkács, which Ilona Zrínyi defended against the imperial troops for three years.

After two months of bloody siege, Buda Castle was also liberated from the Turks in September 1686. Two years later, the Christian army occupied Belgrade. On the death of Mihály Apafi in 1690, Thököly advanced into Transylvania with an Ottoman and Tatar army and, following a victory at Zernyest, had himself elected prince. A few weeks later, however, imperial troops forced him to leave the country forever.

After a few more years of fighting, in 1697 Prince Eugene of Savoy won a splendid victory at Zenta. This sealed the fate of Turkish rule in Hungary. In 1699 the Treaty of Karlowitz was signed. After 150 years of subjugation, Hungary, with the exception of the *Temesköz* area, was finally free from Ottoman dominion.

"I would like our nation not to remain in ignorance"

From the mid-seventeenth century onwards, baroque culture became predominant in Hungary. Establishing close contact everywhere with the Counter-Reformation, this cultural and artistic trend was propagated primarily by the Jesuits. In Hungary, baroque culture became inseparable from the strengthening of ecclesiastical and secular authority, along with the reinforcement of an unchanging feudal society. At the same time, the lack of a Hungarian royal court was felt throughout the period. This would have encouraged cultural aspirations and would have steered them in a uniform direction. Individual aristocratic families had courts of their own (the Nádasdys at Sárvár, for example, and the Batthyánys at Németújvár) but the influence of these was confined to certain parts of the country. What is more, these separate centres divided national culture rather than unified it.

The new ideals, which originated in the Renaissance, first received expression in architecture. Everywhere Catholic churches were built in the baroque style and the palaces of the aristocracy soon bore marks of the new fashion. Of the latter the Esterházys' home at Kismarton (Eisenstadt) was the largest and most splendid. Simplicity was everywhere replaced by rich ornamentation, which often seemed both ostentatious and extravagant. Interior walls were adorned with frescoes (in the castle of Sárvár murals depicting the struggles between Turks and Hungarians can still be seen). Ornamental objects of silver and gold were placed on strongly-coloured pieces of furniture and at the large windows curtains of Venetian brocade were hung. The late Renaissance style lingered on in Transylvania, its best example being Miklós Bethlen's palace at Bethlenszentmiklós.

The first significant art collections also came into existence at this time. The silver, gold, and jewel collection of Ferenc Nádasdy, the lord chief justice beheaded in 1671, was important even by Central European standards. As for Nádasdy's library, this was so comprehensive that the imperial library in Vienna took from it 459 volumes missing from its own collection. It was during this period that the foundations of the famous Esterházy collection of paintings (on which the collection of the Museum of Fine Arts in Budapest was later based) were laid. Rare flowers and ornamental trees were brought from distant lands to the garden of György Lippay, the archbishop of Esztergom, and a whole book was devoted to describing it.

In the palaces of the aristocracy a merry social life was to be found. Feasts, hunting parties, and family celebrations followed each other in close succession. Court orchestras would provide music, and plays, even operas, were performed. Prince Pál Esterházy himself composed ecclesiastically-inspired pieces of music.

The Catholic Church and the Society of Jesus supervised cultural life in aristocratic homes, although Catholic influence extended far beyond these. The Jesuits and Church generally controlled school education and the education of young nobles. Also under their sway were the university at Nagyszombat, which had been founded by Péter Pázmány; the college at Kassa (after 1674); and the colleges at Graz and Vienna, where quite a few young Hungarians studied. Culture was ecclesiastically regulated but was nevertheless closely bound to the old national traditions.

Literature was also inspired by the nobility and the Catholic Church. The poets of the age were, almost without exception, the servants and supporters of aristocrats. Their task was to celebrate the important events in their masters' lives, and to popularize their political principles. The best-known of these writers was István Gyöngyösi, who achieved fame for his narrative poem about Palatine Ferenc Wesselényi's courtship of, and subsequent marriage to, Mária Széchy, the "Venus of Murány". Most Catholic literature in the Hungarian language was religious. Alongside it flourished polemical literature and sermons.

The fine arts had little chance to develop amid the conditions of war, and the goldsmith's craft was the only branch which produced significant works during this period. Painting began to catch up towards the end of the century: its finest representatives were János Kupeczky, who was born near Pozsony, and Ádám Mányoki, who was then just embarking upon his career.

Linking up with Protestantism, intellectual movements of a bourgeois character emerged primarily in Transylvania and in eastern Hungary. The big Calvinist colleges were hotbeds of the new ideas, especially Sárospatak, Debrecen and Gyulafehérvár, the latter having moved to Nagyenyed after the Tatar devastation of 1658. Thousands of Protestant students visited the universities of the Netherlands, Germany, and England where they learned of middle-class aspirations and rational thinking. It was at this time that Puritan ideas demanding a more democratic internal life spread within the Calvinist Church. At the same time, in the wake of Cartesianism, interest in the secular sciences grew substantially. In 1653 János Apáczai Csere wrote the first Hungarian-language encyclopedia, with a view to leading the Hungarian nation out of ignorance. Apáczai wanted to modernize education in schools and to democratize public life. However, his plans were frustrated by the stubborn resistance of the nobility, which regarded any change as a threat to its privileges. The struggle with the nobility, the ruling class at this time, greatly embittered Miklós Tótfalusi Kis, the famous printer of the age who had earned European renown. Despite the fact that Western middle-class aspirations could not strike root in Hungary, knowledge of the latest scholarship (including the investigation of the natural sciences) did nevertheless penetrate the country. Under the surface, new ideas slowly began to shape public opinion. Even the modern medical science of the day found its way to Hungary through the works of Ferenc Pápai-Páriz. However, after 1670 the Counter-Reformation paralyzed Protestant schools. The college at Sárospatak was closed and its teachers and students were forced to go into hiding for years. From 1690 onwards Transylvania also came under Habsburg domination and, accordingly, the possibility of any latitude in Hungarian cultural policy was lost. It was only during the Rákóczi war of independence that a separate line could develop.

"Our countrymen are ready, they lack only a leader"

After 150 years of Ottoman domination, Hungary's territorial unity was restored. However, the country had to pay a high price for the expulsion of the enemy. The Turkish yoke had been removed, only to be replaced by Habsburg oppression.

Emperor Leopold decided that the time had come to destroy Hungary's independence and to make the country one of his family's hereditary provinces. Only a year after the recapture of Buda, the Diet was forced to make political concessions. In 1687 it relinquished its right to elect the country's king and rescinded the clause in the *Golden Bull* which permitted the nobility to rebel against any monarch who infringed the nation's rights. Habsburg rule in Hungary became hereditary and the nobles were no longer legally entitled to take action against a king who violated the laws.

The long decades of fighting had cost a great deal of money, most of which had been exacted from the Hungarian peasantry. At the same time, the country, already the scene of extortion for a century and a half, was almost entirely laid waste. The 60,000–80,000-strong imperial army, together with all its horses, had to be fed, and both officers and men regarded local resources as theirs for the taking. The entire population of certain areas fled to the forests and marshes, and the once prosperous town of Debrecen became impoverished as a result of continual looting. In order to quell nationwide discontent and to acquire more money, General Caraffa, with the approval of his superiors, court-martialled numerous nobles and burghers at Eperjes. After a summary trial on trumped-up charges, they were sentenced to death and their property confiscated.

The Habsburgs regarded Hungary as a conquered province. Imperial generals and military contractors received estates the size of counties, while the Hungarian nobility could only recover its landed property after presentation of documents proving ownership, and after payment of a certain fee. This sum was for "redemption of arms", a reference to the coat of arms of a noble family, and was laid down by the *Neoacquistica Commissio.* All these measures were designed to strengthen Leopold I's absolutist rule as it was felt that "Hungarian blood, which is inclined to revolution and restlessness" could only be tamed by oppression. The *Jászkunság* province was mortgaged to the Teutonic Knights and the free peasants of the area thereby reduced to serfdom. At the same time, those Serbs who had moved to Hungary in 1689 under the leadership of Arsenije Černojević, the patriarch of Ipek, were granted extensive autonomy. It was now that the Serbs' most important town, Szentendre, north of Buda, began to develop, and during the eighteenth century this became the centre of Serbian culture in Hungary. The Court in Vienna began to settle the depopulated regions of the Great Plain and Transdanubia with Catholic Germans, or Swabians as they came to be known. While the Greek Orthodox Serbs acquired complete freedom of religion, the Protestant Hungarian villages were denied it. Another round of enforced conversions began. The country was virtually overrun by various monastic orders—indeed, contemporary folk songs speak of a "reign of priests".

Devastated and oppressed, Hungary was unable to offer much resistance. Although here and there the peasantry rose up against the foreign mercenaries, its attempts to change matters were easily crushed. In 1697, desperate serfs and border-fortress soldiers who had been left without anything to eat launched a surprise attack in the east of the country. They managed to occupy Sárospatak and the castle of Tokaj but, without assistance, were inevitably defeated by the imperial troops. At this point the people's only hope lay with the young aristocrat Ferenc Rákóczi.

Ferenc Rákóczi II was the son of Ferenc Rákóczi I, who died after the Wesselényi conspiracy in 1676, and Ilona Zrínyi, the daughter of Péter Zrínyi, the executed *bán* of Croatia. At the age of twelve Rákóczi was separated from his mother when she finally surrendered the castle of Munkács to the imperial troops (1688). In an attempt to make him loyal to the Habsburgs, the Court in Vienna sent the young Rákóczi to Bohemia, where he was educated by the Jesuits. He later studied at Prague University, and completed his education in Italy. In Vienna, Rákóczi led the frivolous life of a young aristocrat and in 1694 he married. Rákóczi chose his bride from the German Hessen-Rheinfels family, which enjoyed princely rank, and through her became related to the king of France. The couple now moved to Rákóczi's Hungarian estates. The young nobleman dressed in German clothes, had imperial officers as his friends, and was absolutely loyal to Vienna. When rebellious peasants attempted to win him to their cause in 1697, Rákóczi fled to the Habsburg capital.

Even so, when he had become more familiar with Hungary's situation, Rákóczi's enthusiasm for the *status quo* began to wane. His friendship with Miklós Bercsényi, another young aristocrat, was instrumental in this. So, too, was the realization that everyone was expecting him, Hungary's greatest landowner and greatest aristocrat, to defend the country. Together with several high-ranking nobles, he organized a conspiracy against the Habsburgs and turned to King Louis XIV of France with an appeal for help. But his letter to the French king was intercepted and, during the spring of 1701, Rákóczi was captured in his castle at Nagysáros. He was taken to Wiener Neustadt and locked up in the same prison where his grandfather had earlier been executed. Rákóczi's fate was to have been the same, but he managed to escape to Poland. From there he tried to win support for his cause from France and the other anti-Habsburg powers. Rákóczi's appeal for help was rejected everywhere: none of the countries he turned to would trust in the lonely fugitive.

Rákóczi was staying in the castle of Brezani, on one of the remote estates of a Polish friend, when a peasant delegation from the *Tiszahát* finally reached him at the beginning of 1703. Headed by Tamás Esze, the peasants informed Rákóczi that "our countrymen are ready, they lack only a leader". The young prince, who had not sided with the peasantry in 1697 and who up to then had not even thought of leading an army of serfs against Vienna, heeded Esze's call. Having become convinced that the delegation had reported truthfully, in May 1703 Rákóczi sent into Hungary a banner inscribed *Cum Deo pro patria et libertate* (With God for Country and Liberty). At the same time he issued a proclamation calling "every true noble and non-noble Hungarian" to arms. In June 1703 Rákóczi himself set out to take command of his armies and to begin a war of independence.

"With God for country and liberty"

When in June 1703 Ferenc Rákóczi arrived in the northeastern Carpathians, the frontier district between Poland and Hungary, only a few hundred embittered peasants led by Tamás Esze were waiting for him. As this force proceeded down from the mountains, its numbers swelled and, after a few weeks, an army several thousand strong had come into being. The nobles, always fearful of the peasantry, took refuge in their castles and resisted the insurgents. It took some time before they saw that Rákóczi himself was committed to the revolt, and that the uprising was more than a manifestation of lower-class discontent. In the autumn of 1707 the nobility joined the insurrection and the towns soon followed suit. Tamás Esze's peasant delegation of four years earlier had sparked off a national crusade. By the end of the year, Rákóczi's forces had occupied Upper Hungary and the central regions of the Great Plain. In addition, they had advanced not only into Transdanubia but into Transylvania.

The Rákóczi war of independence began at a time when the international situation was favourable to it. In 1701 the War of the Spanish Succession had broken out—splitting Western Europe into two camps. The French Bourbons and the Austrian Habsburgs both made a bid for the rich legacy represented by Spain and its overseas possessions. The maritime powers, England and the Netherlands, supported Leopold of Habsburg, while the elector of Bavaria backed Louis XIV of France. Hungary was therefore a natural ally as far as the French were concerned—indeed, Rákóczi's main hope of victory rested on military co-operation with France. After the initial successes of the war of independence Louis XIV sought contact with Rákóczi, and even gave him money. This was enough only to pay some 5,000 of the 70,000 soldiers who were fighting for Rákóczi at the time: French financial assistance was symbolic rather than substantial.

The early years of the war in Western Europe brought successes for France. In spring 1703 the French army advanced along the Danube towards Vienna while the *kuruc* army headed towards the city from the east. The imperial Court experienced some very difficult weeks; had the two armies linked up and captured Vienna, the Habsburg empire could well have disintegrated.

However, the great hopes of the Hungarians were not to be fulfilled. By the beginning of 1704, the *kuruc* forces had reached the Austrian border but Maximilian Emanuel, the elector of Bavaria, and the commander of the French army did not move directly against Vienna. Instead, the French advanced into the Tyrol, becoming involved there in guerilla warfare. By the time they were again ready to march on Vienna, the English and Dutch armies had organized themselves. At the Battle of Blenheim Eugene of Savoy and the Duke of Marlborough halted the French advance and knocked Bavaria out of the war. After this the French were compelled to fall back and plans to link up the French and Hungarian armies came to nothing: Vienna had been saved.

Rákóczi now suggested to Louis XIV that they join up on the Adriatic and in Croatia. This scheme was unsuccessful, too, and Rákóczi came to appreciate that he could no longer really count on French support. Finding himself in a difficult situation, the French king was unwilling to commit himself to the Hungarians. Louis therefore declined to conclude an alliance with Rákóczi—for all the latter's apparent confidence: since 1704 Rákóczi had borne the title prince-elect of Transylvania and, after the Diet of Szécsény in 1705, that of prince of Hungary.

Rákóczi clearly saw that if the Hungarian cause could not be made a European cause, the war of independece would become isolated and would stand little chance of achieving its objectives. He was anxious to keep international public opinion informed about the cause and purpose of the struggle and, to counter the hostile propaganda put out by Vienna, he issued a Latin-language newspaper entitled *Mercurius Veridicus*. In attempts to drum up support, his envoys called on the king of Sweden, visited the kings of Prussia and Denmark, and negotiated with the Polish Diet and with the Pope. Rákóczi received words of encouragement during these visits but no material assistance was offered. Foreign governments were generally not prepared to antagonize the Habsburgs on Hungary's account. Rákóczi also attempted to win the Turks to his cause—again to no avail. Only Tsar Peter the Great of Russia was willing to make any commitment. Rákóczi concluded a secret alliance with Peter but was unable to derive any military advantage from it. Eventually it became clear that, in its fight for freedom, Hungary could expect no outside help.

In military terms, the Habsburg empire was by far the stronger of the two sides. Rákóczi made tremendous efforts to organize his brave soldiers, who were unaccustomed to the conventional warfare of the day, into a well-equipped and disciplined professional army. However, the young *kuruc* troops were incapable of matching the competence of their opponents, and lost every set-piece battle against the imperial forces. They suffered defeat at Nagyszombat at the end of 1704 and at Zsibó in 1705, in spite of the fact that in these engagements they outnumbered the enemy. Such developments induced Rákóczi to open peace negotiations with Vienna, first in Gyöngyös and then in Nagyszombat. The mediators in these talks were Englishmen and Dutchmen who, as the emperor's allies, were well aware that the 40,000 Habsburg soldiers fighting in Hungary were very much needed in the Western theatre of war. An end to the fighting in Hungary would mean that these troops could be deployed elsewhere and that Hungary could be made to contribute taxes and arms to the struggle against the French. In addition, the English and Dutch sympathized with the Hungarians, whose nation was also opposed to the Catholic Counter-Reformation. Negotiations dragged on for months but produced no results. The *kuruc* rebels would have been prepared to accept Habsburg hegemony, provided that Hungary's constitutional rights were recognized and guaranteed. They also demanded religious toleration within the country, and that this be similarly ensured. Vienna, however, refused to accept foreign states as guarantors of the independence of Transylvania, on which Rákóczi insisted. Although Hungary had become isolated in its fight for freedom, it was, through Rákóczi's efforts, sufficiently strong to reject peace terms which were unfavourable. In 1707 the Diet of Ónod broke internal opposition and dethroned the House of Habsburg. The struggle continued.

"It is my intention to bring about my country's full happiness"

Rákóczi realized that Hungary was backward in virtually every respect, and in his memoirs he laid the blame for this on the Habsburgs. Nevertheless, even while conducting the war for national independence, Rákóczi attempted to strengthen state and society by introducing modern reforms.

In his youth Rákóczi had studied the latest French and Italian works on state theory, and during his imprisonment at Wiener Neustadt he had read extensively. From the very beginning Rákóczi strove to establish national absolutism, attempting to weaken the political power of the aristocracy and to improve the lot of the downtrodden. His programme included a promise of freedom for those serfs who joined his army and, while the Habsburgs attempted to divide the country, Rákóczi struggled to forge national unity. In order to eliminate religious conflict within the country, he returned the Protestants' churches and schools, and ensured equal status for the religious denominations. Non-Magyar minority groups which sided with the war of independence were granted equality with the Magyar population.

Initially, all Rákóczi's close associates were drawn from the ranks of the lesser nobility. The nearest to him throughout the struggle was Pál Ráday, who was also a member of this class. Ráday was first of all Rákóczi's private secretary and later head of the prince's chancellery (and director of foreign affairs). The leader of Rákóczi's court, Ádám Vay, was also a lesser noble, as was Pál Lányi, the government commissioner responsible for armaments. While in the army power was exercised by generals from aristocratic families, Rákóczi kept the military leadership out of politics.

The aristocracy, led by Bercsényi, took offence at its exclusion from decision-making: the Diet of Szécsény, in 1705, witnessed the magnates' first open move to curtail Rákóczi's power. At this a four-member committee was organized to handle government business and an economic council was entrusted with additional tasks. The aristocracy was represented on these bodies; nevertheless Rákóczi retained the power to make the final decisions. This last fact served as a pretext for those nobles who opposed Rákóczi to complain about his total disregard for their privileges. In this they received encouragement from Vienna, and infringement of the nobility's rights was the opposition's main grievance at the Diet of Ónod in 1707.

The war of independence caused serious financial difficulties in the country. Revenues from the Rákóczi estates were by no means adequate to cover expenditure and the collection of taxes was not easy in an impoverished country already under arms. So far the nobles had been exempt from taxation but now Rákóczi introduced a law under which this privilege was abolished. The move constituted a violation of the nobility's outmoded rights.

As Hungary's supplies of silver and gold currency were insufficient, at the beginning of 1704 Rákóczi introduced copper coinage. Industry, however, was primitive and backward (even firearms had to be purchased abroad), and, owing to the war, commerce was also paralyzed. The state was therefore unable to protect the value of the new currency. As a result, traders refused to accept copper coins and the soldiers, who were paid in this money, found themselves in a constantly worsening situation.

The impact of social antagonisms also affected the army. The landowners tried to keep their serfs out of the fighting. They also attempted to force those who had enlisted to return to the land, placing extra burdens on the families of men under arms. The efficiency of the peasant troops suffered accordingly and growing numbers returned home. In December 1708, the Diet of Sárospatak issued a decree which proclaimed the emancipation of serfs fighting in the war of independence, and Rákóczi himself conferred special privileges on several serf villages. These moves, however, were now incapable of reviving morale among the peasants.

In 1708, the *kuruc* army lost the decisive Battle of Trencsén. The long war had produced exhaustion, and economic problems were now compounded by the outbreak of a plague epidemic. Having won the war in the West, the emperor was now able to send more and more troops to Hungary. Accordingly, the *kuruc* forces were gradually compelled to retreat to the northeastern part of the country.

Rákóczi, however, believed that all was not yet lost. He hoped that, through private negotiations, he could persuade Tsar Peter the Great to provide him with military assistance. At the end of 1710 Rákóczi set out for Russia, making Baron Sándor Károlyi supreme army commander during his absence. With Rákóczi's approval, Károlyi entered into negotiations with Count János Pálffy, who had been appointed commander of the imperial armies by Joseph I (1705–11). Rákóczi had intended these talks to be a means of gaining time but Károlyi, who realized that the military situation was now hopeless, signed the Treaty of Szatmár with the Habsburgs on April 29, 1711. Under its terms the *kuruc* soldiers once again became loyal subjects of the emperor, who made a number of concessions. An amnesty was promised and Vienna pledged to uphold not only Hungary's feudal constitution but also freedom of religion within the country. On May 1, 1711 the *kuruc* forces laid down their weapons.

Rákóczi refused to recognize the Treaty of Szatmár, which did not guarantee Hungary's independence and which swept away the social achievements of the war. He went into voluntary exile, first to Poland and later to the French Court at Versailles. From there Rákóczi eventually moved to Turkey—in the hope that the liberation struggle could be restarted from that country. He died in Rodosto in 1735. The diary written in letter form by his page, Kelemen Mikes, gives a moving account of Rákóczi's last years and the life of those in exile with him.

Settlement and reorganization in the eighteenth century

Joseph I died while negotiations for the Treaty of Szatmár were still under way and was succeeded as emperor by Charles VI, his younger brother. The new ruler was the last male member of the Habsburg family and became king of Hungary as Charles III (1711–1740). Originally, Charles had been heir to the Spanish throne but the prospect of Spain and Austria united under one monarch caused alarm among other European states. In order to preserve the European balance of power against the threat of Austrian hegemony, England and the Netherlands both renounced the war. The Treaty of Utrecht (1713) confined the Habsburgs to their Danubian provinces. The settlement of Hungary's internal affairs was now vital if Austria was to retain its status as a major power.

After Rákóczi's war of independence, Vienna dared not continue Leopold's policy of forced assimilation. In theory Hungary retained its autonomy within the empire but in practice the supreme organs of the state operated from the Austrian capital and their independence was merely illusory. Major issues were decided by the *Hofkriegsrat* or the *Hofkammer*, neither of which had Hungarian members. Public administration was entrusted to the newly-organized Council of Lieutenancy in Buda with the palatine at its head. Since Charles III had no male heir, in 1722 the Diet was forced to accept a law known as the Pragmatic Sanction. By doing so, it recognized the right of succession through the female line of the House of Habsburgs. Also accepted was the "indivisible and inseparable" unity of the countries united under Habsburg rule. However, the Pragmatic Sanction simultaneously confirmed Hungary's constitutional autonomy.

The 150 years of Turkish occupation and the fighting which took place during this time had claimed a heavy toll in human lives. Hungary's population had been four millions when Matthias was king, but the figure was now down to three and a half millions. In the same period, the number of Europe's inhabitants had increased from 80 millions to 130 millions. The devastation had primarily affected the Magyar inhabitants of the Great Plain and the river valleys. Some southern regions of the Plain, which had previously been densely populated, were now empty wastes.

The population which had earlier fled to Upper Hungary from the Turks began to return at the end of the seventeenth century. Nevertheless, those areas which had become deserted were resettled by the Habsburgs. Vienna recruited Catholics in Germany and brought them into the country. This policy to some extent served political purposes, designed as it was to reduce the concentration of Hungarians. The German settlers were provided with newly-built and fully-equipped villages and were exempted from tax for years, especially on the Crown estates in the Temes region. In the course of the eighteenth century, the number of Germans in the Banat (who were known as Swabians) topped the one million mark. It was at this time that the German villages of the Bakony and Vértes regions emerged, along with those near Buda. These years also witnessed the creation of German blocks in Tolna and Baranya counties, and in the *Bácska*.

Spontaneous large-scale immigration also took place. The Southern Slavs, under pressure from the Turks, began to move northwards. It was now that the Croatian villages of Transdanubia and some of the Serbian settlements of the south came into existence. At the end of the seventeenth century, 40,000 Serbian families fled to Hungary from the Ottomans and were granted extensive privileges by Leopold I. While the emperor had reduced the free Hungarian peasants of the *Jászkunság* to serfdom and did everything possible to prevent the practice of Protestantism in the Hungarian villages, he granted full freedom of worship and wide autonomy to the Greek Orthodox Serbs.

Romanian shepherds from Wallachia also came to Hungary in large numbers —fleeing to Transylvania from the tyranny of Turkish-appointed local rulers. Slovak settlers moved from Upper Hungary to the vicinity of Pest and to Békés county.

By the end of the eighteenth century, Hungary's population had risen to eight millions. At the same time, however, the Magyars found themselves in a minority. In the Middle Ages, they had made up 80–85 per cent of the country's inhabitants but this figure had now fallen to 40 per cent. A multinational Hungary had emerged and this development was not unimportant in shaping the country's subsequent history.

The Hungarian aristocracy had previously headed the national movements and now Vienna made great efforts to win it over. Aristocratic families moved in growing numbers to the Habsburg capital and intermarried with their Bohemian and Austrian counterparts. They seldom visited their estates in Hungary and their contact with the Hungarian people became almost non-existent. The Court was also successful in its efforts to recruit leading Catholic clergy from those aristocratic families loyal to the dynasty. The Counter-Reformation had brought a new status to the Church, making it attractive to career-minded nobles. Increasingly, the country's upper classes backed the Court's policy.

The fact that the Rákóczi estates were given exclusively to Austrian and Bohemian families also contributed to the weakening of internal resistance. The Diet obediently naturalized these families and in southern Hungary a large military frontier zone was established and placed directly under Vienna's control. The now defunct Principality of Transylvania remained separated from Hungary. Instead, it was governed as a grand duchy and subordinated to Vienna.

Increased taxation and the necessity of reconstruction work added to the burdens on the serfs. The oppression they suffered was almost limitless. In 1735, peasants from Békés county joined forces with disaffected Serbian peasants in the military border zone and staged an uprising in Rákóczi's name. (This is known to history as the "Pero Uprising" after the Serbian captain who led it.) The insurrection was suppressed and the organizers ruthlessly punished.

The fact that Hungary was unaffected by war for three generations meant that the country could be rebuilt. The population doubled and agricultural production began again on the Great Plain. The baroque townscapes, which can still be seen today, also came into being at this time.

"Our life and our blood"

On October 20, 1740, King Charles III died and the male line of the Habsburg dynasty became extinct. Charles III was succeeded by his daughter, Maria Theresa. However, the new ruler's right to the throne was challenged by those powers wishing to expand at the expense of the Habsburgs, and the War of the Austrian Succession resulted. Having concluded an alliance with the elector of Bavaria, Frederick the Great of Prussia attacked the Habsburg empire from the north and west. At the same time, the Spaniards and Venetians launched an offensive from the south. In 1741 the enemy was already on Austrian territory and occupied Prague, and it seemed that Habsburg power might well be at an end. In this difficult situation Maria Theresa—who had been crowned "king" of Hungary at Pozsony in June 1741—turned to the Hungarians. On September 11, the nobility, which had gathered to attend the Diet, offered its "life and blood for our king, Maria Theresa" (*vitam et sanguinem pro rege nostro Maria Theresia*). The appearance of Hungarian regiments marked a turning-point in the conflict. The enemy was driven from Austrian territory and in the peace which followed (1742) the Habsburgs lost only a part of Silesia.

In 1757, Maria Theresa made an attempt to recover the territories she was forced to give up fifteen years earlier. In the struggle which now developed (the Seven Years War) Hungarian troops again fought alongside those of the Habsburgs and General András Hadik's hussars even captured Berlin. But the fighting did not achieve its purpose and Silesia came under Prussian rule. At the first partition of Poland, however, Maria Theresa obtained Galicia, together with the town of Cracow. Later the Bukovina, which had previously been under Ottoman control, was also added to her dominions.

Historians have often wondered why the Hungarian nobility, which only a generation earlier had fought for national independence under Rákóczi, now sided with Maria Theresa. The answer lies in the fact that the world had changed considerably since 1711, the year the Treaty of Szatmár was signed. The Court no longer wished to curtail the rights of the nobility and was prepared to grant to the Hungarian élite almost unlimited exercise of its ancient privileges. This state of affairs suited the Hungarian nobility, which in return was willing to lend its support to the dynasty. Indicative of how satisfied the nobility was during this period is the saying of the time: "There is no life outside Hungary" (*Extra Hungariam non est vita*).

Maria Theresa, whose highest rank was "King of Hungary" (her husband, Francis of Lorraine, bore the title "Emperor"), was one of the greatest members of the Habsburg dynasty and implemented her policies with caution and feminine tact. To contemporaries it seemed that she was guided by benevolence towards, and indeed sympathy for, the country. She re-annexed the thirteen Szepes towns that had been pawned to Poland and also reclaimed for it the port of Fiume and the Banat of Temes, which had been under military administration. In Vienna she organized a corps of Hungarian bodyguards made up of members of the Hungarian nobility, and she also founded a Hungarian decoration (the Order of St Stephen). Several Hungarians were awarded the Maria Theresa Military Medal. This all demonstrated that Maria Theresa had broken with the anti-Hungarian policy of her predecessors.

Maria Theresa's aim was to establish a united Danubian empire. Since Hungary constituted the largest territorial unit among her dominions and since almost half of her subjects lived within this, it was of paramount importance that the country be developed and strengthened. This was done not out of love for the Hungarians but out of recognition of the interests of the Habsburg empire.

Maria Theresa's measures were already affected by the spirit of the Enlightenment. The aim of these was to bolster the power of the monarchy and the state. Wenzel Anton, Prince von Kaunitz-Reitberg, Maria Theresa's chancellor and chief adviser, played an important role in this process. The curtailment of ecclesiastical and aristocratic power, the protection of the serfs, the implementation of social welfare measures, the encouragement of education, and the raising of the cultural level—all served to reinforce central authority. So, too, did those economic measures, often criticized later, which used tariffs to strengthen Austrian and Bohemian industry while allocating to Hungary the role of agricultural commodities and raw materials supplier.

Naturally, the ruling class was very jealous of its privileges, and when Maria Theresa wanted to tax the nobility the Diet turned against her. After this Maria Theresa resorted to government by decree in Hungary. In 1769 she issued a patent regulating the dues and labour requirements for the serfs. There was only one area in which the Enlightenment failed to influence Maria Theresa's policies, and this was religion. Throughout her forty-year reign, non-Catholics remained second-class citizens. They could practise their religion only in the context of considerable restrictions and they could not enter state service. Some Romanians and Ruthenians of the Greek Orthodox faith were forced to join the Greek Catholic Church, which recognized the Pope's authority. However, attempts to force Greek Orthodox Serbs to do the same were unsuccessful. Rather than yield to pressure, many emigrated to Russia.

From Hungary's standpoint, Maria Theresa's reign was a period of consolidation. It was during these years that the country was rebuilt and the devastation wrought by the Ottomans made good.

"Every nation became learned in its own language"

In the eighteenth century culture was still in the hands of the clergy, which control-led the schools, literature, and the arts. In Hungary the Roman Catholic Church enjoyed a unique position on account of its vast estates and the support it received from the Habsburgs.

Baroque was the dominant artistic style of the age. The monumentalism of baroque buildings, the inner pomp of the churches, and the spectacular richness of forms all proclaimed the dominance of the ecclesiastical and secular power. During this period the baroque cathedrals of the bishops and archbishops were built, together with their elaborate palaces. Also constructed in the baroque style were the palaces of the aristocracy and the churches of the newly-populated villages. The homes of the landowning classes no longer served defence purposes, but comfort and extravagant tastes. In quite a number there were theatres and concert halls in which actors and musicians entertained the owner and his distinguished guests. The rooms were furnished with expensive furniture and adorned with statues and paint-ings. The parks around these palaces imitated the gardens at Versailles.

Catholic baroque left its mark on eighteenth-century painting and sculpture as well. In Transdanubia and in northwestern Hungary, churches were decorated with frescoes which portrayed Biblical scenes. Franz-Anton Maulbertsch, an Austrian, and István Dorfmeister, who founded a dynasty of artists, were the greatest masters of baroque painting in Hungary. Murals in aristocratic palaces no longer took their inspiration from the national past, but from classical mythology. Most were painted by Hungarian masters but their quality was often very provincial.

The language of scholarship was Latin, and the vernacular, which had begun to flourish in the seventeenth century, lost its prominence. As regards approach and method, however, the eighteenth century saw great progress. A discipline known to contemporaries as *Staatskunde* (a blanket term for geography, history and ethnogra-phy) underwent considerable development. In his *Notitiae Hungariae...* Mátyás Bél, the rector of the Lutheran grammar school in Pozsony, presented a complete survey of the country, although up to 1742 only five volumes of this work were pub-lished. The Jesuit school of historiography which emerged in the second half of the century (Gábor Hevenesi, György Pray and István Katona) was the first to work on the basis of the modern, critical approach to source material. The Jesuit historians were, however, strongly biased in favour of the Habsburgs.

Most literature in the Hungarian language was in the form of religious works written for the people. Catholic publications were brought out by the Jesuit printing press at Nagyszombat, while Protestant works were published in Debrecen and in the towns of Upper Hungary.

Everywhere the language of tuition was Latin—with the exception of village primary schools. Most Catholic secondary schools were in the hands of the Jesuits. Around 1750, the Society of Jesus ran thirty grammar schools and six colleges, the latter being known as academies. The Jesuits also controlled the university at Nagyszombat. Elementary education they neglected: the teaching of villagers was not their chief concern. The Piarist grammar schools, now increasing rapidly in number, represented a more up-to-date approach to education. At these schools the natural sciences were taught in addition to the other subjects. Protestants were debarred from education at university level but their colleges (at Debrecen, Sáros-patak, Nagyenyed, Pápa, Eperjes, and Pozsony) provided a high-quality training in theology and philosophy. The Protestants devoted considerable attention to small village schools, although in these only reading, writing, Biblical stories and, occasionally, arithmetic were taught.

The government attached great importance to the development of schools. A faculty of medicine was added to the university at Nagyszombat, the mining school at Selmec was awarded the status of an academy, and an institute for the training of engineers was established in Pest. When the Jesuit order was dissolved in 1773, the government established from its assets an educational fund for the support of primary education. In spite of these efforts though, the number of rural people able to read and write was very low in Hungary, as indeed it was elsewhere in Europe. The new cultural trends barely touched the peasantry. However, the peasants did preserve their traditional folk culture, Hungarian language, and ancient melodies in a period when the nobility and the middle classes were preoccupied with other things.

In 1772 György Bessenyei's *Ágis tragédiája* (The Tragedy of Agis) was published. This marked the beginning of the Enlightenment in Hungary and of the manifestation in literature of a national awakening. Bessenyei, a member of the Royal Hungarian Lifeguard in Vienna, had become acquainted in that city with the ideas of the French Enlightenment. In his works, Bessenyei advocated certain social reforms and the development of a vernacular culture. "Every nation became learned in its own language," ran Bessenyei's slogan. Things began to liven up first in literature and later in politics, and the masonic lodges played a highly important role in this process. The members of these—aristocrats, nobles and even a number of burghers—held meetings during which they familiarized themselves with the spirit of the Enlightenment. The view was expressed that social changes were necessary. Within a few decades, Hungarian society was transformed and backwardness in culture, thinking, and attitude to life was, to some extent, remedied.

The first servant of the state

Maria Theresa died on November 29, 1780 and was succeeded by her thirty-nine year-old son, Joseph II. Joseph had become Holy Roman emperor in 1765, although by this time the office amounted to little more than the title. His mother had not allowed him to involve himself much in the affairs of the Habsburg dominions. During his long years as heir to the throne Joseph had travelled extensively in his territories, although taking good care not to reveal his identity. The new ruler had also visited Hungary, and the experiences and impressions he gained were important. They helped to shape his conception of government and his plans for reform.

Joseph II was raised in the spirit of enlightened absolutism. He regarded himself on the one hand as absolute lord of the empire and, on the other, as the principal servant of his peoples. The goal of his political philosophy—known as Josephinism—was to forge a united and strong empire from its multilingual and vastly-differing component regions. He wished to create a state capable of matching the rival European powers. Modernization of government would not, however, be sufficient in itself. Social reforms designed to eliminate backwardness would also be needed. Since Joseph believed that the masses lacked the maturity to order their own affairs, he wished to act on their behalf. His ruthless interference provoked resistance even where his intentions were good. His motto ran as follows: "Everything for the people, nothing by the people."

After his accession, Joseph II immediately embarked upon the path of reform. He wished to strengthen society and the state by reducing the power of the privileged and by allowing the lower classes a freer life. Joseph II refused to be crowned king of Hungary, thereby avoiding the obligation to observe the privileges of the nobility. What is more, Joseph had the Hungarian Crown, as the symbol of a bygone age, transferred from Pozsony to a museum in Vienna. He governed by decree and did not convene the Diet. His proclamations regulated the individual and society from the cradle to the grave, and down to the smallest detail.

Joseph's first measures were aimed at curbing the power of the Catholic clergy—a body which had grown excessively large. He took censorship, in other words the right to supervise and to veto the publication of printed material, out of the Church's hands and restricted the political role of the bishops, as well as the Pope's right to interfere in the country. Joseph also dissolved all monastic orders not involved in teaching or in caring for the sick, using their assets primarily for educational purposes. In 1781 he issued a decree granting freedom of worship to his Protestant and Greek Orthodox subjects, who were now allowed to fill the higher positions in the state. Pope Pius VI personally called on Joseph in Vienna to persuade him to amend his decrees, but to no avail. Joseph II was a devout Catholic and his policy stemmed not from a lack of faith but rather from practical considerations. The emperor realized that the state could not do without the expertise and work of the non-Catholics, and that creed should not limit the rights of a citizen.

Although his religious policy was welcomed by society at large, Joseph II's administrative reforms created discontent in the ranks of the nobility. In the interests of the empire's unity, Joseph II abolished Hungarian autonomy. Officials in Hungary were now appointed by the monarch and the country was divided into ten administrative units, each headed by a commissioner. Even more unpopular as far as the nobility was concerned were Joseph II's decrees aimed at protecting the serfs. Joseph abolished the manorial law courts in which the landowners themselves passed judgement on their serfs. Also done away with was punishment by flogging. In addition, freedom of movement was ensured for serfs and even the term "serf" abolished officially. At the same time, Joseph II made preparations for the taxation of the nobility. He ordered the land to be surveyed and this was followed by a general census and the registration of estates. But the government's measures gave rise to exaggerated hopes among the peasants. In 1784, the Romanian serfs on a Crown estate at Zalatna, in Transylvania, rose in arms. Under the leadership of Horia and Closca, the rebellion mobilized some 20,000 serfs against the bailiffs and the landowners. Joseph II ruthlessly suppressed the peasant uprising and, as a deterrent, had its leaders broken on the wheel.

The emperor's religious and social reforms antagonized the Church and the nobility respectively, but more general provocations were to follow. In 1784, German was made the official language throughout the Habsburg empire, and this move turned the entire Hungarian people against Joseph. As a result of the relevant decree, the language of public administration, jurisdiction, and higher education in Hungary changed accordingly. The nation became united in its indignation. Joseph's attempt to germanize the country contributed appreciably to the subsequent revival of Hungarian literature, the Hungarian language, and Hungarian national traditions.

The implementation of Joseph II's reforms proved more and more difficult. The emperor's problems were compounded by other developments. In 1788 Joseph launched a military campaign against the Turks but this was not successful. Domestic opposition increased as a result, and the compulsory delivery of produce was sabotaged in many places. In 1789 revolution broke out in France and there was a national uprising in the Austrian Netherlands, a distant Habsburg province. In Hungary the nobility began openly to organize a conspiracy. In 1790, a few weeks before his death, Joseph withdrew all his reforms, with the exception of his decrees on religious toleration, on the monastic orders, and on the abolition of perpetual serfdom.

THE RISE OF CAPITALISM
IN HUNGARY

The Impact of the French Revolution and the Age of Reform

"The line of Habsburg succession will be broken"

Although Joseph II revoked most of his decrees, this was not sufficient to calm discontent in his dominions. His death only served to increase ill-feeling, and the return of the Holy Crown from Vienna to Buda in February 1790 was almost a triumphal procession. The Crown was escorted by the private armies of the nobility arrayed in Hungarian national dress. Entire villages turned out for the spectacle and in Győr, the bishop himself headed the assembled burghers. In Pest-Buda, cannons thundered and the whole city celebrated. Old Hungarian costumes were taken out, Hungarian dances re-appeared at balls, and there was merry-making to the strains of the Rákóczi March.

Hungary was celebrating a "new-found liberty". County organization was restored, former officials returned to their jobs, and the land survey documents were publicly burnt. The movement was led by the lesser nobility which believed that the time had come to re-establish an independent Hungarian state. Its leader, Péter Ócsai Balogh, formulated the lesser nobility's demands. The cornerstone of these was that by refusing to be crowned, Joseph II had violated the social contract between the Hungarian nation and the House of Habsburg, thereby breaking the line of succession. The nation was therefore entitled to conclude a new contract and to elect a new king. The lesser nobility's candidate for the throne was a son of the Prussian monarch and its most radical members had already established contact with the court in Berlin. These reformists also drafted a new constitution, under which the lesser nobility would play a prominent role. Lesser nobles would enact legislation at the Diet and between Diets the government of the country would be carried on by a senate made up of them. Royal power would therefore become nominal.

The leading groups in the nobility, among them a part of the aristocracy, favoured enlightened reforms. Unlike Joseph II, however, they did not subordinate these to imperial needs, but wished to realize them in accordance with Hungarian requirements. However, the greater part of the nobility thought shortsightedly in terms of its own narrow interests, in other words the preservation of its privileges. Gradually, the conservatives gained the upper hand. While they were dreaming of a republic dominated by the upper classes, the serfs and the burghers featured less and less in their plans. There were some who considered unlimited power over their serfs to be

85

natural. As Szabolcs county put it: "Fate has willed it that some are born kings, others nobles and still others servants."

The new ruler was Leopold II, the younger brother of Joseph II. Leopold succeeded to the throne at a difficult time. The Austrian Netherlands were on the verge of seceding, the nobles in Hungary were arming themselves, and there was discontent in the Polish territories as well. The war against the Turks remained unfinished and the Habsburgs' old rival, the king of Prussia, had deployed his troops along the Silesian frontier on the pretext of a military exercise. The Habsburg empire was again on the brink of disintegration.

Leopold had previously headed the Grand Duchy of Tuscany, which he had turned into a state modelled on the ideas of the Enlightenment. Like his brother, Leopold favoured reforms, although he also favoured a more tactful approach. In Hungary Leopold convened the Diet and announced that he wished to rule the country in accordance with the constitution. At the same time, he started to isolate the Hungarian nobility's reform movement from possible outside help. Leopold concluded a peace treaty with the Turks and, with some loss of prestige, reached agreement with the Prussian king in the Convention of Reichenbach, 1790. In this way, the Hungarian nobility was denied assistance from the two powers which were in a position to give it support, and the imperial army was freed from foreign commitments. News of the treaties and the fact that imperial troops were now heading towards Hungary had a calming effect on the Diet. There was no more talk of electing a new king and gradually the demands of the nobility were dropped. In November 1790 Leopold II was unconditionally crowned king of Hungary. At the same time, Archduke Alexander Leopold, the king's fourth son, was obediently elected palatine, the Habsburgs' chief officer in the country.

Leopold II knew how to intimidate the nobility, and his agents had previously encouraged the peasantry to rise against their landlords. At the same time and also at the instigation of the king's agents, the towns were also demanding self-government and representation at the Diet. Leopold also used the non-Magyar minorities, whose national consciousness was now awakening. For the Serbs he established an independent Illyrian chancellery and convened a Serbian national assembly at Karlóca. In Transylvania Leopold supported the national demands of the Romanians. All of these moves made the Hungarian nobility reconsider its position. The influence of the French Revolution was important in convincing the greater part of the nobility that it must forge an alliance with the monarch against the lower classes.

Nevertheless, the Diet of 1790–91 enacted important legislation. It stated again that "Hungary is a free and independent country" which should be governed in accordance with its own laws and customs, and through independent government organs. Freedom of religion, together with Maria Theresa's and Joseph II's serf decrees, received codification.

In the summer of 1791 Leopold believed that the time had come to continue his reforms. This he intended to do not by issuing decrees but through legal means, by compelling the Diet to act in accordance with his wishes. The creation of a constitutional monarchy was Leopold's ideal, and above all he wanted to organize the peasantry's representation at the Diet. However, his sudden death on March 1, 1792 put an end to these ambitious plans.

"Hungarian citizens,
let us take an oath for liberty or death"

The accession of Francis I marked the beginning of a new era in the life of the Habsburg empire and in that of Hungary. Whereas Joseph II and Leopold II wished to introduce changes inspired by the Enlightenment, Francis was a staunch conservative. With the French Revolution well under way, Habsburg policy was also determined by fear of similar events at home. While Leopold had attempted to "steal the thunder" of the radicals by introducing reforms, Francis was preparing to crush opponents of the existing order. Leopold had wanted the peasantry represented at the Diet but Francis set up a cabinet composed of conservative aristocrats. With the stubbornness of the ungifted, he refused to countenance even minor changes. He established a police state, in which informers operated everywhere. Indeed, even suspected sympathy with bourgeois aspirations often brought retribution. To turn attention away from domestic problems, Francis entered into war against the French Republic.

During this time, discontent was growing in Hungary as well. In particular, the intelligentsia, which had finally lost its feudal character and recently grown in strength, gave increasingly powerful expression to its grievances. The bitterness of the intellectuals was, however, now mixed with a growing determination partly inspired by the French Revolution. As regards social background, ideology, and opinions, this group was rather heterogeneous. It did agree on one point though, namely that the existing situation was unacceptable and had to be changed.

The intelligentsia found an ally in that section of the lesser nobility which believed that growing absolutism was detrimental both to the country's interests and to its independence. This part of the nobility was willing to accept certain reforms. Contact between the nobility and the intelligentsia was established primarily in the masonic lodges, where opportunities for discussion were provided.

For a while discontent remained beneath the surface. In the towns, reading circles and clubs were formed where intellectuals could meet and read *Le Moniteur*, the official paper of the French Revolution. The most prominent figure among these intellectuals was József Hajnóczy, who had served as a reform *alispán* under Joseph II but who, as a non-noble, had lost his job in 1790. Hajnóczy was a man of great erudition who pointed out in print that conditions in Hungary were intolerable and that reform was of paramount importance. However, nobody at this time thought of taking action to change the situation.

All this changed at the beginning of 1794, when Ignác Martinovics became leader of the malcontents. Martinovics had pursued his university studies as a member of the Franciscan order, and had afterwards become an army chaplain. He later worked as professor of physics at the University of Lemberg (Lvov). Martinovics was a talented and cultured man who nurtured immense ambitions but who, at the same time, lacked self-discipline. Not satisfied with his scholarly achievements, he aspired to a political career as well and, in 1791, entered Leopold's secret service. For appearances' sake Leopold appointed him Court chemist and abbot of Szászvár but his real task was to travel through the country and report the prevailing mood.

Martinovics hoped that, by serving the monarch, he could play a leading role in bringing about change in Hungary but Leopold's death frustrated his plans. The new ruler, Francis I, did not trust Martinovics and sacked him immediately. Soon Martinovics became the leader of those he had previously reported on to the authorities. These included the group of dissatisfied intellectuals who rallied around Hajnóczy and who wished to see a democratic transformation in Hungary.

In spring 1794, Martinovics established two secret societies. The first, the Society of Reformers, rallied the discontented elements in the nobility. The main goal of this society was to set up an independent republic in Hungary, but at the same time it also advocated moderate social reform. The second was the Society of Liberty and Equality, and was intended to continue where the Society of Reformers left off. The Society of Liberty and Equality was made up of the Hungarian Jacobins, the advocates of radical transformation. After seizing power from the Society of Reformers, the latter would abolish the privileges of the nobility and would introduce the achievements of the French Revolution. Naturally, the Society of Reformers was to be kept in the dark about the existence of its would-be successor. Martinovics appointed leaders to head these secret societies. These were Count Jakab Sigray for the Society of Reformers and Hajnóczy; János Laczkovics, a former hussar captain; and Ferenc Szentirmay, a young radical; for the Society of Liberty and Equality. The nobility was to play a decisive role in the first part of the two-stage struggle and the peasantry a decisive role in the second. The conspirators had no clear plans for the period after their revolution, and formulation of these would have been difficult considering the level of development of Hungarian society at this time. In any case, the peasants, who were counted on as allies, were told nothing of the conspiracy.

After a few months of organizing, the two societies had some three hundred members between them. In summer 1794, however, the police in Vienna arrested Martinovics in connection with another plot. Martinovics revealed the details of the Hungarian conspiracy to the investigating committee. Vienna was not entirely surprised, but still reacted with panic. The government put fifty people on trial in Hungary, charging them with high treason. Whoever had seen or taken the secret oath was considered guilty. The rules of criminal procedure were made more strict and the hands of the defence were tied. An intimidated court passed eighteen death sentences on the accused, of whom seven were actually put to death. Martinovics and the four leaders were executed on May 20, 1795. On June 3 they were followed by Sándor Szolártsik and the young lawyer Pál Őz on the grounds that there was no hope of these two ever reforming their ways. The others were given long prison terms, among them the finest representatives of contemporary Hungarian literature—Ferenc Kazinczy, János Batsányi, László Szentjóbi Szabó, and Ferenc Verseghy.

"An example had to be made to intimidat the country," wrote Kazinczy later. However, the yearning for progress could not be suppressed in the people's hearts. In the nineteenth century the Hungarian reform movement continued where the Hungarian Jacobins left off.

The Napoleonic Wars

When the leaders of the Hungarian Jacobin movements were beheaded, Europe was already at war. However, the fighting between the armies of revolutionary France and those of the so-called First Coalition took place in Northern Italy and in the Rhineland area far to the west of Hungary. However, in 1796 General Bonaparte took the command of the French forces in Italy and the situation changed. After dealing heavy blows to the Austrians, at the end of the year the French were in a position to dictate peace to Vienna. The Habsburgs were on the defensive.

During the next years, England and Austria attempted to organize coalitions against France but these were doomed to military failure. It was during this period that Napoleon scored his greatest victories and became emperor of the French. In 1806 the Holy Roman empire was formally abolished and the Austrian Empire came into existence. Hostilities extended to Central and Eastern Europe (Napoleon occupied Vienna twice) but when, in 1805, the war reached Hungary's western border, the Treaty of Pozsony (Pressburg) halted the fighting. In 1809 the French army actually entered Hungary but only a comparatively narrow strip of Transdanubia witnessed battle and occupation. Napoleon's decline started only in 1812–13, after the failure of his Russian campaign, and by 1815 he had been defeated.

The French wars lasted for almost two decades and naturally exerted great influence over political life in Hungary. That small section of the nobility which had grown up during the period of the Enlightenment, together with part of the bourgeoisie and the intelligentsia, sympathized with Napoleon, even when it became clear that he was not following the democratic course of consistent bourgeois transformation. In this stratum aversion to feudalistic conditions was far more powerful than any disenchantment felt. Dániel Berzsenyi wrote: "Napoleon had promised liberty, the soul of the age, but failed to keep his word. His fall was the revenge of 'humanity's cause'." The poet's words, however, could not lessen Bonaparte's appeal. There can also be no doubt that even at the end of the eighteenth century other sections of the nobility still entertained ideas of extending their struggle. Accordingly, they attached great hopes to the probable waning of Habsburg power. But whereas in private conversations and at county assemblies they strongly and sincerely criticized Court policy, sooner or later they came to the realization that they and the Habsburgs shared common interests. The great mass of the nobility from the very beginning had correctly felt that Napoleon's victories posed a serious threat to the feudal order and to feudal privilege. This was the view not only of the tens of thousands of impoverished nobles who for the most part, led a peasant existence, but also that of the overwhelming majority of aristocrats.

The reaction of the peasant masses to the Napoleonic phenomenon cannot be precisely determined, although a certain amount of information undoubtedly reached them concerning world affairs. This arrived in the villages through the accounts of those who returned home from the war, either for good or on leave. For the time being, however, there were no consequences of this awareness.

The changing political attitude of the nobles explains why Napoleon's appeal to the Hungarians in 1809 met with almost no response. In this he offered Hungary the chance of breaking with Austria and the opportunity was allowed to pass. Throughout the Napoleonic Wars, the Hungarian Diets were more than prepared to accede to the Court's every wish, be it the granting of money, produce, or new recruits. Indeed, nobles were even willing to play a part in the fighting themselves. Their involvement took the form of *levées en masse*, financed at their own expense, and service with the colours, either with the infantry or with the cavalry. The wealthiest undertook to provide fully-equipped soldiers, the number depending on the size of their estates. Many impoverished nobles also volunteered and were equipped out of contributions levied on commoners by the counties. The *levées en masse* of the nobility in 1797, 1800, and 1809 mobilized some 135,000 men but only the last one played a part in the war. This was at the Battle of Győr, where the imperial army, under the command of traditionally untalented officers, was seriously defeated by French troops advancing into Hungary from Italy. (This engagement was considered important by the French: Győr's German name—Raab—was inscribed on the Arc de Triomphe in Paris.) Although they had not received proper training, the Hungarian troops fought courageously for quite a time. However, as in the case of previous *levées en masse*, they were demoralized by the fact that the arms they received from the army were old-fashioned or of poor quality. The military failure of the 1809 *levée en masse* shed harsh light on the increasingly weak moral basis of the nobility's exemption from tax. It also contributed to significantly greater awareness of the anachronism represented by feudal conditions.

Loyal gestures on the part of the Hungarian nobility, however, did not dissipate lack of trust on the part of Vienna. The Court regarded the *levées en masse* as an attempt to establish an independent nobles' army and not merely as a manifestation of solidarity. At the same time, Vienna considered it irreconcilable with the absolutist policy of the day that the monarch should be compelled to bargain with his subjects at the Diet and that the latter should grant his wishes only for something in return. As soon as the Court felt the nobility's support was no longer needed (in 1809 Napoleon married Emperor Francis's daughter and in 1813 his star began to wane), it began to ignore feudal constitutional forms and excluded the nobles from the business of politics.

From 1814 onwards Vienna held things increasingly under control. After the fall of Napoleon the Congress of Vienna strengthened the Court's position. The Congress based its settlement on conservative and anti-revolutionary criteria, and the Holy Alliance, which was initiated by the Russian tsar and supported mainly by the absolutist Austrian and Prussian monarchs, established military and political guarantees for the maintenance of the new *status quo*. No amount of coercion, however, was able to disguise the fact that the new arrangements could not last.

Towards the Age of Reform

The collapse of Napoleon's power, the conservative territorial and political settlement in Europe, and the establishment of the Holy Alliance by the absolutist powers—all made it superfluous for the Habsburgs to co-operate with the Hungarian nobility in accordance with the rules of feudal constitutionalism. The Court undoubtedly had good reasons for a more authoritarian approach. After 1800 the only way the Habsburgs could finance their vastly expensive wars was to issue paper money. However, as this paper money lost its value, inflation increased rapidly. To avoid bankruptcy, Vienna was compelled to take drastic steps. In 1811 paper money was devalued by 80 per cent and by a further 60 per cent in 1816. This was catastrophic for the Hungarian nobility. It meant the ruthless tapping of the modest wealth that this class had accumulated from the increased trade made possible by the war. Accordingly, as early as 1812, the nobility questioned the right of the monarch to issue paper money without the approval of the Diet and tried to escape the consequences of the devaluation.

Vienna, however, did not even convene the Diet after 1812. Instead it reverted to government by decree, dismissing the remonstrations of the counties. Hungary was again flooded by the "informants" of the reorganized secret police. The counties came under growing administrative pressure and in 1822 the king issued a decree under which tax was to be paid in silver money. Although this measure primarily affected the peasantry, indirectly it further curtailed the revenues of the nobility. When, in 1821, Vienna demanded the immediate presentation of a backlog of 28,000 recruits, a majority of the counties openly refused to comply. Vienna found it difficult to counter the increasing resistance, which threatened to paralyze the public administration entirely. It resorted to threats, corruption, and even military force where necessary. The poet Ferenc Kölcsey wrote the words of the Hungarian National Anthem on January 22, 1823, at the height of the antagonism. Giving an evocative image of liberty that cannot flourish "from the blood of the dead", the poet points out the anachronism and weakness of purely ancient rights in a changed world, thereby indicating the need for new political attitudes.

The time for this soon arrived. Vienna, despite its hard-won victory, had to realize that in Hungary it would still have to rely on the counties for a number of reasons. It therefore could not dispense with them if it wished to maintain the feudal social order. The convening of the Diet and the suspension of the implementation of the offending decrees were essential for consolidation. Accordingly, the Diet was convened in 1825 after an interval of thirteen years. This was a victory over absolutism for the Hungarian state and recalled the triumph of 1790, after the death of Joseph II. Twenty years later, Chancellor Metternich dated the beginning of his troubles with Hungary from 1825. Liberal Hungarian historiography describes the period which now began as the Age of Reform. The original question in the conflict, the legality of the paper money issue, could no longer be disputed, and it was unlikely that the victims of the devaluations would be compensated. However, Hungary had, during the Napoleonic Wars, at last entered the mainstream of Europe's economy and there was now an increasing foreign demand for Hungarian grain, wool, and even tobacco. This provoked new political demands in the nobility which were demonstrated by the two main achievements of the Diet—the foundation of the Academy of Sciences and the ordering of renewed discussions on reform. These discussions were to be conducted by a broadly-based committee charged with examining the plans originally drafted at the beginning of the 1790s but which had then been shelved by Vienna.

The founding of the Academy of Sciences (after this the name of Count István

91

Széchenyi became inseparably linked with the national reform movement) indicated that a part of the nobility and aristocracy wished to place contemporary science at the service of development in Hungary. An eighty-one member committee (the members were delegated by the Diet) discussed the proposals for two and a half years while the whole country looked on. In the end, the various ideas and proposals were reported in a conservative spirit. Public opinion, however, expected more than this, demanding that the proposals be discussed throughout Hungary at county level. By summer 1830 there existed numerous suggestions which all aimed at improvement, and by the end of the year Vienna was forced to allow the published findings of the committee to be considered by the counties after all. Merely a unifying concept was now missing, one around which everything could be organized. This was soon provided and quickly became known: on January 28, 1830 Széchenyi's *Hitel* (Credit) was published.

István Széchenyi and the Reform Movement

The fact that during the first half of the nineteenth century Hungary gradually entered the mainstream of European economic life demonstrated to the landowners that in a predominantly agrarian country the expansion of agricultural commodity production offered them a good opportunity to augment their wealth. But at the same time it also revealed the preconditions necessary for this, i.e. intensive cultivation of the land together with animal husbandry of a high order. For these the forced labour of the serf and the existing expertise of the stockman were increasingly inadequate. It soon became clear that, on the one hand, better work could only be demanded of the free wage labourer and that, on the other, Hungarian landowners lacked not just the capital needed for the regular employment of wage labourers but also access to the credit which could make this available. The reason for this lack of credit was that the landed estates of the Hungarian nobility could not be seized to recover debts. Under the medieval institution of entailment (which dated from 1351) such estates were inalienable as long as a member of the family in possession was alive. However, capital was vital for the development of the economy and this was true for industry, commerce, and banking—as well as for agriculture. Credit was needed and this would not be forthcoming while the land remained unavailable to guarantee loans.

Count István Széchenyi was the first to draw attention to the importance of all this. In 1825 he offered a year's revenue from his estates to found a learned society, the Academy of Sciences. The Széchenyis were no strangers to such public spiritedness: in 1802 István's father, Ferenc, had donated his collections of books and *objets d'art* to the nation (thereby laying the foundations of the Széchényi Library and the National Museum), and in 1797 an uncle, Count György Festetics, had established the Georgikon, the first agricultural college on the continent of Europe, at Keszthely. István Széchenyi had begun his adult life as an army officer but after the Napoleonic Wars he abandoned soldiering and started to manage his vast estates. His private life and inner world were shaped by Romanticism, the dominant philosophy of the age. On economic questions, however, Széchenyi read the Western European economists with whose works he had become acquainted in the course of his foreign travels. Therefore, when a bank in Vienna rejected his application for a small loan, Széchenyi was able to see that this shed light on the fundamental problem of the Hungarian economy. Széchenyi's *Hitel* accordingly proposed the abolition of entailment as a first step towards credit-worthiness for the Hungarian landowner.

Later on Széchenyi was to compare the feudal order to a knitted stocking that could be unwound as soon as the first stitch was undone. In point of fact, in *Hitel* Széchenyi went beyond the abolition of entailment and made further proposals which inevitably pointed towards bourgeois transformation. These included the total separation of the land of the nobility from that of the peasantry; the abolition of the ninth, which was paid in kind to the landowner out of the serf's produce; the disbanding of the guilds; the establishment of a ceiling on prices; and the abolition of internal tariffs. Economic and institutional development was not, however, to be an end in itself: as Széchenyi saw it, these merely served the prosperity of the nation, which also required "a multitude of educated people".

Széchenyi's approach was a new one in Hungarian politics. Not only did he address problems in a more bourgeois way, but he also proposed reforms which did not involve a deliberate challenge to the government. Admittedly, the fundamental issue, the lack of credit, was a problem that chiefly concerned the big landowners (in other words, not those groups which had been forced into the opposition). Széchenyi regarded these big landlords—undoubtedly the most powerful group in the Hungarian economy—as the possible leading force of the transformation. However, the very fact that *Hitel* sought the solution outside the feudal framework was sufficient to prompt sharp attack from several quarters. In 1831 Széchenyi responded —primarily to Count József Dessewffy's *Taglalat*, an analysis of *Hitel*—by publishing *Világ* (Light), in which he clarified those parts of *Hitel* which were open to misinterpretation. In the same year Széchenyi wrote *Stádium* in which he put forth twelve proposals for a basic programme of transformation. Széchenyi held that the granting of credit must be independent of the social status of the party concerned. Entailment, which obstructed a free market in land, needed to be abolished, along with the treasury's right of inheritance after families had died out. The right to own land must be conferred on non-nobles and everyone should be made equal before the law. The nobility (and not just the peasantry) should contribute to the expenses of operating the county administration and of sending deputies to the Diet. Feudal barriers to industry and trade needed to be removed and Hungarian made the official language of public administration. The Council of Lieutenancy, which governed the country from Buda, should be given broader powers (in order to reduce Vienna's interference in the country's internal affairs). Consultations and jurisdiction must be made public. All this amounted to more than just reform—at least as far as the government was concerned—and it was no surprise that the censors withheld permission for the book to be published. However, *Stádium* was printed abroad and smuggled into the country. In November 1833 copies discovered in Hungary were seized, although too late. For more than a decade Széchenyi's programme became the sole model for reform in Hungary.

Széchenyi was not content to raise the problems of transformation on a theoretical level only. He was also the instigator of, and participant in, a whole series of practical economic enterprises. His activities were extensive, ranging from the organization of horse shows designed to promote better blood-stock through the support of shipping on the Danube to the construction of Budapest's Chain Bridge across the same river. This bridge was built between 1842 and 1848 by a capitalist joint-stock company. Széchenyi was also involved in the Pest Rolling Mill (1846), the first high-performance steam mill in the country. Széchenyi not only organized these modern ventures, but was also one of the largest shareholders in them. In Pest he owned valuable residential accommodation, and this increased in value as the city grew. By 1848 the greater part of Széchenyi's income came from capitalistic sources and not from feudal dues. To further his plans, at the end of the 1840s he became a member of the body which supervised Hungary's public administration. As such, he undertook the state supervision of work which aimed to regulate not only the river Tisza (to prevent flooding) but also the Danube at the Iron Gate. The aim of these projects was to link the grain-producing areas of the Great Plain to domestic and foreign markets. But co-operation with the government or even the avoidance of conflicts became more and more unwelcome, and by the mid-1840s Széchenyi's popularity had declined. This could not alter the fact, though, that in 1830 *Hitel* had provided a convincing analysis of Hungary's increasingly difficult problems, as well as definite proposals for solving them. Although Széchenyi did not explicitly say so, what was involved was the crises of the entire feudal order, the only way out of which was development. This was a decisive realization and its truth was underlined a few months later. In the wake of the 1831 cholera epidemic, a peasant uprising broke out in Upper Hungary and the dreadful events which followed shed light on the great tensions which had built up in the masses, tensions which were ready to erupt generally at the slightest slackening in the social order. This convinced the liberal representatives of bourgeois transformation that they must follow in Széchenyi's footsteps.

"Liberty and property"

Széchenyi's proposals were only one possible answer to the growing crisis of feudalism in Hungary: in the long run, even the traditional landowning aristocrat who disposed of the vast revenues from his estates could eventually hope to borrow capital. Széchenyi was a member of the political élite which governed the Austrian empire, and his reform ideas did not include the radical transformation of the existing political order; indeed, Széchenyi counted on government assistance in the realization of his plans. The great majority of Hungarian landowning nobles were not satisfied with the answers he gave. New generations of lesser nobles were increasingly threatened by the break-up of their estates, and neither their income nor the size of their properties made any major investment possible. These nobles therefore felt that if they wished to exploit effectively the opportunities afforded by the economic boom then occurring, they must take control of the whole state. Once they had done this, positions of power would be redistributed. More importantly, changes would also have to be made in the tariff system, which hindered the marketing of their produce. However, this path would ultimately have led to the total annihilation of Habsburg absolutism—the goal that was contemplated in 1790. Just as in the eighteenth-century, pro-reform nobles had used the ideology of the Enlightenment to back their demands, so their descendants now applied the ideology of liberalism, which characterized the consolidated Western European systems that had now emerged. In the majority of the reform proposals that cropped up in such great variety during the course of the 1828 debates, there surfaced not only anti-absolutist ideas, but also liberal ideas and demands pointing towards bourgeois transformation.

The experiences of the 1831 uprising had made those sections of the nobility which advocated reforms conscious of their need for large-scale peasant support in the event of conflict with Vienna. With this aim in mind they worked out a strategy, that of the "reconciliation of interests". Under this the nobles tried to create an opportunity primarily for the landed elements of the peasantry, the serfs with small plots, to pay off their feudal dues once and for all with cash. These peasants would then become free and, at the same time, the landowners would acquire money. "Liberty and property"—this was how the poet Kölcsey defined the common interest that bound every inhabitant of the land to his country.

The opportunity to implement reformist plans arose during the Diet of 1832–36. The central issue there was the passing of reform legislation which took account of the conclusions arrived at during the earlier county debates. The advocates of reform made an attempt to develop further the recommendations made by the committees, to make the proposals more liberal in spirit, and to enact legislation appropriate to them. However, Vienna succeeded in frustrating the reform hopes. In this it was able to rely on the traditionally conservative Upper House, the majority of whose members were loyal to the Habsburg dynasty, and also on the impoverished mass of lesser nobles. Their representatives in the Lower House were thus persuaded to modify the instructions issued to the pro-reform deputies. This victory was not, however, entirely unequivocal.

It turned out that the traditional opposition of the nobility to Vienna had taken on a new, totally different, and more dangerous form. At the Diet there now emerged a consciously liberal political grouping which was favourably disposed towards embourgeoisment and which was capable of steadfastly advocating an opposition reform policy. Simultaneously there also emerged new politicians to organize and lead this opposition. Mention can be made of three such figures. First and foremost was Baron Miklós Wesselényi, a Transylvanian aristocrat who entered politics as Széchenyi's friend and follower but who soon turned against the government. Wesselényi became the most influential and most zealous organizer of the liberal opposition. In a book entitled *Balítéletek* (Misjudgements), he addressed himself to bourgeois transformation as well as to economic and political changes. Kölcsey, a poet, was capable of formulating the central issues of reform with unparalleled lucidity, while the young Ferenc Deák, an excellent tactician, unravelled the internal contradictions of the system and used them to further the reformist cause. Around these leading politicians there gathered a large group of young opposition deputies.

Finally, the frequently acrimonious and sharply-worded arguments between the

Diet and the government were brought before the public for the first time. Lajos Kossuth, a young lawyer from Zemplén county, reported events at the Diet, and especially the ideas put forward there, in his *Országgyűlési tudósítások* (Dietal Reports). These he published in the form of private letters in order to evade the censorship. Kossuth's efforts were not without consequence: more and more people were now informed concerning important questions of the day.

This was too much for Vienna. On March 2, 1835, Francis I died and was succeeded by his son, the mentally-retarded Ferdinand V. The small ruling clique controlled by Metternich continued to do everything possible to maintain rigid absolutism. In May 1836, a few days after the Diet was closed, the leaders of the younger deputies were arrested and sentenced to several years imprisonment, and Kossuth was prohibited from carrying on with his *Törvényhatósági Tudósítások* (Municipal Reports), in which he wrote about the municipal authorities and local government. When he defied this order in May 1837 he, too, was arrested and sentenced to four years in jail. After a treason trial which began in 1835 and lasted four years, Wesselényi was also sent to prison—for a three-year term.

The country was again overwhelmed by bitterness and fear, although this state of affairs would not last for long.

On the road to capitalism

The national and social reform movement scored its first major successes at the Diet of 1839–40. A law was passed under which serfs were entitled to buy freedom together with their plots of land. A law on bills provided security for creditors, the preconditions for commercial and industrial development were created in the capitalist spirit, and the Jews—formerly without rights—were allowed to settle freely in the towns and to set up businesses in trade and industry. As a result of the reform opposition's persistent and skilful efforts, in May 1840 the political prisoners were released. Wesselényi, now blind, and László Lovassy, the youth leader who went insane, did not return to political life. The new head of the movement, Lajos Kossuth, made a triumphant comeback and immediately became the main spokesman for the opposition.

The opposition's struggle under Kossuth's leadership can be divided into three phases and was carried on in three different forums. It began on the pages of *Pesti Hírlap*, a paper edited by Kossuth which was first published in January 1841. This was the first modern political newspaper in Hungary, and did not merely inform but also served as a means of agitation and organizing. The paper also had provincial correspondents. Extremely well-informed, Kossuth wrote forceful articles on a wide range of subjects, from the question of poverty, basement flats in Pest, prison conditions and the injustices of soke, to the pressing economic issues of railway construction and the settlement of the tariff question. He criticized and ridiculed, but at the same time put forward a programme. This advocated the general abolition of the serfs' feudal dues, and the abolition of the privileges of the nobility, including its exemption from tax. The main goal of Kossuth's programme was the creation of a bourgeois middle class, thus ensuring the possibility for a constitutional and independent national existence. To this end it was necessary to pursue a policy of co-ordinating the interests of the nobility, the middle class, and the peasantry.

The antagonism which developed between Széchenyi and Kossuth in the 1840s was not chiefly over the primacy of agricultural as opposed to industrial development, indeed not even over the order in which modernization and independence should be achieved. The argument was over "method" and tactics. By this, Széchenyi primarily understood Hungary's relationship with Vienna. Széchenyi wanted to introduce reforms in co-operation with the government, and not in defiance of it. Kossuth knew that genuine change could only be accomplished by opposition to absolutism. Ultimately, "method" came to signify conflict between the more moderate, i.e. aristocratic, path to bourgeois transformation and the more radical, liberal one.

In 1843 the absolutist government removed Kossuth from his post as editor. This could not, however, stop the opposition movement from making great strides. At the Diet of 1843–44 Hungarian was declared to be the official language of the state. In the years that followed Kossuth organized the reform movement in a new area—the economic—and organized the *Védegylet*, which aimed to organize a boy-cott of foreign (i.e. Austrian) goods and so encourage Hungarian industry. Kossuth also attempted to establish a factory-founding society and a commercial society, but these achieved little. In the course of this economic and political struggle, Kossuth developed his plan for an independent tariff area.

During the third phase, in spring 1847, the opposition organized itself into a political party. In response to the conservatives' programme of autumn 1846, Ferenc Deák drafted the "Proclamation of the Opposition". This was inspired by Kossuth and served as the party's programme. Its chief demands were taxation for all social groups, equality before the law, the abolition of serfdom with state compensation, the free sale of the landed estates of the nobility, freedom of the press, the introduction of parliamentary government and a responsible ministry, and union between Transylvania and Hungary—demands which were later codified in March 1848.

The opposition party drew support from some of the country's best politicians, writers, and scholars—a reform generation that excelled in intellectual prowess, courage, and moral integrity. One of its leaders was Ferenc Deák, whose proposal for a new penal code in 1843 was the most progressive of the time. Another prominent figure was the writer, scholar, and politician Baron József Eötvös. Eötvös's two novels, *A falu jegyzője* (The Village Notary), which unveiled feudal backwardness, and *Magyarország 1514-ben* (Hungary in 1514), which re-told the story of György Dózsa's peasant uprising, had a great impact. Eötvös's circle included the writer Zsigmond Kemény and the historian László Szalay, both of whom were advocates of centralization and capitalism. Count Lajos Batthyány was another outstanding leader of the opposition. He, his cousin Count Kázmér Batthyány, the Károlyis and the Andrássys, patriotic liberal aristocrats, and the majority of the lesser nobility all supported reform.

In the course of the fierce struggles of the 1840s it became clear that the Viennese government would frustrate any attempt at genuine change and that it was opposed

97

to progress and national revival in Hungary. At the same time the conservatives, now organizing themselves into a political party to counter the liberal reformists, could neither provide a meaningful programme nor produce any results. The pro-government clique gradually became isolated. All this made things easier for Kossuth and the opposition.

Ultimately, the opposition's success derived from the fact that, in the wake of the economic boom of the 1840s, more and more Hungarians desired modernization and bourgeois development. The landowning nobility grappling with economic difficulties, the non-noble intelligentsia, the urban and rural lower bourgeoisie, the fledgling industrial and agricultural wage labour force, and the rising Jewish burghers were all united in a desire for reform. The most diverse elements rallied behind Kossuth's programme—all those, in fact, whose existence and opportunities were threatened by the outmoded feudal and absolutist order. Literature, music, and the fine arts all gave expression to expectations of radical change. "Young Hungary", a circle of youthful writers headed by the revolutionary poet Sándor Petőfi, deserves special mention in this respect.

In the autumn of 1847 the last feudal Diet convened in Pozsony at a time of economic difficulty, tensions, and a mounting discontent which permeated the whole of society.

Hungarian culture
in the first half of the nineteenth century

European politics and European economic development played a part in the undermining of feudal conditions and the absolutist political order in Hungary. Primarily as a result of economic development, the demand grew for the utilization of certain modern scientific discoveries for industrial and other purposes, despite the fact that the preconditions for independent scientific and technical progress, along with money and qualified experts, were still largely lacking. Nonetheless, noteworthy results were achieved at Pest University in the agricultural sciences (including botany and zoology), in hydraulics, and in medicine. In 1828 Ányos Jedlik built an electric motor and in 1832 the Bolyais discovered absolute geometry. Both of these steps were highly important contributions to international science, although owing to backward technical conditions in Hungary they could not be put to practical use at home. At the same time, however, social sciences and culture developed quickly, as did culture in the broadest sense of the term.

The decisive cultural achievement of the time was the renewal of the Hungarian language which began at the end of the eighteenth century. In the wake of a new orientation in society and the economy, the horizons of the average person began to expand: new objects and phenomena entered his daily life, along with increasingly complex relationships. The perfection of a new handicrafts industry, changes in agriculture, the first modern Hungarian-language works on commerce and science —all required that a Hungarian equivalent be found for innumerable new terms. At the same time, in an ever-widening world it became increasingly clear that people were unable to express precisely such things as the more intricate and contradictory feelings of love, passion, sadness and joy. Since these were rooted in the more developed parts of Europe, it is not difficult to see that the renewal of the language indirectly made people familiar with the conditions prevailing in those countries. This was why the renewal of the language triggered off a fierce struggle, and one that lasted for many decades, between those who would have been satisfied with merely increasing the vocabulary and those—led by Ferenc Kazinczy—who, through a renewal of style and behaviour, wished to introduce middle-class tastes, values, and sensibilities.

Supplemented with tens of thousands of new words and expressions, by the first quarter of the nineteenth century the Hungarian language had become suitable not only for the expression of the new ideas in economics and science, but also for the adoption of new literary genres. This enabled writers to convey new emotions to their readers, together with the ideals of enlightened and romantic behaviour. In the early nineteenth-century Hungarian writers and poets were already producing outstanding work: János Batsányi, Mihály Csokonai Vitéz, Mihály Vörösmarty, Ferenc Kölcsey, and Ferenc Kazinczy all made powerful contributions to Hungarian literature. The greatest Hungarian play to date, *Bánk bán* by József Katona, was written during this period. Literature still reflected the political demands, outlook, historical consciousness, and mentality of an overwhelmingly noble readership but also bore the stamp of authors' social origins. At this time most writers came from the lesser nobility, generally from its impoverished strata.

However, cultural change was not confined to the great literary figures and their educated readership. It began to permeate the lower strata of society as well. The rapid spread of literacy was the chief catalyst in this. Maria Theresa's education decree of 1777 (the *Ratio Educationis*) had aimed to organize elementary education for the people, and the number of peasants who could read had subsequently increased. A second *Ratio Educationis*, in 1806, made school attendance compulsory for children, although this was not achieved for some time. Naturally, not everyone became literate even when they did attend classes but nevertheless a number of people benefited. It was precisely for these persons that the primitively-illustrated cheap publications which started to proliferate at the turn of the nineteenth century were intended. This period also witnessed the birth of the Hungarian-language press in Hungary. The early nineteenth-century Hungarian-language theatre responded to the new requirements of society and began to acquaint even illiterates with the new models of behaviour and emotion. After the establishment of some provincial theatres (in Kecskemét, Miskolc, Székesfehérvár, etc.), the first Hungarian-language theatre in Pest was opened in 1837. Travelling theatre troupes tried to meet the demand for their services in the countryside. As a result, from the mid-1840s onwards a more radical mentality and the more definite tastes of a rural, small-town, and partly non-noble lower middle-class intellectual stratum began to emerge. This layer, developing during a period of economic upswing, produced figures who started to play an increasingly important role in determining the course of literature, and it was at this time that Sándor Petőfi and János Arany appeared on the literary scene. The voice of literature was brought to a wider and wider readership by several different kinds of literary and cultural journal, while the first popular plays made their highly-successful appearances on the stage. Thanks to good translations, the works of not only Shakespeare, Schiller, and Molière found their way to Hungarian theatres, but also those plays which depicted the modern European middle-class world of the age. The cult of the actor emerged, and so did the role of the primadonna.

The first quarter of the nineteenth century brought about a change in Hungarian musical life as well. Primarily amongst the urban middle class and well-to-do nobility, interest in contemporary European music widened. Vienna's musical culture, now at its height, influenced Hungary as well. On the other hand, it was during these years that a special Hungarian style of music, the *verbunkos*, evolved. This soon became extremely popular—appealing to the nobility and peasantry alike. Traces of its influence could also be perceived in the classical genres of contemporary Hungarian music. Eventually new elements also appeared in the musical culture of the people generally. In the wake of increased social mobility, new motifs, often originating from distant lands, were added to the previously closed melodies of the village, and a new type of folk song appeared. After a quarter of a century of unsuccessful attempts, 1844 witnessed the birth of the first modern Hungarian opera, *Hunyadi László* by Ferenc Erkel (who also composed the music for the National Anthem). *Hunyadi László* was a great triumph, and not just because of its patriotic theme.

The spread of bourgeois *mores* brought about the awakening of a demand for, and a receptiveness to, fine art. The number of artists and buyers of art grew. The walls of rural manor-houses were adorned with portraits and engravings, and even in peasant homes pictures grew rapidly in number, although these were, for the most part, primitive. In the 1830s a more sophisticated art appeared. Its first masters, Brocky and Markó, soon went to live abroad, but Miklós Barabás achieved fame in Hungary—primarily through his portraits. In addition, romantic historical painting, which reached its high point only after 1849, also slowly emerged. Exhibitions organized by the Pest Art Association attempted to spread contemporary European artistic taste, as did the first art dealers in the capital. Illustrations in books and periodicals made their contribution to this process. It was during these years that the sculptor István Ferenczy, who had studied in Rome, created the first great pieces of Hungarian neo-classical sculpture.

The face of Hungarian architecture also changed in the wake of the modest and periodical economic booms. The growing number of new buildings, primarily aristocratic palaces, town houses, manor-houses and, in some places, even peasant dwellings, showed the influence of the neo-classical style, the leading contemporary artistic fashion. The same may be said for the churches and, generally speaking, the public buildings erected at this time. The great Hungarian architects of the age (especially Mihály Pollack and József Hild) put up impressive structures (e.g. the National Museum, Pest County Hall, and the Vigadó) in Pest, which was now the centre of the national economy, culture, and the state administration. They also laid out impressive squares as well as entire streets. Attractive neo-classical building complexes were laid out in several country towns as well.

The diverse elements of the consciously Hungarian national current now emerging in culture were integrated by a politically-conscious behaviour which by this time had taken its first steps to initiate bourgeois transformation. This behaviour advocated the primacy of the "national" element and from culture it expected the expression and interpretation of what was at the same time a concept and a demand. The demand was difficult to define but it could now rely on historical research—the discovery of sources and syntheses that had been going on since the mid-eighteenth century. Contemporary Hungarian culture therefore became markedly historical in character. The National Anthem and the *Szózat* (Appeal) were poems which were just as much summaries of Hungarian history as were those works of music and fine art which attempted to interpret the present through history, by means of theme and analogy. It was to meet this demand that Mihály Horváth's great four-volume history of Hungary was written in the years 1842–46.

This close interconnection between culture and politics imparted popularity and social significance to the former, and penetrating force—the widening of popular understanding—to the latter. This was the decisive precondition for the success of a broad-based political struggle pointing in the direction of capitalist development.

The awakening of the nationalities
in the Danubian region

The process which took place amongst the Magyars at this time, and which resulted in the emergence of the modern Hungarian nation, also occurred amongst the non-Magyar peoples of Hungary. Of course, there were many differences in the way this happened.

These differences essentially derived from the social structures of the various nationalities. Only the Croats resembled the Magyars in the way their society was made up, and in any case contemporaries regarded the Croats as different from the rest. Croatian society was strongly reminiscent of Hungarian society, with its sizeable landed aristocracy, large body of lesser nobles, and broad peasant masses. Some of the Croat peasants were not even serfs but freemen who could cultivate their land in exchange for army service in the so-called Military Border zone.

In Transylvania, Saxon society was fundamentally bourgeois in character, although feudal privileges also kept it closed. In Hungary the German urban middle class had already started to assimilate and the peasant masses were not yet affected by incipient nationalism.

The Romanians, Serbs, Slovaks and Ruthenes were basically characterized by the fact that their nobility, through enjoying feudal privileges, had assimilated with the Magyar nobility, and by the fact that magyarization had already begun to affect their national languages. The bulk were peasants who lived the life of serfs, but there were the urban lower middle-class strata as well. In the case of the Serbs and Romanians, a small proportion also served as free soldier-peasants in the Military Border zone. For the most part, the Serbs became merchants in the royal free towns situated along the main trade routes. They also settled in the southern areas, the Bácska and the Banat. The Serbian burghers achieved a certain prosperity, especially after the regulation of the Danube at the Iron Gate. That river accordingly became the principal trade route to the east, at the expense of those routes which went through Transylvania. This change brought business to the Serb settlements.

Although numerically small, the intelligentsia, and above all the clergy, played a major part in the life of all the national minorities. In a sense the Eastern Orthodox and the Greek Catholic Churches served as national churches for these peoples. In the case of the Serbs, the Orthodox Church played an especially significant role. The privileges granted to it in 1690 permitted Church congresses to be held, and these, which were convened from time to time, also served as political forums. The Serb National Congress held at Temesvár in September 1790 raised for the first time the demand of territorial autonomy for this particular ethnic group. Also indicative of the political and secular role of this congress was the fact that it was also attended by Serb officers from the Military Border. In 1842, the Congress of Karlóca elected Josip Rajačić as metropolitan. Rajačić was to be an important figure later on, at the time of the 1848 Revolution.

The Serb intelligentsia was the first to proclaim its secession from the Hungarians, and its belonging to another nation. It believed that this nation had always existed, but that it was asleep and needed to be woken up. In this way even contemporaries spoke of national awakening and revival.

The first and most important task of this awakening was the creation of a national language which could be used to address the people and to make them conscious of belonging to the nation. At the beginning of this period none of the nationalities possessed a national literary language. The Slovak Lutherans used Medieval Czech as their literary language, the Catholics used various dialects, and the Serbs Russian interspersed with Serb words—which they called Slaveno-Serb. The Croats also used dialects. Towards the end of the eighteenth century Greek Catholic (Uniate) Romanian priests started to raise the vernacular to the rank of a literary language, and to purge words of non-Latin origin from it. In the case of the Croats Ljudevit Gaj accepted as the Croatian literary language the dialect closest to Serb, which Vuk Stefanivić Karadžić had already elevated to the rank of a Serbian literary language. Owing to the conservatism of the Serbian burghers, it was more difficult to attain recognition for the new tongue, but nevertheless Slaveno-Serb gradually disappeared from usage. After some experimentation L'udovit Stúr made the Middle Slovakian dialect the literary language of the Slovaks. The languages which emerged at this time have remained the literary languages of these peoples to this day. Only the more backward Ruthenes were incapable of creating their own literary language in this period. Poetry, short stories, novels, and plays were written in the new Serbian literary language, and the outlines of a national culture began to take shape. In 1826 the Serbs founded *Srpska Matica* in Pest, a public education society which later served as a model for other Slav peoples. Primarily concerned with cultivating the Serb language, *Srpska Matica* also published literary works. The urban middle class was very active among the Serbs: in 1791, it founded a Serb grammar school in Karlóca and another in Újvidék nineteen years later. In 1812, a teachers' training college was established in Szentendre, a major Serb ecclesiastical centre.

Literary works also dealt with the historical past of the ethnic group concerned, although historiography also proclaimed the former glory of the nationalities. A good example is the chronicle written by the Romanian Gheorghe Sincai. The Slovak Ján Kollár sang of the great past and sad contemporary situation of the Slavs in an impressive series of sonnets (*Slávy dcera*—The Daughter of Glory) to stimulate their self-awareness. Theories of glorious origins also served to emphasize a historical past. For instance, the Slavs were said to be related to the Scythians, and the Romanians tried to prove their purely Roman ancestry. The historians of every nationality stressed their people's entitlement to the area it then inhabited. During the mid-eighteenth century, Jovan Rajic wrote a history of the various Slavic peoples, dealing especially with the Bulgars, Croats, and Serbs. He completed this work in 1768 and it was published in Vienna in the years 1791–95. A revised edition came out in Buda in 1823, demonstrating the interest in Serb history which then existed. Rajic, too, believed in the kinship between the Scythians and the Slavs. Apart from this, however, he strove to base his work on original sources, towards which, to some extent, he adopted a critical approach.

The cause of language and literature was also served by the establishment of separate theatre for the nationalities. Owing to unfavourable conditions, however, for the time being this meant no more than amateur dramatics and travelling theatre companies. The Serbs, too, had theatre troupes which travelled to towns with Serb populations and which used theatrical performances in efforts to arouse national self-consciousness.

During these decades the cultural development pressed for by the intelligentsia undoubtedly achieved considerable success, even though it still only reached the urban lower middle-class elements of society. Reference could, however, be made to this cultural development, to its achievements, and to the separate identity of the nationality in question. Moreover, the demand could now be raised that the nationalities' languages be granted equal status with Hungarian.

The Croats were in a more favourable position because they had their own feudal institutions—counties and a provincial assembly (the Sabor). Croatian deputies also attended the Hungarian Diet. Accordingly, it was the Croatian national movement that first put a political demand—namely, the removal of Hungarian authority in the areas inhabited by Croats. Croatian leaders regarded their own people as too weak by themselves: it was thus in the name of all the South Slav peoples that they launched the idea of "Illyrism". This advocated the establishment of a common South Slav state, naturally within the framework of the Habsburg empire. In 1832 Count Janko Drašković, the Croatian Széchenyi, wrote a work (*Dissertatio iliti razgovor*) in which he also raised social issues.

Although to a lesser extent, the Serbs, too, were in a better position than most other nationalities living in Hungary. This was not just because of the religious autonomy they enjoyed. The fact that they lived for the most part in either the royal free towns or in the Military Border area meant that the magyarizing measures of the counties did not affect them. Prior to 1848, therefore, no serious conflicts existed between the Serbs and the Hungarians. The prosperous Serb merchants were also represented in the town magistracies in Southern Hungary, and, indeed, even in the county administration there. The 1840s witnessed the forming of the *Omladina*, the youth organization of Serbian students enrolled at colleges and lycées, which played a significant role in arousing political and linguistic consciousness. Important *Omladina* branches functioned in Pest, Pozsony, and Szeged. It is interesting from the viewpoint of Serbian national development that, from the early nineteenth century onwards, large numbers of intellectuals and officials originating from Southern Hungary worked in the state apparatus and cultural institutions of the Principality of Serbia, which existed outside the borders of the Habsburg empire. This embryonic Serbian state was still part of the Ottoman empire but enjoyed a large measure of self-government.

On the whole, though, prior to 1848 the national movements were predominantly cultural in character. Their principal demand was the free use of their national languages.

The Bourgeois Revolution

The outbreak of the Revolution in March 1848

When in November 1847 the emperor Ferdinand opened the Diet at Pozsony, no one could have imagined that this would be the last feudal Diet in Hungarian history.

Admittedly, those advocates of bourgeois development who appeared in Pozsony to attend the Diet had higher hopes than ever before. They enjoyed a small, albeit undoubted, majority in the Lower House and, for the first time, Lajos Kossuth was also present as the chief spokesman for the opposition deputies there. His influence in the Lower House could not be rivalled by anyone on the conservative side. Although the conservatives still possessed a majority in the Upper House, here, too, there were powerful advocates of change led by Count Lajos Batthyány, the chairman of the opposition party.

All this was to no avail, however. As the months passed the signs grew that once again the liberal opposition would fail to achieve a solution to urgent issues, including the most pressing one—the need to abolish serfdom. The Diet of 1840 had made it possible for serfs to purchase their freedom and their plot of land but very few serfs had found the money to liberate themselves in this way. During the early months of the Diet not only conservative resistance stood in the way of tangible results. The fact that the liberals did not act consistently and in concert also served as an important obstacle.

Most of the middle nobles were contending with an oppressive shortage of money. These people therefore had no alternative but to oppose the idea of liberating their serfs without compensation, at least until they were able to make good in some other way the losses that such a move would involve. In other words, an economic policy which encouraged domestic industry and which rapidly expanded the domestic market would have to be introduced before the general liberation of the serfs could take place. Such an economic policy would make the business opportunities of agricultural producers much more favourable, and would boost profitability.

However, the introduction of such a policy was inconceivable as long as the government of the country was not in the hands of the liberal opposition. For their part, the liberals could only contemplate the idea of making a bid for political power *after* the liberation of the serfs, so that, in the ensuing power struggle, the peasant masses would side with them and not against them. This contradiction, implicit in the landowners' circumstances, had a paralyzing effect on even the best of liberal politicians.

105

This was the state of affairs until March 1848, when, suddenly, the situation underwent a complete change. In the course of the preceding weeks a wave of revolution had swept half of Europe and this spilled over into the Habsburg empire. On March 13 Vienna became the scene of fervent revolutionary activity, as did Pest, Milan, and Venice a few days later. This sudden turn of events created an opportunity for the Hungarian liberals to make an immediate bid for domestic political power, even without ensuring in advance the backing of the peasant masses. Kossuth and his associates availed themselves of this opportunity right away: on March 15 they dispatched a dietal delegation to Vienna which returned two days later. The Court had issued a rescript appointing Batthyány prime minister and had promised that the monarch was ready to sanction in the course of the following weeks all legislation passed by the Diet.

The liberal leaders were, however, well aware that sooner or later they must take steps to win the goodwill of the peasantry. Accordingly, and as early as March 15, the Diet expressed its support for the emancipation of the serfs with the state treasury assuming the entire burden of compensating the landowners. This was a crucial statement to make, as the radicals rallying around Petőfi in Pest soon demonstrated. To exert public pressure on the Diet, they summed up their principal liberal demands in twelve points. These were worded more radically than ever before (e.g. although they demanded the liberation of the serfs, they made no mention at all of any compensation for the landlords). When news of the Vienna disturbances reached Pest, Petőfi and his group also embarked upon the path of revolutionary action. Within a few hours they mobilized the people of the city, as well as the tens of thousands of rural folk who had flooded in to attend the national fair on St Joseph's Day. Without prior permission from the censors, they had the "Twelve Points" printed, and also Petőfi's *Nemzeti dal* (National Song), thereby establishing the freedom of the press in a single day. They then forced the Municipal Council of Pest and the Council of Lieutenancy—the supreme body responsible for public administration in Hungary—to grant their demands. Finally, they succeeded in obtaining the release from prison of Mihály Táncsics, the radical politician representing the peasants.

On receiving news of the developments in Pest, the Diet stated on March 18 that the serfs must be immediately freed from the obligation to perform their feudal services even though the compensation of landowners would not follow right away. Thus, the Diet finally settled the peasant question. This extremely important decision at Pozsony was, however, only the first of many which followed each other in rapid succession and which created a framework for transformation. Legislation enacted by the Diet included provisions for putting the legislature on a representative basis, for the creation of a responsible ministry, for Hungary's total political independence within the empire, for the equality before the law of nobles and nonnobles, for the abolition of the censorship, for the setting up of a National Guard, for general and proportionate taxation, for the abolition of Church tithes, and for the reunion of Hungary and Transylvania. By enacting such legislation, the Diet made it possible for the millions of people living in Hungary to embark upon the path of prosperity despite their numerous differences of interests, and to join ranks in creating a modern society.

The revolutionary camp and the counter-revolution

After the closure of the last feudal Diet, most members of the Batthyány government set to work convinced that the implementation of the March Laws would be
fairly smooth. This was, however, too optimistic an assessment, primarily because it
was based on an underestimation of the Crown's counter-revolutionary hopes. For
although the Crown had been compelled to retreat in March, it still possessed formidable instruments of power (including the army), and was by no means willing to
accept the March settlement as final.

Admittedly, by this time the anti-Habsburg camp in Hungary was far stronger
than it had been at the end of the eighteenth century and, for this reason, the country
could no longer be pushed back into its former oppressed state. However, the anti-
Habsburg group did not yet wield sufficient power in Hungary to ensure permanently that measure of independence for a government which it could undoubtedly guarantee in March. At the same time, the difficulties which were temporarily preoccupying the Habsburgs concealed, for the moment, the counter-
revolutionary threat. From March onwards, the best units of the imperial army were
tied down by the struggle for independence waged by the provinces of Northern
Italy, which were fighting for complete secession. Also, for quite a while revolutionary mass movements also erupted in Vienna itself. Not even these difficulties made
the Crown accept the changes in Hungary as permanent. On the contrary: a secret
court conference decided as early as March 26 that, although the Crown temporarily
had to present a friendly face to the Batthyány government, as soon as "the time was
right" it would have to clamp down on Hungary as well.

The Batthyány government was already having to grapple with a growing number
of domestic problems. The flaring up, again, of the peasant issue presented one of
the greatest difficulties. For although initially the peasants were grateful for the
abolition of serfdom, afterwards a growing number began to demand exemption
from service obligations which were not strictly feudal, obligations incurred
through use of land outside their "urbarial" holdings. The demands were often
accompanied by militant sabotage movements and attempts to seize land. On the
other hand, the government could make no further concessions to the peasantry that
would place additional burdens on the state treasury. It soon became obvious that,
owing to inadequate financial resources, even the payment of compensation for the
abolished feudal services would take far longer than had been expected—something
which rather dampened the spirits of the landed nobility. For the time being, therefore, the political leadership of the Revolution rigidly opposed peasant aspirations.
This in turn had an adverse effect on the peasantry and again there developed a real
possibility that the liberal nobles would sooner or later lose the sympathy and support of the peasant masses.

The rapid sharpening of the nationalities issue, however, posed an even greater
problem for the government. Although most of the liberal and radical politicians
welcomed the news of the March Laws (unlike the right wing of the movement),
from the very beginning they demanded that full equality be granted to the country's non-Magyar population. For its part, the government wished to comply with
cultural and religious demands only, and rejected requests to recognize non-Ma-

107

gyars as the sons of separate nations and to grant official status to national languages in those territories where non-Magyars lived. As a result, those nationality politicians who had initially supported the Hungarian Revolution very soon turned against it. Since these politicians immediately gave their backing to the demands of the peasantry, that stratum quickly rallied behind them. This was especially true of those whose situation—for example, the Croatian, Serbian or Romanian border-guards—had not been improved as a result of the liberation of the serfs in March. Moreover, these peasants immediately started to voice national slogans which previously expressed only the sentiments of those politicians claiming to represent them. As a result, the situation deteriorated—rapidly and irrevocably. In June a Serbian uprising occurred in Southern Hungary and during the autumn months Croatians, Slovaks, and Romanians also rose in arms against the Hungarian Revolution.

The deteriorating nationalities situation compelled the government to begin organizing armed units for the protection of the Revolution as early as May. There was indeed a pressing need for this.

In the course of the summer the Habsburgs gradually consolidated their position; and by early August the imperial armies had succeeded in suppressing the war of independence in Lombardy. In the meantime, the Crown had also introduced parliamentary government in Austria and made a number of other concessions there. These moves had the effect of winning over the Austrian bourgeoisie which in March had played a revolutionary role and which was concerned at the possibility of Hungary's secession. In August, therefore, the Habsburgs were ready to take active steps against revolution in the eastern part of their empire.

The beginning of the War of Independence

By the middle of August even the most moderate politicians in the Batthyány government realized that the country would soon arrive at a crossroads. Up to then only Petőfi and a few other radicals had stressed this. Hungary would either have to relinquish voluntarily the most important achievements of the March Revolution, or would have to undertake the difficult task of defending those achievements, with arms if necessary. Even at this stage Batthyány made one last attempt at resolving the conflicts. The prime minister travelled to Vienna, intending to offer, as a last resort, a substantial curtailment of the Hungarian government's independence.

In more concrete terms, Batthyány planned to propose the abolition of the separate Austrian and Hungarian defence and finance ministries and their replacement by common Austro-Hungarian ministries. This would undoubtedly have suited the relative equilibrium then existing between the opposing parties. But such a compromise was now unacceptable to the Crown, just as previously, during the promising March days, it would have been rejected by the Hungarian liberals. Therefore, Batthyány had to return to Hungary on September 10 with his mission unaccomplished. The next day units of the imperial army stationed in Croatia invaded Hungary. These were commanded by Lieutenant-General Baron Jellačić, the *bán* of Croatia and an officer absolutely loyal to the dynasty.

The liberal nobility, which had been induced to emancipate the serfs only by the hope of achieving self-government for Hungary, was now compelled to meet the challenge that presented itself. The Batthyány government resigned. Power was transferred by the first representative parliament, which assembled in July, to the Committee for National Defence, which was more left wing in character than Batthyány's administration had been. The committee and its president, Kossuth, began to mobilize the population. Efforts were concentrated on the peasantry, which had become rather disenchanted during the previous months.

To the surprise of many, this action was successful. Only four days after Jellačić invaded Hungary, Parliament passed a resolution abolishing the obligation of the peasants to pay tithes from their own vineyard produce. It thereby created an unfounded hope amongst the peasantry that if made a successful effort in defence of the Revolution, it would be granted further concessions. Moreover, the fear spread among the people that, in the event of the Revolution's defeat, not only reform in the direction mapped out in the March Laws would be endangered, but also that the emancipation of the serfs might be revoked. In addition to these influences, the Hungarian peasants were now also swayed by the zealous national slogans that had previously only affected the leading political stratum. These were suddenly made credible to the peasantry by the fact that the non-Magyars were the first to take up arms against the Hungarian Revolution.

On September 29, the armed forces of the Revolution caused Jellačić to flee at Pákozd. In mid-December, though, the main forces of the imperial army under the command of Field-Marshal Prince Windischgrätz set out against Hungary. On this occasion the enemy succeeded in capturing not only Buda and Pest, but also Kolozsvár, in Transylvania. However, this was not the end of resistance: the Committee for National Defence, now in Debrecen, continued to organize additional fighting units and soon its efforts brought about a dramatic change in the military situation. Under the command of the Polish General Bem, the revolutionary Army of Transylvania launched a counter-offensive and, having inflicted heavy blows on the imperial forces from Csucsa to Nagyszeben, liberated almost the entire territory of Transylvania in three months. At the end of March 1849 an offensive was launched by the main forces of the Hungarian army in the vicinity of Eger. Under General Görgei's command, these forces scored splendid victories at Hatvan, Tápióbicske, and Isaszeg, and cleared the region between the rivers Danube and Tisza. After this they pressed forward along the left bank of the Danube, thereby liberating the castle of Komárom, which had been under siege since December, and compelling the enemy to pull back. The imperial army evacuated Pest without fighting and had retreated as far as the western frontier by the end of April 1849.

It is, however, certain that from this time on the military successes of spring 1849 served not to consolidate the Revolution but to undermine it. The fact that the Hungarian army succeeded in forcing the enemy to retreat but failed to inflict crushing defeat on him made stalemate inevitable. Neither side could score a decisive military victory over the other and it followed from this that neither side could force its will on the other. The situation gradually convinced the nobility that it should give up the idea of continuing the struggle to protect all the achievements of the March Revolution, and instead try to reach a compromise agreement with the Habsburgs based on mutual concessions. Previously this view had been confined to the right wing in Parliament and to Görgei. It was in vain that the radicals and the more sober-minded of the liberals warned that so far Vienna had shown no readiness to negotiate. Attempts at reconciliation were, according to them, bound therefore to produce disappointing results. Most liberals were firmly convinced that the previous successes of the Hungarian army provided an adequate basis for the initiation of peace talks.

On December 2, 1848 the eighteen year-old Francis Joseph became emperor of Austria and by early March 1849 he had imposed an absolutist "constitution" on his territories—a constitution in which he listed Hungary, Transylvania (to be detached from the former), Croatia, and the Military Border among those lands of the "Austrian Empire" which possessed only a semblance of autonomy. In response to this arbitrary step the Hungarian Parliament adopted a rather ambivalent course of action. On April 14 it dethroned the House of Habsburg-Lorraine at Kossuth's suggestion and, under pressure from the Debrecen citizenry, proclaimed Hungary to be a totally independent country. Kossuth was elected provisional head of state and given the title of governor-president. On the other hand, he was deprived of executive power, which was transferred to a new government led by Bertalan Szemere. This advocated a compromise with Vienna—the line of the majority of deputies in Parliament.

The collapse of the Revolution

The more consistent and devoted advocates of transformation viewed the internal political changes of spring 1849 with growing concern. More and more arrived at the conclusion that another favourable development comparable to that of the previous September could only be hoped for if the Revolution succeeded in enlarging its popular base. The precondition for this, however, was the satisfactory settlement as soon as possible of the unresolved peasantry and nationality problems. In the ranks of the peasants there were growing signs of disenchantment. This was quite understandable considering that during the months that had elapsed since September two things had become clear. The first was that Vienna (which did not wish to incur the wrath of millions of their number) would not, after all, revoke the emancipation of the serfs, and the second was that the leadership of the Revolution, composed as it was of nobles, did not intend to proceed along the path it appeared to be advocating when it did away with the grape tithe in September.

In the course of the spring months, therefore, a number of revolutionary radicals proposed that Parliament quickly effect the abolition of feudal service obligations, which still constituted a serious burden for the peasantry. In May and June Mihály Táncsics, who advocated the most radical steps in this respect, put forth the demand that all estates over 2,000 *hold* (863 hectares or 2,133 acres) and in the possession of secular landlords be appropriated and distributed amongst those in need. The majority of liberals, however, rejected initiatives of this kind—even the most modest ones. The fact that the peasantry's demands remained entirely unsatisfied increasingly handicapped the Revolution.

An even more serious problem was the still-outstanding nationality issue. Indicative of the scope of this were the countless plundered towns and villages in the areas of mixed population and the thousands of civilians who had been ruthlessly killed. Soon, therefore, not only the radicals but also many liberals came to realize that reconciliation was necessary. In April representatives of the governing circles entered into negotiations with Iancu, the head of the Romanian national movement's left wing and also the commander of the Romanian insurgent army in Transylvania. In May Hungarian representatives held talks with Baron Kušlan, a prominent Croatian liberal, and, at the beginning of June, spoke with Stratimirović, the leader of the Serbian liberals. However, these negotiations were fruitless. In spring 1849 the Hungarian government dropped its earlier policy and signalled its readiness to grant municipal autonomy to the inhabitants of non-Magyar areas, although it continued to refuse to recognize the non-Magyar peoples of Hungary as constituting separate nations. The liberal leaders of the Hungarian Revolution completely disregarded the opinion expressed both by Albert Pálfi, a member of the "March Youth", and by Count László Teleki, a leading opposition figure and by now a member of the radical left, that if the Hungarian Revolution wished to prevent the victory of reaction it would have to recognize the separate nationhood of the non-Magyar peoples and would have to grant them territorial autonomy as well—thereby transforming Hungary into a federal republic.

Finally, in July, the Hungarian government changed its nationality policy. Around the middle of that month, Bălcescu, the most open-minded leader of the 1848 revolution in Wallachia and now an exile in Hungary, came to an agreement with Kossuth. This recognized the separate nationhood of the Romanian people and granted—much to the satisfaction of Iancu—self-government at county level for Romanians in counties where they constituted a majority. At the end of the month Parliament extended these concessions to every national minority in the country. By doing so, it laid the foundations, at least in theory, for a sizeable change in the balance of power between the forces of the Revolution and those of reaction.

By this time, though, the days of the Hungarian Revolution were numbered. The military developments of the spring made the Habsburgs realize that they could not defeat the Hungarians unassisted. This realization did not, as the Hungarian "peace party" had expected, prompt Vienna to conclude a settlement on the basis of mutual concessions, but rather to seek help from "the gendarme of Europe", the Russian army. At Francis Joseph's request, a vast Russian force under the command of Field-Marshal Prince Paskievich invaded Hungary in June 1849. In co-operation with the imperial troops, now under the command of General Baron Haynau, this force suppressed the Hungarian Revolution. Less than two months after his arrival, on August 13, 1849 the prince could report to Tsar Nicholas I that "Hungary lies at the feet of Your Majesty..."

The Period of Absolutism and Dualism

The years of despotism

The defeat of the Hungarian War of Independence in 1849 was followed by military occupation and bloody reprisals. The sentence passed on the Revolution by the emperor and his government was carried out by General Haynau. "I shall have the leading traitors hanged . . ., I shall have the officers who went over to the Hungarians executed. I shall pull the weed up by its roots, and shall set an example to the whole of Europe of how rebels should be treated, and of how order, peace and tranquillity can be ensured for a century," boasted Haynau. During the dark autumn days of 1849, one execution followed another. On October 6 Count Lajos Batthyány faced a firing squad. Thirteen generals, veritable heroes, were executed at Arad. The names of Lajos Aulich, János Damjanich, Arisztid Dessewffy, Ernő Kiss, Károly Knezić, Vilmos Lázár, György Lahner, Károly Leiningen-Westerburg, József Nagy-Sándor, Ernő Pöltenberg, József Schweidel, Ignác Török, and Károly Vécsey all serve as a reminder and as proof that Magyars, Germans, and Serbs fought together and died together for liberty.

The executions were followed by harsh sentences. Imprisonment in chains and under extremely bad conditions was meted out to many who had participated in the Revolution. Confiscation of property and forced conscription into the army were also common. In its blind desire for revenge, Habsburg tyranny went well beyond the limits within which some sort of reconciliation could have been possible. If the War of Independence created heroes, then its aftermath created martyrs whom the nation never forgot.

After 1849 Hungary was divided up: Transylvania was detached and Crown provinces were created under the names of the Serb Voivodina and the Banat of Temes. The main body of the country was divided into five districts which were first administered by soldiers and subsequently by district *főispáns* and so-called country chiefs who were their subordinates. Archduke Albrecht, the emperor's uncle, was placed at the head of the occupied and incorporated country. Real power, was, however, in the hands of the Vienna-based Alexander Bach, the minister of the interior. Officials recruited by him, the army of so-called "Bach hussars", flooded the country.

Defeated Hungary was thus "pacified" by military occupation and complete—political, administrative and economic—incorporation into the Habsburg empire. All of this was intended as punishment; Hungary was considered to have forfeited its constitutional rights by rebelling against the Habsburg dynasty. Hungary's treatment was by no means exceptional: it was meted out to all the peoples of the empire. It was a bitter irony of the age that the nationalities loyal to the Habsburg dynasty received as a reward those very same things given to the Hungarians as a punishment: harsh tyranny and deprivation of rights. Of the 1848 reforms Habsburg absolutism accepted only the emancipation of the serfs and equality before the law. It abolished every other achievement of constitutionalism and liberty. The national autonomy promised in the 1849 Olmütz constitution was not forthcoming. Indeed, the constitution itself was soon shelved and on the last day of 1851 unlimited imperial absolutism was proclaimed.

The young emperor, Francis Joseph, was the son of the ambitious Archduchess Sophie, and a pupil of Metternich and Felix von Schwarzenberg. He had been brought up in an autocratic atmosphere characterized by remoteness from the people and indifference to nationality aspirations as such. Francis Joseph considered his power to be sanctioned by God. As a ruler, he was mediocre, irresolute and cold, more of a dull bureaucrat in fact, but nevertheless one who was industrious and dutiful. Relying on a large and apparently strong army, a well-disciplined force of civil servants, a strong gendarmerie and police, and a whole host of spies and informers, he tried to consolidate a rigidly centralized empire. He wished to germanize the national minorities within the empire and to maintain the absolutist government he had introduced. In addition, he also confirmed the privileges of the Catholic Church in the concordat of 1855.

The vast majority of Hungarians hated absolutism and opposed the Bach regime. Although the aulic aristocracy remained on good terms with the Habsburgs, the staunchly conservative group of influential aristocratic politicians were dissatisfied with bureaucratic centralization, the shelving of Hungary's ancient constitution, and the spurning of their services. But quite a few nobles, especially the impoverished, accepted office and served absolutism, although an even larger group of brave patriots strove to prepare an insurrection. In the years following the defeat, secret organizing started in Pest, Transdanubia, the Mátra hills, and especially in Transylvania. Counting on the exiled Kossuth and his associates, the conspirators intended to stage a surprise multinational uprising. However, the Austrian authorities discovered these secret conspiracies and executed their leaders. Even harmless social events, such as balls, were banned.

The majority of well-to-do landowners and small gentry chose the path of passive resistance. They retired to their estates, did not accept office, withheld their taxes, and wherever possible duped the authorities. "To despise absolutism, to know nothing of its slaves, as though they did not exist"—this was the general aim. "Austrians should feel at home nowhere [in Hungary] ... They should be and should remain foreigners in this land... Austrians should not be accepted socially... Let them be like plague victims who are shunned by everybody—people of whom everybody is afraid."

Passive resistance meant not only retirement from public life, but also a lack of ambition as far as modernization and embourgeoisment were concerned. As a policy, passive resistance was therefore unsatisfactory considering the grave conditions

113

created by absolutism. The greater part of the nation continued to nurture the seed sown by the War of Independence. During 1857 the poet János Arany wrote *A walesi bárdok* (The Bards of Wales). In this he alluded to a visit by Francis Joseph to Hungary:

> Around him silence which way he went
> In his Welsh lands over the border.

"The nation shall endure"

Haynau and Bach failed to ensure "peace" for even a decade. Absolutism proved to be a weak, alien, and anachronistic edifice. Its internal base was extremely narrow and rested—leaving aside the obedient bureaucrats and the aulic aristocracy—on arms only. However, such a creation was bound to be short-lived in a Europe where liberal parliamentarism had already spread and where plans to unify Italy and Germany had implications for the continued survival of the Habsburg empire.

The first blow came from without. On June 24, 1859 Austria was heavily defeated at Solferino by Italian and French troops. Austria lost Lombardy, which subsequently went to Piedmont, and the equilibrium of the Habsburg empire was upset. In the wake of defeat, latent discontent and resistance erupted with great force in Hungary and in other provinces. Francis Joseph tried to stem the tide by sacking Bach, by removing Archduke Albrecht, and by promising concessions. These moves did not placate the population. In 1860, March 15, the anniversary of the Revolution, was celebrated for the first time. Students clashed with police.

In this situation the old conservatives—the opposition element nearest to the Habsburgs—came out with plans for a moderate new settlement. More importantly, István Széchenyi made his voice heard once again. Having suffered a nervous breakdown, in September 1848 Széchenyi had gone into a mental hospital in Döbling, near Vienna. Recovering from his condition, he was horrified to see the damage done by a decade of absolutism, and the sad fate of his country. When, in 1857, Bach boasted in an anonymous pamphlet about the achievements of "pacification" in Hungary, Széchenyi put pen to paper. Published in London in 1857, his ruthlessly accurate and ironic critique of absolutism dispelled any notions of its "civilizing" effects. The Viennese police did not overlook Széchenyi's renewed public activity. On March 2, 1860 they searched his quarters at Döbling and threatened him. On April 8 an extremely distressed Széchenyi committed suicide. His death was followed by national mourning and by another wave of national resistance.

In that memorable summer of 1860, when Garibaldi's redshirts liberated Southern Italy and when Hungarian patriots already imagined Kossuth's and Garibaldi's legions along the banks of the Danube and Tisza rivers, Francis Joseph was forced to make major concessions. In the October Diploma, which was based on the plan of the conservatives, he granted a constitution to his peoples. In this he attempted to temper absolutist rule with a certain measure of constitutionalism. The October Diploma set up a *Reichsrat* with a very restricted sphere of authority and with a number of appointed members. The emperor wished to establish moderated centralism by promoting limited provincial autonomy and to placate the Hungarians by partially restoring the pre-1848 system. This attempt was, however, doomed to failure. By far the greatest section of the Hungarian public wanted more than this, demanding the restoration of the 1848 achievements. At the county meetings and during the re-election campaigns of officials this sentiment received expression.

The Austrian bourgeoisie was not satisfied with the October Diploma either. It demanded more constitutionalism but, at the same time, stronger centralization as well. The February Patent was accordingly issued in February 1861. This increased the size and sphere of authority of the *Reichsrat* but simultaneously strengthened centralization, too. The new constitution triggered off even greater protests in Hungary, especially at the time of the dietal elections which took place in early spring.

From the Diet which convened on April 6, 1861 Vienna expected acceptance of the new constitution and the election of deputies to the *Reichsrat*. However, the Diet was imbued with the spirit of 1848. Francis Joseph had not been crowned king of Hungary and the majority of deputies did not recognize him as the country's legitimate sovereign. They accordingly wanted to reject the emperor's rescript by means of a simple resolution. This party faction was led by László Teleki, an outstanding politician and friend of Kossuth. (Teleki had, in fact, been captured abroad while meeting a lady friend in Dresden but had been released in Hungary.) The group rallying around Ferenc Deák recognized Francis Joseph as *de facto* ruler and wished to respond to the rescript with a traditional petition. In the days leading up to the vote Teleki committed suicide. Some of his followers interpreted this as a symbolic warning that they should give their support to the petition idea, which left open the way for a compromise.

Deák's two petitions were legal and political masterpieces in defence of the 1848 constitution. "Your Highness," one of them ran, "as King of Hungary... (You) cannot abolish any part of our sanctioned law arbitrarily, without the country's consent." The inviolability of Hungary's independence and constitution was closely connected with recognition of the right of succession: "We cannot sacrifice the country's ... constitutional independence ... to any consideration or any interest, and we insist on it as the fundamental precondition for our national existence."

The full restoration of the 1848 achievements was unacceptable to Vienna, which insisted on its policy of integration. The Diet was dissolved in August 1861 and absolutist government restored. Solemnly remonstrating against coercion and the breach of legality which had taken place, the deputies broke up peacefully. Legal resistance did not develop into revolutionary insurrection, and unfavourable developments internationally also played their part in this. Italy did not launch a new war against Austria, and Hungary could not count on foreign assistance. Kossuth, who organized opposition abroad and led the Hungarian exiles, himself recommended that negotiations be rejected. At the same time, the landed nobility also feared peasant discontent at a time when the reintroduction of labour services was being considered. It was also worried by the reorganized nationality movements of the non-Magyar peoples and their growing demands for autonomy. The leading stratum which organized Hungary's struggle became isolated both inside and outside the country.

The landed nobles therefore had no choice but to return to passive resistance and to play a waiting game. Again, it was Deák who provided guidance in a warning delivered when the Diet was dissolved: "If need be, the nation shall endure ..., for that which force and power take away, time and good fortune may restore. The recovery of that which the nation ... itself relinquishes is always difficult and always uncertain."

Lajos Kossuth in exile

After the defeat of the War of Independence, the Ottoman government offered refuge to Kossuth and several thousands of his followers. Protection was, however, more personal than political. Kossuth and a small group of his supporters were first settled in Sumla, in what was afterwards Bulgaria. Later, in spring 1850, Kossuth was sent to Kütahya in Anatolia following demands for his extradiction by the Russian and Austrian governments. Almost completely isolated from the outside world, Kossuth worked on the organization of a new uprising and on a new democratic constitution. Finally, in September 1851, the American frigate *Mississippi* released him from banishment—a gesture symbolic of European and American public sympathy.

The hero of popular liberty was given a rapturous welcome in Italian, French, and English ports. His arrival in London, Manchester, and Birmingham occasioned the showing of tremendous appreciation. His tour of the United States, between December 1851 and July 1852, brought even more celebration and homage. At the memorable New York, Philadelphia, and Boston receptions Kossuth was called "The Demosthenes of the Modern Age", "The Hungarian George Washington", and even "The Greatest Man Since Jesus Christ". In the figures of Washington and Kossuth the people saw the champions of Western and Eastern liberty respectively. At the beginning of January 1852 Kossuth was received by the Senate and the House of Representatives—the first Hungarian to be honoured in this way. In a Ciceronian speech to the Congress, Kossuth pleaded for the active support of the United States in the attainment of Hungarian liberty. This bold dream could not be realized at this time, however, and the White House offered Kossuth no more than courteous words. Nonetheless, during his six month trip through America, Kossuth won enormous popularity and substantial financial backing.

In his early years of exile Kossuth regarded the organization of an uprising and the continuation of the War of Independence as the main priorities. He settled in London and maintained close contact with Mazzini and the other leading European revolutionaries. From London he promoted secret conspiracies in Hungary but did not realize—contemporaries rarely see at once changes in the historical climate—that the time for revolutions and uprisings was over for many years. Only a string of failures and serious losses could make him understand that he would have to wait for the right moment, the moment when Habsburg absolutism was shaken both at home and abroad. This came at the end of the 1850s, when a Franco-Austrian war erupted in Northern Italy. The conflict filled exiled Hungarian politicians with new enthusiasm, and in 1859 Kossuth, László Teleki, and György Klapka formed the *Magyar Nemzeti Igazgatóság* (Hungarian National Directorate), a kind of a government-in-exile. Kossuth concluded an agreement with Emperor Napoleon III of France by which, in exchange for French support, this body could organize a Hungarian Legion in Italy. Kossuth, Teleki, and Klapka would then give the signal for an uprising in Hungary, but only when French and Piedmontese armies actually appeared on the country's soil. However, after two important French victories (Magenta and Solferino), the war suddenly ended—without the unification of Italy and without assistance being given to Hungary. Italy was now in ferment; Kossuth therefore moved first to Genoa and finally to Turin to be near the scene of decisive events.

Large numbers of Hungarian officers and soldiers participated in Garibaldi's campaign to liberate Southern Italy in 1860. They fought courageously against the Neapolitan troops in the capture of Palermo and the skirmishes outside Naples. István Türr was promoted to the rank of general and became one of Garibaldi's deputies. At this time Kossuth concluded a military alliance with Cavour, the Piedmontese premier who was leading the drive to unify Italy. In the summer of 1860 external help for Hungary appeared to be a realistic proposition. Moreover, revolutionary organizing and resistance were, under Kossuth's supervision, making considerable progress in the country. The following year, however, brought disappointment. Another war against Austria failed to materialize, Cavour died, and in the end the Hungarian Legion was disbanded.

During the third phase of his activities in exile, Kossuth invested his hopes not in the promises of the Great Powers, but in the coming together of the smaller Danubian peoples. After Klapka, Teleki, and others had conducted talks with Romanian and Serbian politicians, in 1862 Kossuth published his plan for a Danubian Confederation. Under this, Romania, Serbia, Croatia, and Hungary would establish a confederation in which foreign affairs, defence and the economic matters would be managed in common. A federal council would be responsible for these and would be accountable to a federal parliament. "Unity, understanding, and fraternity among Magyars, Slavs, and Romanians—these are my most fervent desires, my sincerest advice. They offer a happy future for all these peoples." However, under the international and domestic political conditions then prevailing, the plan was incapable of implementation.

Since Kossuth's utopia did not offer a realistic alternative, the majority of Hungarian leaders gradually came to accept the idea of reconciliation with Austria on the basis of a compromise agreement.

In 1866, Prussia challenged Austria for hegemony in German affairs. The early and impressive victories of the Prussian army raised hopes in Kossuth of military assistance from Prussia and hopes of Austria's disintegration. With the conclusion of peace Kossuth devoted all his energies to prevent such a compromise. In a series of studies, articles, and letters, Kossuth argued that for Hungary to link her fate with a Habsburg empire doomed to extinction would be tantamount to national suicide. "Hungary will be the stake at which the inexorable logic of history will burn the Austrian eagle," he maintained. Even at the last moment, in May 1867, Kossuth entreated his one-time friend Ferenc Deák to reconsider and not to commit the country to an arrangement in which it would not be master of its fate.

After the Compromise of 1867, Kossuth gradually retired from active politics. He delved into botany and astronomy, arranged his papers, and consoled himself with history. Kossuth's once-fervent desire to accomplish things vanished on the southern slopes of the Alps and on the shores of the Ligurian Sea, where he searched for thyme and cudweed. On occasion Kossuth spoke out for independence and liberty. "The hand of a clock indicates the passage of time but does not regulate it," he said. "My name is a clock hand, it indicates the time that shall come, . . . if fate holds any future for the Hungarian nation. That future has a name: a free homeland for the free citizens of Hungary."

After forty-five years in exile, Kossuth died in Turin on March 20, 1894. His burial turned into a great national demonstration, indicative of the times.

The Compromise

Although the 1848 revolutions in Central Europe were defeated, the revolutionary process forged ahead irresistibly. Two things gradually became clear. The first was that the consolidation of absolutism, which blocked the path to all progress, was impossible, and the second that its overthrow by means of revolution was similarly unlikely. This was borne out by the unification processes which developed under dynastic leadership first in Italy and afterwards in Germany. Especially important, though, was the Russian tsar's suppression of the Polish revolutionary uprising of 1863 while a liberal and sympathetic Europe merely looked on. Austria, too, felt the need for change, but neither the semi-constitutionalism introduced in the western part of the empire, nor the feeble attempts to win over the "reliable" nationalities produced the desired results. Austria became increasingly isolated internationally, and her credit and finances fell into disarray. Moreover, Hungary, the resisting "province", could under no circumstances be integrated into the imperial edifice. Slowly, the idea established itself in Viennese political circles that some sort of agreement must be reached with the Hungarians if the empire was to survive.

The willingness to consider a compromise also grew within the ranks of the Hungarian political leadership, the landed class, and the bourgeoisie. The fate of Poland served as a warning, as did the menacing possibility of German unification. A Germany united under Prussian leadership and directed by Otto von Bismarck might even swallow up the western half of the empire. In such an event Hungary would be caught up between two great powers, Germany and Russia. The prominent politicians of the age were very aware of Hungary's geographical position: the country could well be crushed between Germany and Russia, the former pursuing a *Drang nach Osten* policy, and the latter expanding westwards under the banner of Pan-Slavism. Deák and his supporters believed that it was not only impossible to overthrow the Habsburg empire given the circumstances, but also that such a development was not even desirable. It was preferable, they thought, to remain within the framework of a constitutional Monarchy and to reach agreement with its ruler rather than to fall prey to two expansionist powers as an independent, but weak, state.

In Turin, the exiled Kossuth drew radically different conclusions. His view was that the Hungarians should reach a compromise with the national minorities rather than with the Great Powers or the Habsburgs. Kossuth formulated his conception in a draft for a Danubian Confederation, a draft previously mentioned. Although ideologically important, this plan was both utopian and unfeasible at the time. Not only was it opposed by the Great Powers, but also by those whom it most directly concerned. Hungarian public opinion, and even most of Kossuth's supporters, rejected it.

Meanwhile, the economic situation acquired importance. The markets opened up as a result of railway construction and the desire to participate in the great European boom also prompted the leading stratum to opt for an agreement, as did aspects of the settlement reached between Austria and the national minorities, such as the winning over of the Transylvanian Romanians. The liberals who rallied around Deák in Hungary therefore welcomed initiatives for a compromise which came first from Austrian liberal deputies and then from the Court itself. During several months of secret negotiations, Deák worked out the conditions for such an agreement which at a suitable moment—at Easter 1865—he made public in a famous article. If Vienna would recognize the territorial unity of Hungary, recognize the 1848 laws, and appoint a responsible Hungarian government, Deák was willing to concede that foreign affairs and defence matters were common to both Austria and Hungary and would be handled accordingly.

As a sign of goodwill, Francis Joseph suspended the February Patent of 1861 and convened the Hungarian Diet for the end of 1865. It was while the Diet was assembled that war broke out between Austria and Prussia in June 1866. Bismarck intended to use Prussian troops to drive Austria out of Germany before unifying that area and subordinating it to Berlin. On July 3 Austria suffered a grave defeat at Sadowa (Königgrätz) and was forced to make peace on Bismarck's terms.

The defeat at Sadowa was of decisive importance from the point of view of the Habsburg empire. Deeply shaken, it could now only restore its equilibrium and authority by reaching agreement with Hungary. Finally, after much wrangling and numerous modifications, Deák's proposals were accepted. The empire was to be transformed into a dualist state with two centres, Vienna and Budapest. Common foreign and defence ministries were to be set up, as well as a common finance ministry to defray their expenses. Two separate governments and two separate parliaments were also to come into being. The Compromise (*Ausgleich*) was born. Common affairs would be supervised by delegations seconded by the two parliaments. The tariff and commercial alliance between Austria and Hungary, as well as the charter of the Austro-Hungarian Bank, would have to be renewed by both governments and both parliaments every ten years. The Austrian empire would become the Austro-Hungarian empire.

On February 17, 1867, Francis Joseph appointed a responsible Hungarian government headed by Count Gyula Andrássy, the former exile condemned to death *in absentia* in 1851. After lengthy debates, on May 29 the Diet passed the Compromise into law with a large majority. Kossuth's numerous warnings were in vain. He regarded the Compromise as "the death of the nation", with Hungary becoming attached "to the towrope of foreign interests". In May 1867, Kossuth wrote in his famous *Cassandra Letter* that the Compromise would turn Hungary's neighbours into its enemies and would "make impossible the satisfactory solution of the nationalities question...". Kossuth added, ominously, that "...European complications which clearly threaten will make our country the target of rival ambitions".

The leading groups, together with the majority of the middle class, did not listen to Kossuth. They welcomed the Compromise and the reconciliation it brought about. On June 8 Francis Joseph and his wife Elizabeth, herself sympathetic to the Hungarians, were crowned with great pomp in the presence of numerous aristocrats and prelates at the Matthias Church in Pest-Buda. By a curious irony of history it was Andrássy, the hussar colonel sentenced to death in 1851, who placed the Hungarian Crown on the head of Francis Joseph, who had earlier signed Andrássy's death warrant and who was now dressed in the uniform of a hussar general. The celebrations were widespread.

Austria–Hungary—an empire of contradictions

The Austro-Hungarian empire was vast: it spread from the Swiss Alps to the snow-capped mountains of Brassó, from the Dalmatian coast to the Polish Carpathians—indeed even beyond, to the onion domes of Lemberg. Its area exceeded 600,000 square kilometres; its population was 35 million at the time of the Compromise and 50 million when the First World War broke out. As regards size and population it was the third largest power in Europe but in political influence it ranked either fifth or sixth. In Austria-Hungary public institutions were "imperial", "royal", or "imperial and royal". In German this last phrase was *kaiserlich und königlich*, abbreviated to *k.u.k.* Robert Musil, a prominent writer on the Austro-Hungarian empire, spoke of "Kakania", and Heinrich Benedikt, a historian who knew it well, called it "the empire of contradictions".

On the surface, Austria-Hungary appeared to be a constitutional state. There could be discerned within its territory modest signs of progress, good roads, attractive cities, schools and barracks, a bureaucratic apparatus to keep watch over its citizens and a large army on which vast sums of money were lavished but which nevertheless remained among the weakest in Europe. The empire embraced eleven nationalities. Within its frontiers, there were Germans, Magyars, Czechs, Slovaks, Poles, Ukrainians, Romanians, Serbs, Croatians, Slovenes, Italians and a dozen other small ethnic groups, including Yiddish-speaking Jews, multilingual Gypsies, Armenians, Bulgarians, and Serbo-Croatian Muslims. The Austro-Hungarian empire was indeed a modern Babel of peoples and the more educated these peoples became, the less they understood each other.

The state was officially called the Austro-Hungarian Monarchy, although it was commonly referred to as Austria, a practice about which the Hungarians constantly complained. They held that the empire was an alliance of two independent states in which a united Hungary stood opposed to "His Majesty's Other Countries". These other countries, admittedly, did not have a collective name. They were not known as "Austria" because the Czechs, Poles and Southern Slavs would have resented this, and the leading Austrian circles did not use this term either, as it would have implied giving up the idea of a united empire. Thus, Cis-Leithania, the non-Hungarian part of the empire, was named "the kingdoms and provinces represented in the *Reichsrat*". The two parts matched each other, said Musil, "as a red, white and green coat matches black-and-yellow trousers; the coat was all right on its own, but the trousers were only half of a black-and-yellow suit torn apart in 1867". With some sarcasm we could say that this empire was the only creation in world history that "died of its own ineffability".

The empire thus consisted of two states, with two governments, two parliaments, and two separate public administration systems. The two halves of the empire often frustrated each other's aims and paralyzed each other's measures, although they could not interfere in each other's "internal affairs". The unity of the empire was represented by its ruler, Francis Joseph, and by the common ministers—the ministers of foreign affairs, defence and finance. Not burdened by too many duties, these ministers also governed Bosnia-Herzegovina after its occupation in 1878. The common ministers did not constitute a government and were responsible only for their own portfolios, primarily to the emperor-king. The separate "Austrian" and Hungarian governments had little influence over foreign affairs, and still less over the army. These common ministers could not exert any constitutional influence over internal affairs in either half of the empire. The final decision on important matters always rested with Francis Joseph, the commander-in-chief of the armed forces, and appointments remained his prerogative. Despite heated public debate, the Habsburg dynasty for the most part preserved its former absolutist power, and although Austria-Hungary had a liberal constitution, it was "governed in a clerical spirit". Although every citizen was equal before the law, not everyone was considered a citizen. Parliament made ample use of its liberty and because of this remained closed for most of the time. By declaring a state of emergency, it was possible to govern by decree. However, "every time absolutism was applauded, the Crown ordered the reinstatement of constitutional government".

Serious antagonisms placed the empire's socio-economic structure under growing strain. Despite the flourishing of capitalism, a powerful aristocracy survived. Leading aristocrats possessed landed estates the size of half a county and had an army of bailiffs and farm labourers to run them. The material and spiritual assets of the Catholic Church also remained intact, as did its political influence.

In Hungary public administration continued to be very much the preserve of the nobility. The impressive cities of Vienna, Budapest and Prague, with their universities, clinics, shops, motor-cars and railways, contrasted keenly with the results of centuries of backwardness and oppression in rural Galicia, the Bukovina, Upper Hungary, Transylvania, and Dalmatia. The countryside contained millions of landless, destitute people, large numbers of whom were compelled to emigrate.

The nationalities issue was at the root of most of the antagonisms within the Austro-Hungarian empire. Of the two ruling nationalities, the Austro-Germans were in the better position and Austria was economically superior to Hungary. Fifteen provinces of Austria enjoyed a certain degree of autonomy. The Poles had the most privileges, while the Czechs were the best off materially, although they, too, were subordinated to Austrian hegemony. In 1868 the Hungarian ruling class reached an agreement with Croatia. Under this, the Croats were granted a large measure of autonomy and a parliament. The other nationalities had even fewer privileges and now became subject to increased political and cultural oppression. The structure of the Austro-Hungarian empire was thus characterized, in addition to the survival of the bastions of absolutism and feudalism, by a system of hierarchical dependence amongst the nationalities. This facilitated the application of the "divide and rule" principle of government. Nonetheless, instability generated by nationality tensions undermined the apparently solid edifice of the Dual Monarchy from the very beginning.

At the time of the Compromise, and afterwards as well, the plan for a federal settlement, which would have suited the nationality structure, was also raised. In 1871 the Hohenwart government drafted a plan for a Czech compromise. Under this, Bohemia would have been granted equal status with Austria and Hungary in a trialistic arrangement. The scheme was, however, opposed by Austrian leading circles, Hungarian leading circles, and by the German chancellor, Bismarck. Nothing came of the proposals.

This multinational and multifaceted empire could have been the experimental laboratory of history had not its leaders, who insisted on nationality and class oppression, frustrated every attempt at serious change. It was their intransigence which eventually brought about the collapse of the entire system.

A Hungarian minister at the Ballhausplatz

Count Gyula Andrássy the Elder (1823–1890) was the descendant of a prominent aristocratic family and was fortune's darling. He was just twenty-five when the Revolution of 1848 appointed him to head Zemplén county. He participated in the War of Independence and was present at the Battle of Schwechat. Andrássy was promoted colonel when Kossuth sent him to Constantinople on a diplomatic mission. Having been forced into exile, he spent a number of years in Paris where he lived affluently and in the limelight. The fact that he had been hanged in effigy in 1851 made Andrássy even more appealing in high society. This handsome aristocrat, who was a brave soldier, a courageous horseman, and a captivatingly witty cosmopolitan, became popular everywhere he appeared. His rich family eventually procured him an amnesty from the emperor, making his return home a possibility.

In 1858 Andrássy came back to Hungary and in the years of constitutional experimentation he entered public life as an advocate of compromise and as a supporter of Deák. He enchanted his associates, Francis Joseph and his wife Elizabeth, and even Deák himself with his appealing manners and diplomatic skills. It was not without reason that Deák recommended Andrássy for the post of prime minister. It was in him that Deák saw "the providential statesman given us by the Grace of God". What exactly did Deák mean by "providential"? Andrássy was certainly a skilful politician and diplomat, although many contemporaries considered him a man of remarkable talent rather than a genius. Certainly, he owed a great deal to his family background, his rank and to his patriotic past. However, Andrássy's greatest asset was that he was able to win the confidence and sympathy of the imperial couple who lived in the cold atmosphere of the Hofburg. One could also describe as providential the qualities which awakened a deep affection in the young queen towards Kossuth's one-time officer, this "fine hanged man". The day after Austria's defeat at Sadowa, Elizabeth recommended to Francis Joseph that he appoint Andrássy foreign minister, or at least minister for Hungary, "because what is now most needed is that the country calm down".

As Hungarian prime minister, Andrássy lived up to the highest expectations. He achieved territorial unity for the country, reincorporated Transylvania and the Military Border, and set up a separate Hungarian army. The establishment of the army was a great achievement twenty years after the War of Independence, even though it differed vastly from its predecessor of 1848–49. Insignia and banners were changed, and its equipment and combat-readiness were greatly inferior to those of the "common" Imperial and Royal Army. The Andrássy government hammered out the compromise with Croatia and organized public administration, together with a judiciary. It also gave financial assistance for the promotion of railway construction and for the development of the economy.

Important legislation is linked with the name of the scholar and writer Baron József Eötvös. The Nationalities Law of 1868 declared that, politically, Hungary's citizens belonged to the "united Hungarian nation", that is to say it did not recognize the national existence and right to autonomy of the non-Magyar peoples. Yet this act was a liberal piece of legislation by contemporary standards. It guaranteed the nationalities free use of their mother-tongue at the lower levels of litigation, public administration, and education. It also ensured their freedom to organize culturally and politically. The Education Law of the same year made elementary schooling compulsory and placed it under state supervision. However, this act did not make any changes in the nationalities' right to education in their mother-tongue, or in their right to use their own languages.

At the same time the government suppressed the peasant movements on the Great Plain and in Transdanubia. Worker leaders who had demonstrated in favour of the Paris Commune (1871) were put on trial charged with treason. The government also dissolved democrat circles, disciplined those army associations which adhered to the spirit of 1848, and even wanted to forbid in public life any praise of the exiled Kossuth. It helped to strengthen a liberal system that protected the interests of the landowners and the upper middle class and, by doing so, helped to consolidate the Austro-Hungarian empire.

In 1871 the German Empire was proclaimed in the Hall of Mirrors at Versailles. German unity posed something of a threat to Austria-Hungary and in this sensitive situation Francis Joseph made Andrássy the Monarchy's foreign minister. Formerly, Andrássy's appointment was attributed to his pro-German stance, although the facts indicate that Andrássy did not like Bismarck at all during the early 1870s. The Hungarian minister, who nurtured the foreign policy traditions of 1848, regarded tsarist Russia to be the principal enemy. At first, Andrássy considered that his main task was to push Russia into the background; Bismarck, on the other hand, wished to bring it into European affairs.

Andrássy initially tried to win England as an ally, but failed. Having comprehended, however, the realities of the European balance of power, he decided that a different policy was necessary. Alliance between the emperors of Russia, Germany and Austria—all bastions of the conservative order—represented the only guarantee of the Monarchy's security. Having moved to the foreign ministry in Vienna, Andrássy followed in the footsteps of Metternich and Beust. He understood more quickly than his predecessors that there was nothing for Austria-Hungary in the West: its nationalities policy and expansionist ambitions pointed towards the Balkans.

Originally, Andrássy had not opposed the aspirations of the small Balkan peoples for autonomy, provided these aspirations did not undermine the *status quo* and lead to Russian supremacy in the area. One by one the peoples of the Balkans now rebelled against Ottoman tyranny and, in spring 1877, Russia took up arms to help them.

In the Russo-Turkish War of that year the sultan's crumbling empire suffered total defeat. By the Treaty of San Stefano (1878) Russia acquired Bessarabia and most of the Caucasus. Bulgaria—widely seen as a potential Russian puppet state—acquired not only full independence but also an Aegean coastline. Andrássy's hour then struck: he succeeded in creating a united front of England, Germany and France, all of whom were unhappy at the prospect of excessive Russian influence in southeast Europe.

Andrássy scored his biggest success at the Congress of Berlin in 1878. The Great Powers cut down Russia's annexations and reduced Russian influence in the Balkans. To counter that which remained, they commissioned Austria-Hungary to occupy Bosnia and Herzegovina, two South Slav provinces formerly under Turkish rule. These territories were the empire's first territorial gains since 1815, and even though their actual occupation was accomplished only after serious losses and considerable fighting, they did represent a conquest. Andrássy was quick to capitalize on the favourable turn of events and to consolidate the Monarchy's international position. In 1879 he concluded a defensive military alliance with the Germans. Under this, the Dual Alliance as it became known, Germany was obliged to render military assistance to Austria-Hungary in the event of a Russian attack on the latter.

Thus, Andrássy partially accomplished his foreign policy goal of counterbalancing Russian expansion in southeast Europe. The price he had to pay was rather high. Hungarian public opinion was averse to the Bosnia-Herzegovina occupation. Pro-Slav sentiment had obliterated memories of the one-time Ottoman occupation of Hungary and gave rise to a wave of sympathy for Turkey which permeated even the lower chamber of Parliament. On the other hand, the Dual Alliance was not regarded favourably by the ruling circles in Vienna and this feeling of antipathy also extended to the Hofburg. Popularity at the bottom and confidence at the top both ebbed.

Andrássy signed the German treaty on October 7, 1879. Francis Joseph dismissed him the following day.

"Let sleeping dogs lie"

Hardly had the "stone-hearted man", the imperial administrator of Bihar county, died, than his sons swore an oath to the Revolution and to the War of Independence. The Baradlay family of Mór Jókai's gripping novel was modelled on the real-life Tiszas. The elder son, László Tisza, died on the battlefield at Mór, while the younger son, Kálmán, who had a poorer physique, served the revolutionary government to the very end. He endured the vicissitudes of exile, joined the great remonstrations against the persecution of Protestants, and participated in the struggles to re-establish constitutionalism. Nobody would have thought that this gaunt, nondescript Calvinist, whose spectacles and full beard made him look much older than he was, would one day become a party leader.

Tisza owed his position in politics to a number of misfortunes and national afflictions. After his uncle, László Teleki, committed suicide, Tisza became a leader of the opposition at the Diet of 1861 and subsequently a leader of the national resistance. He did not join Deák after the conclusion of the Compromise, regarding the concessions it involved as too many, and their resulting unpopularity too great. "If we accept the Compromise," he said in March 1867, "I believe that we shall be happier and shall have fewer difficulties. We, who live in our country today, shall enjoy greater liberty, but we ourselves will make the re-establishment of a legitimate independent Hungary impossible." Tisza was not against the Compromise itself but rather the terms on which it was agreed. As the leader of the left-centre faction in Parliament, Tisza issued a party programme, the "Bihar Points", in 1868. In these he called for the abolition of the delegations and the common ministries. He also demanded the establishment of an independent army, together with entirely independent finances and commerce for Hungary.

Tisza and his party did not remain on the opposition benches for long. Growing internal opposition in the years following the Compromise, the demands of the nationalities for equality, threatening developments in the Balkans, continual deficits and serious financial difficulties—all undermined the governing Deák Party. Things were made worse by the fact that this was not a true political party but rather an alliance of factions which shared political power. After Andrássy's move to Vienna, Eötvös's early death (in 1871), and the retirement of the ailing Deák, this party began to disintegrate. When the situation became serious enough to undermine the entire dualist system, Tisza came to the rescue. His party merged with the government party in spring 1875 and Tisza soon became prime minister. Tisza was accused by contemporaries of "dropping the Bihar Points" and of becoming a renegade. The new premier rejected these charges, saying that it was his patriotic duty to take control of the country at a time of crisis. There was some truth in what his opponents said, but Tisza's response was more than an attempt at self-justification. To Tisza, "the country" meant the estates of the landed nobility, and "patriotic duty" signified the protection of the dualist system which could best preserve the existing political order and which, according to Tisza, also ensured the survival of the Hungarian people.

As prime minister (1875–90) Tisza showed excellent tactical skill in surviving crises and in avoiding pitfalls that would jeopardize the dualist system. At considerable sacrifice to the country, he put state finances in order and renewed the economic Compromise in 1877 and 1887. Despite strong public opposition, he also supported the occupation of Bosnia-Herzegovina. How could he do all this in a multinational country where the population was predominantly made up of peasants and where the inhabitants were strongly opposed to the government?

Kálmán Tisza's name is linked with the establishment of the political system of the dualist state. The franchise had been extremely limited ever since the first settlement in 1848 and was dependent on property and educational qualifications. Yet, as far as the system was concerned, the number of peasants and lower middle-class people entitled to vote was too high. To prevent supporters of the opposition from being elected to Parliament, Tisza cleverly altered constituency boundaries, introducing "electoral geometry" to favour the government. Canvassing in return for public administration posts, the bribing of voters, corruption, getting people drunk, and intimidation were all features of the electoral process. By the time the Lower House convened, the government party always had a majority among the 413 members. However, it was not enough that the government party could outnumber all the others in the chamber. Government deputies had to be moulded into an obedient squad, and Tisza knew how to do this. By means of kind words, strict discipline, appointments, and patronage generally, Tisza put the government party under obligation to him. The MPs followed the leader, "General Tisza", like guardsmen: contemporaries referred to them as "Mamelukes" for this very reason. In addition, Tisza gave jobs to sons of the impoverished landed nobility, employing them at state, county, and municipal level in an ever-expanding public administration system. By demanding a certain degree of professionalism from these employees, he strengthened public administration and therefore the government. In the countryside Tisza set up a gendarmerie and established a police force in the capital.

What, then, was the purpose of parliamentarianism? Why was there such an emphasis on constitutionalism? Would not absolutism have been a more appropriate political form? The answer is that constitutionalism was quintessential to Austro-Hungarian dualism, and the product of the struggle against Habsburg absolutism. Constitutionalism protected Hungary against Vienna and at the same time legalized the domination exercised by the leading Hungarian political strata over Magyars and non-Magyars alike. "Every country has an ideal crucial to its existence. Hungary has ... survived primarily through adherence to its constitution." This ideal would be embodied in "the monumental building to be constructed for the two houses of Parliament", said Tisza in 1883, when the money for the new edifice was voted.

Intolerant nationalism strengthened during Tisza's term as prime minister—on both a social and governmental level. Tisza closed down the Slovak Cultural Association, crushed the autonomous political movements among the nationalities, put their leaders on trial, and developed a magyarizing educational policy. As a liberal politician coming from the ranks of the nobility, Tisza was insensitive to the need for a social welfare policy, demanded by the new times. He regarded the labour movement as the work of "callous" agitators, but at the same time was convinced that the semi-feudal dependence of farm servants on their landlord was natural. For Tisza this represented the age-old relationship between master and servant, something he attempted to conserve by legislative means as well.

No major reforms were introduced during Tisza's term of office. *Quieta non movere*—let sleeping dogs lie—this was Tisza's principle of government. During the 1880s, the "happy time of peace", this principle seemed to work well in practice, too.

There was one, and only one, issue that Tisza was unable to handle—that of the common army. The Imperial and Royal Army constituted a state within the state. It still treated Hungary as a conquered province and showed scant respect for the country's national traditions and independence. Public opinion, which was slowly adapting to dualism, could not come to terms with the presence of its domineering soldiery. Incidents involving the officers of the Imperial and Royal Army were everyday occurrences and kept the public in a state of constant tension. It was in such an atmosphere that at the beginning of 1889 Tisza put forward new proposals for the Hungarian army. In addition to increasing its strength, the various points would have curtailed Parliament's right of control over it and would have prescribed a German-language examination for officers.

The proposals provoked a general outcry and were followed by innumerable demonstrations. In the end the government was compelled to make modifications but, in spite of this, it lost prestige. In a matter of weeks, the year 1889 revealed how superficial and fragile this decade of peace had been. Kossuth, living in seclusion in Turin, sensed "the spontaneous pulsation of national aspirations". To manifest themselves as history, all they required was a favourable climate. "When all is said and done, great historical problems cannot be suppressed. They must be resolved," wrote Kossuth at the beginning of 1890.

In March 1890 Kálmán Tisza fell from power.

"We're heading towards the land of liberty..."

The most peaceful years of the "happy time of peace" had arrived: noisy campaigns for election to Parliament, extravagant festivities, frenzied business activity, spectacular company crashes, notorious games of cards, gallant adventures, and secret duels. The upper classes were enjoying the post-Compromise boom. Why worry about the twelve-hour day of tens of thousands of workers and the unspeakable destitution of a few million farm servants and day-labourers? Who cared about a few dozen workers who occasionally met in workshop corners or in poorly-lit pubs to organize and set up societies? Only the police, in fact, and with exemplary thoroughness. Having completed his apprenticeship, a worker either travelled abroad for a time or took a job. If he joined a friendly society on beginning work he was immediately subject to police attention. The guardians of law and order were especially afraid of workers who had just returned from foreign countries. They might have learned a trade certainly, but they might also have become acquainted with socialistic ideas—very dangerous ideas as far as the vigilant police were concerned.

Prior to the Compromise, only a few dozen friendly societies existed. These rendered certain assistance to a worker or his family in case of the former's illness or death. In a constitutional system the organizing of workers could not be prevented and associations specializing in self-help and self-education proliferated. Those which, under the cover of "self-education" and "assistance", were also involved in politics and the protection of workers' interests, were called trade associations. After the Compromise, these served as the basis for the development of the working-class movement. Founded in 1868, the *Általános Munkásegylet* (General Workers' Association) was the first umbrella organization for these associations and workers' circles. This association co-operated closely with its German and Austrian counterparts.

According to its first charter, the aim of the *Általános Munkásegylet* was "the intellectual advancement of the working class, the safeguarding of its material interests, and its development with a view to enabling the worker not only to become a useful inhabitant of the state, but also to become one of those citizens capable of enjoying its liberal constitution". It wanted to lead the working-class army of slaves out of "the Egypt of the labour wage" and take it to the "Promised Land". Ferdinand Lassalle was the guiding star at this time. Before long, the Hungarian sections of the First International were set up, the teachings of Marx became known, and Social Democrats began organizing within the association.

In a few years the *Általános Munkásegylet* had increased its strength in Budapest and in the major industrial towns of the provinces. Mihály Táncsics, the renowned democrat and member of Parliament, joined the association, as did a number of intellectuals concerned about social problems. The activity of the association was especially intensive at the time of the Paris Commune. It organized successful strikes and demonstrations and staged a funeral procession after the defeat of the Communards. For this the government put the leaders of the association on trial for "high treason". Those tried were Károly Farkas, an iron worker and one of the organizers of the International; Antal Ihrlinger, a printer; András Essel, an iron worker; and Viktor Külföldi and Lajos Szvoboda, both journalists. Zsigmond Politzer, a university student and newspaper editor, was also charged with the same offence, along with twenty-two others. Although only Politzer was sentenced, the *Általános Munkásegylet's* activity became paralyzed. The organization dissolved in 1872.

After the defeat of the Paris Commune, a campaign was launched against socialist workers and labour organizations throughout Europe. In Hungary, undercurrents of the movement survived in the few trade associations that maintained a low profile, while socialist ideas were advocated by the labour press. In 1873 the *Munkás Heti-Krónika* was published, followed by the *Népszava* in 1877. The economic slump of 1873 and the lengthy recession which followed it also handicapped the movement, which picked up again only towards the end of the 1870s. In this revival a major role was played by Leó Frankel, one of the leaders of the Paris Commune who returned to Hungary in 1876 and who became one of the organizers of the labour press. An experienced revolutionary and a trained Marxist, Frankel clearly saw the tasks that lay ahead—linking the economic and political struggles and expanding the movement's size. Together with his associates, he founded the *Magyarországi Általános Munkáspárt* (General Workers' Party of Hungary) in 1880. This was essentially a social democratic party, although because of a government ban, it was unable to adopt such a name. The party's programme openly formulated the socialist goal: the nationalization of landed estates and all means of production, the abolition of the capitalist system of wage labour, and the liberation of the workers.

The General Workers' Party of Hungary did not accomplish great feats, indeed, circumstances were not conducive to this. The 1880s were characterized by calm and the Tisza government took good care lest unruly proletarian agitators should disturb the tranquil life of the propertied classes. The working class itself was still going through its formative years; its numbers barely topped the 100,000 mark, and the better-paid skilled workers constituted the majority of those organizing.

At the end of the century, the strengthening of the socialist movement was facilitated by three factors. Firstly, industrialization in Hungary had speeded up during the previous two decades. Budapest especially, and the areas near it, underwent rapid industrial development and there was a corresponding growth in the industrial population. In a matter of a few decades the capital was encircled by factories whose chimneys emitted thick clouds of smoke. Secondly, the 1880s witnessed a slump in agriculture and, accordingly, the position of the agricultural population deteriorated substantially. Poverty, unemployment, the hopelessness of life on the land—all made people receptive to socialist ideas that now permeated the village as well. Thirdly, the socialist movement generally was making progress throughout Europe. In many countries socialist parties were formed at a national level. In the summer of 1889, on the hundredth anniversary of the French Revolution, the representatives of the socialists convened in Paris to form a new international organization. Once again the *Marseillaise* was heard in Paris, now with socialist words. This time Vienna, Prague, and Budapest echoed in unison:

> Capital shall not dominate us.
> He who lives in the past shall be lost.
> We are heading towards the land of liberty.
> Justice is our goal...

The "Age of Founders"

Hungary was founded several times. It was founded by King Stephen I after the Magyar conquest of the Carpathian Basin and by Béla IV after the Mongol invasion of 1241. Modern Hungary was founded by the generation of Széchenyi, Kossuth, and Deák. They were followed by others, with spades, industrial equipment and business sense. This last group established banks and factories, built railways, towns and water-mains. The half century that followed the Compromise was the age of such founders.

Between 1867 and 1918, the dualist period, Hungary's population rose from 15.4 million to 21 million. Arable land increased from 25 million hectares to 27 million hectares. Vast areas of the country were reclaimed, the Danube and Tisza rivers were regulated, and the Ecsed marshes and other swamps drained. At the beginning of the period a quarter of arable land remained fallow, but at the end only 8 per cent. Since the area of arable land grew by one-third and since average yields rose between two- and threefold, harvests trebled. Wheat production rose from 14 to 42 million quintals, potato production from 8.5 to 50 million quintals, and sugar beet produc-

129

tion from 2.3 to 16 million quintals (1 quintal = 100 kg). As the country consumed only half of the grain produced, between 15 and 20 million quintals were exported annually by 1900. Increasingly, grain was sent abroad in the form of fine, albeit gluten-rich, flour. The expansion and prosperity of the milling industry in Hungary was based on this enormous grain production. In the 1870s Budapest's milling industry was the largest of any city in the world and was overtaken only at the end of the century by those of Minneapolis and Cincinnati.

New equipment and machines helped the work of agriculture. The use of the steam-driven threshing machine became widespread and a great many new machines were introduced in land cultivation and harvesting. Examples were the steel plough, steam ploughing, and various small devices.

During the decades of prosperity, Hungarian agriculture was strong enough to stand up to competition from overseas grain, although farmers were badly hit by two decades of falling prices. Hungarian viticulture survived the phylloxera attacks which destroyed excellent vineyards at the end of the century, reducing the grape harvest to a quarter of what it had been previously. This crisis was overcome shortly after 1900 when new vineyards were planted. To offset the decline in the profitability of grain, intensive livestock breeding was started. During this period the cattle population rose from 4.5 million to 6.2 million head, in spite of the fact that the exports of cattle for slaughter rose between two- and threefold. More importantly, the grey longhorn Hungarian cattle kept outside all the year round were, for the most part, replaced by the redspeckled breed, which produced much good milk. As a result, there was an enormous growth in the quantity of dairy produce. During these decades Hungary's stock of pigs doubled, topping the seven million mark in good years. Pig killing in the winter became a national custom, indeed something of an occasion.

The upswing in agriculture was helped by improving communications and credit facilities. The chronic shortage of credit and good transportation about which Széchenyi so bitterly complained in 1830 now became things of the past. While at the time of the War of Independence there were only two railway services, one to Vác and one to Szolnok, and while even in 1867 trains ran only to Vienna, Debrecen, and Arad, between the Compromise and 1913 the length of track increased from 2,200 kilometres to 22,000 kilometres. Freight carried rose from 3.5 to 72 million tonnes and the number of railway passengers from 3.5 to 200 million. While in 1867 only some sixty small credit institutions functioned with a total of 700 million koronas, prior to the First World War a network comprising 5,000 institutions and with over 13,000 million koronas at its disposal had been established. Five major banks played a key role in the Hungarian economy.

The numerous disadvantages of the common tariff zone and the powerful competition from Austrian and Czech firms notwithstanding, the process of industrialization accelerated in Hungary. As one would expect from the country's natural resources, the food industry—especially the milling industry, the sugar industry and distilling—prospered most. The engineering industry was on a par with that of the other areas of the Austro-Hungarian empire. Hungary's progress was especially impressive in the most modern branches of production—the electrical and chemical industries. In these Hungary started at the same time as her Western neighbours.

The facts and figures speak for themselves. After the Compromise, the time new businesses started to mushroom, there were 170 industrial joint-stock companies and a few hundred private firms in Hungary. Their employees numbered fewer than 100,000. By the end of the century as many as 2,700 industrial plants were registered, employing 300,000 workers and with an annual output worth 1,500 million koronas. The next decade and a half witnessed even more dynamic development: 5,500 plants operated just before the war with 600,000 workers and an output worth 3,300 million koronas yearly. At the beginning of the period, machinery developing 9,000 horsepower was employed in industry, but by the end such machinery developed 900,000 horsepower, a hundredfold increase. Industrialization made especially great strides in Budapest, with its trams, railway stations, huge factories, smoke, and labour force. The population of the suburban Újpest, Kispest, Erzsébetfalva and Csepel factory districts—districts which had been just farmland before—rose from a quarter of a million to over one million in the course of half a century. Manual workers accounted for over 40 per cent of these people.

Hungary's national income multiplied threefold during the period and, at 2.5 per cent, the average annual growth rate was significant even by international standards. It indicated that Hungary, once a backward agricultural country, had become a fast-developing agrarian-industrial state.

What were the social factors behind this great leap forward? Mention must first and foremost be made of the leading liberal stratum which recognized the necessity and usefulness of modernization and encouraged the evolution of the capitalist system. Gábor Baross, who founded the Hungarian State Railways thus creating modern transportation in Hungary, was one of its members. Secondly, there was a large group of excellent businessmen and entrepreneurs who operated on a large scale. These men were not sentimental philanthropists. They ruthlessly exploited and oppressed the workers but nevertheless achieved something. Henrik Haggenmacher established the beer industry and, to some extent, the milling industry; Sándor Hatvani-Deutsch the sugar industry; Manfréd Weiss the Csepel factory complex; and Leó Goldberger the best textile complex in the country. Engineers, technicians, inventors, innovators, and a large number of devoted experimenters made substantial contributions to advancement. In this relation special mention must be made of András Mechwart, the brilliant chief engineer of the Ganz factory; Tivadar Puskás, the inventor of the telephone exchange; Károly Zipernowsky, Ottó Bláthy, and Miksa Déri, the inventors of the transformer; Donát Bánki, the inventor of the turbine; János Csonka, who invented the carburettor; and hundreds of others.

Last, but not least, credit for this great boom must go to those industrial workers, agricultural workers, and peasants who were compelled to accommodate themselves to capitalist labour discipline, who learned trades, who became familiar with materials, and who really got to know what work meant. It was from their expertise and diligence that modern Hungary was built.

The decline of Romanticism

During the hectic period of the Age of Reform and the Revolution, and then in the difficult years of absolutism, the national consciousness and the public mood were in complete harmony with Romanticism. The poems of Petőfi, the paintings of Barabás and Madarász, the operas of Erkel (*Hunyadi László* and *Bánk bán*) gave appropriate expression to the struggles of the War of Independence, and to joy and sorrow. The doubts that arose after the defeat and a search for the meaning of human existence were formulated in *Az ember tragédiája* (The Tragedy of Man), a profoundly philosophical play written by Imre Madách in 1860. Even János Arany, who belonged to the popular-national grouping, drew on Romanticism for inspiration in the epics and ballads he wrote in this period.

The year 1867 marked the end of the revolutionary phase. The greater part of the leading classes became reconciled to the Compromise, and moved into the historicist public buildings of Austro-Hungarian dualism. The sober epoch of founding and construction had arrived. Baron József Eötvös, the distinguished writer, thinker, and education minister, laid the foundations of a capitalist educational system. Ágoston Trefort continued Eötvös's work in this field. The number of elementary schools rose from 13,000 to almost 17,000 during the period, and standards improved substantially. The number of teachers doubled, while the proportion of state and village schools rose from 3.5 per cent to 28 per cent of the total. While at the time of the Compromise, over half the 1.1 million children of school age received no schooling, in 1914 this was true for only 10–15 per cent of the 2.5 million eligible to attend. The number of secondary-school students also doubled. At the beginning of the period Hungary's only, somewhat provincial, university was enlarged, and prominent politicians and scholars of the period established a modern network of colleges. The medical and arts faculties of Budapest University earned a high reputation in Europe. Budapest's Technical University was founded in 1871. A year later the Francis Joseph University in Kolozsvár was set up, and at the end of the period the universities of Pozsony and Debrecen also. These years also witnessed the foundation of the Academy of Fine Arts (1872) and the Academy of Music (1875)—not to mention the colleges of law and veterinary science, the museums, the libraries, and the string of Budapest and provincial theatres which followed the opening of the National Theatre during the Age of Reform.

In sum, cultural standards rose substantially: the proportion of illiterates dropped from two-thirds to one-third of the population. Yet the content of culture changed only very slowly. In poetry, the popular-national trend established by Petőfi and Arany was continued in the work of untalented epigones, while the novelist Mór Jókai wrote and popularized romantic works. His novels *A Rab Ráby* (The Strange Story of Rab Ráby), *Egy magyar nábob* (A Hungarian Nabob), *Kárpáthy Zoltán*, *Az új földesúr* (The New Landowner), *A kőszívű ember fiai* (The Sons of the Stone-hearted Man), *Az arany ember* (The Man with the Golden Touch), *Fekete gyémántok* (Black Diamonds) gave expression to the finest patriotic and heroic virtues. These included a passionate love of liberty, unselfishness, and chivalry. Jókai's novels were naturally laced with innumerable anecdotes, cheerfulness, and patriotic grief. Jókai achieved unprecedented popularity. He was more than just a writer, editor and politician: he was a representative of the nation, its greatest story-teller and educator for half a century. There were many fine and noble things in this period, as well as a great deal of self-deception. It was a period which would have benefited more from sober self-awareness than from Romanticism.

Jókai's outstanding successor Kálmán Mikszáth also started out by writing short stories and exciting tales in the Romantic tradition: *Tóth atyafiak* (The Slovak Yokels), *A jó palócok* (The Good Palots), *Szent Péter esernyője* (St Peter's Umbrella), *Beszterce ostroma* (The Siege of Beszterce). In these works the plot is woven around an anecdote and a huge fraud stands at the centre of everything. Later, however, Mikszáth's anecdotes became increasingly bitter and turned against a decaying and profligate gentry. The short stories and novels written by Mikszáth at the end of the century often portrayed, in a satirical vein, the decline of the once-powerful Hungarian noble.

Romanticism also flourished on the stage, and not only at the National Theatre. In those theatres where the popular play scored its great successes, Romanticism was also well established. The sympathetic portrayal of life for ordinary people tended towards Romantic idyll, even in the late works of this genre's initiators, Ede Szigligeti and József Szigeti. In the 1870s the popular play turned into a song-and-dance peasant "musical" which smoothed over the set-back in the embourgeoisment of the peasantry and presented a spectacular and bogus folkishness of sorts. The only thing that can be said for such productions is that Lujza Blaha, "the nation's nightingale", rose to prominence through them. In fame and fortune she was on a par with the great tragic actresses of the day, Mari Jászai and Emília Márkus.

For three decades the famous historical tableaux of Viktor Madarász, Bertalan Székely, Mór Than, and Gyula Benczúr evoked patriotic enthusiasm for Hungary's past, and did so with great artistic force. However, even in painting the appeal of Romanticism slowly began to wane. It was no accident that the great popular painter of the post-Compromise period was Mihály Munkácsy, who used naturalistic techniques and whose genre paintings—*Siralomház* (Condemned Cell) and *Tépéscsinálók* (Lint Makers)—and whose religious and historical tableaux—*Krisztus Pilátus előtt* (Christ Before Pilate) and *Milton*—contained some impressive realistic elements. In his late works—*A magyarok bejövetele* (The Arrival of the Hungarians) and *Ecce homo*—not even Munkácsy's brilliant painting skills could conceal the empty theatricality of late Romanticism. The truly modern painter of the *fin de siècle* was the then almost-unknown Pál Szinyei Merse, who in his great paintings—*Majális* (Picnic in May) and *A csalogány* (The Nightingale)—discovered air, light and colours almost at the same time as the masters of French Impressionism.

Ferenc Liszt, the great genius of the age, worked until the mid-1880s. His Hungarian rhapsodies, Hungarian sketches, and the *csárdás* made Hungarian melodies known the world over and pointed ahead to the appearance of folk music in formally-composed works. Ferenc Erkel was still active at the beginning of the period, although his new operas, *Dózsa György* and *Brankovics György* did not gain popularity. Musical life became stale at the end of the century and Hungarians found it difficult to choose between Western-type musical culture and recently written, pseudo-Hungarian folk songs.

Late nineteenth-century Hungarian culture presents a varied picture. The important achievements of mass education and the establishment of a network of cultural institutions notwithstanding, there were signs of stagnation and decline in many areas. Admittedly, men of great talent such as Jókai, Erkel, Munkácsy, and especially Liszt introduced and maintained high artistic standards. However, the class that fostered culture, the one-time landed nobility, was decaying—along with national Romanticism. The Romantic sun still shone, but the evening hours had already arrived.

By the end of this period Budapest had grown into a big metropolis. It had a sizeable middle-class population, an intelligentsia with a European outlook, and a working class. These strata were no longer satisfied with the antiquated tastes and empty culture of a nobility which looked to the past.

The Millennium

Around 1890 important developments began to affect the history of this peaceful time. The strong prime minister, Kálmán Tisza, fell from power, and opposition in the country increased. The Social Democratic Party was formed in Hungary and socialist ideas penetrated to the remote villages of the Great Plain. Bloody riots broke out in Békés and Csongrád counties, the "Stormy Corner" of the southeastern region, and the towns of Orosháza, Békéscsaba and Hódmezővásárhely were all caught up in these disturbances. The landless and destitute—for example, day labourers and harvesters—demanded higher wages, better conditions, and rights. These people formed socialist organizations and swore an oath of allegiance to the red flag. The government's first response was to declare a state of emergency on the Great Plain and to use coercion. However, it also tried a more sophisticated approach. As finance minister, Sándor Wekerle began to put the state's monetary affairs in order, continuing this work even after becoming prime minister in 1892. Adopting the gold standard, he stabilized the Austro-Hungarian empire's uniform currency, the korona. (One U.S. dollar was now 4.935 koronas.) These years witnessed the last revival of the Hungarian liberal traditions dating from the Age of Reform, and despite fierce opposition from Francis Joseph, the Viennese Court, influential conservatives, and leading churchmen, the Wekerle government was able to enact important liberal legislation. Civil marriage was made possible and state registration of births, marriages, and deaths introduced. In addition the free practice of religion was guaranteed, as was the equality of Judaism with other faiths.

Wekerle was a talented economic policy maker and popular also, as was Dezső Szilágyi, the liberal justice minister of great erudition. The same held true for Count Albin Csáky, the education minister. Also highly thought of was the railway-building transport minister Gábor Baross, who died in 1892. Nevertheless, the Wekerle government remained in office for only two years. At the burial ceremony of Lajos Kossuth on April 2, 1894, the real feelings and discontent of the nation were expressed in no uncertain terms. At the same time the Romanians also revealed their grievances to the world when students at the University of Bucharest issued a memorandum on the plight of their kinsmen in Hungary. Every conservative grouping, political party, and religious denomination now turned against Wekerle. His permissive and liberal policy had become unacceptable generally, and Francis Joseph himself was dissatisfied. The equilibrium of the past had been upset: on January 14, 1895 Baron Dezső Bánffy was appointed prime minister.

In 1896 the thousandth anniversary of the Magyar conquest of the Danube Basin was celebrated. The festivities, for which the country had been preparing for a whole decade, took place with great pomp but also served to restore balance and to obscure problems.

The country now looked back on a millennium full of struggle. Situated between stronger peoples and at the crossroads of Europe, its very survival had often been in jeopardy. Hungary's position among states, peoples, and cultures had always been peripheral and this had led to oppression. Despite all the vicissitudes of history the Magyars had fought simultaneously for survival, acquisition of European culture, and acceptance for their own. At the end of the nineteenth century Hungary could look back on a period of peace characterized by economic development, hectic construction work, and fine cultural achievements. The nation could indeed commemorate with pride the thousand years of its history, and its half century of capitalist development.

The organizers of the celebrations, though, overplayed this pride, as did the authorities, official institutions, and the press. The events soon turned into bluster on an enormous scale. *Fin-de-siècle* nationalism used the Millennium to popularize Hungarian state power and, in stone, iron, and words, to perpetuate the illusion of a Hungarian empire.

At midnight on New Year's Eve, 1895, bells rang out simultaneously throughout the country. Every town and every village, no matter what its size, greeted the anniversary year. In April, Parliament, at a gala session, commemorated the Magyar conquest of the Carpathian Basin, giving thanks to Providence, Prince Árpád, and Francis Joseph for their gracious contributions. On May 2 the king—amid great splendour and in the presence of the chief dignitaries of the Austro-Hungarian empire—opened the Millenary Exhibition in the present-day City Park, which had been designed and laid out especially for the occasion. The exhibition was certainly impressive and demonstrated Hungary's great material and cultural progress, as well as its relative affluence. The effect was heightened still further by the large number of important construction projects which were launched. The *Nagykörút* (Grand Boulevard) was opened to traffic, the first electric underground railway on the continent of Europe was put into operation, and the Francis Joseph Bridge (today's Liberty Bridge) was inaugurated. At the same time reconstruction work started on the Royal Palace in Buda and in Heroes' Square, where the Millenary Memorial Column and the Museum of Fine Arts were built. One splendid celebration followed another. A thanksgiving service featuring Liszt's Coronation Mass was held in the Matthias Church during which an address was delivered by the prince-primate.

On June 8 homage was paid to the anniversary of King Stephen I's coronation. This was a particularly grand affair. The representatives of the counties and towns appeared with mounted escorts, along with members of the aristocracy in Hungarian gala-dress. Together with representatives of institutions and associations, this

THE AUSTRO-HUNGARIAN MONARCHY IN 1890

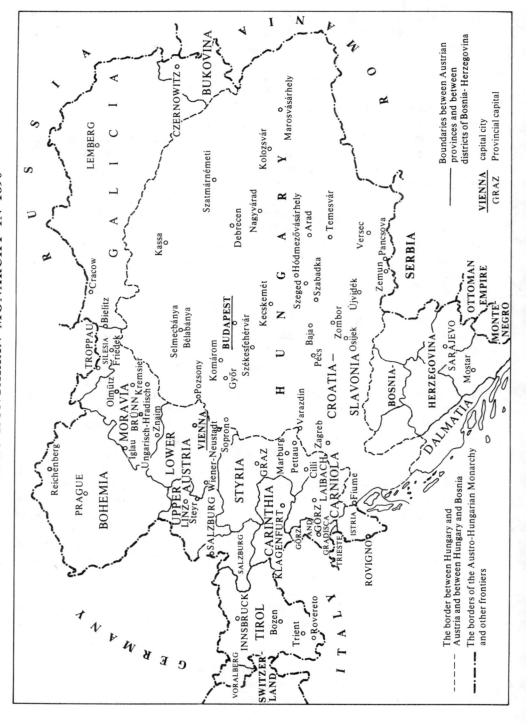

Boundaries between Austrian
provinces and between
districts of Bosnia- Herzegovina

VIENNA   capital city
GRAZ   Provincial capital

RUSSIA

BUKOVINA

GALICIA

LEMBERG

CZERNOWITZ o

Marosvásárhely o

Kolozsvár o

Szatmárnémeti

Kassa o

Debrecen o

Nagyvárad o

Cracow o

SILESIA

TROPPAU

Bielitz
Friedek

Selmecbánya
Bélabánya

Szeged o Hódmezővásárhely

Arad o

Temesvár o

Versec o

H U N G A R Y

BUDAPEST

Kecskemét o

Kőmárom

Pozsony o

Olmütz o

MORAVIA

BRÜNN o
Ungarisch-Hradischo

Iglau o

Znaim o

Győr o

Székesfehérvár o

Szabadka o

Zombor o

Zemun Pancsova o

SERBIA

Osijek

Újvidék o

CROATIA—

SLAVONIA

BOSNIA-

HERZEGOVINA

SARAJEVO o

Mostar o

MONTE-
NEGRO

OTTOMAN
EMPIRE

DALMATIA

Reichenberg o

PRAGUE o

BOHEMIA

LOWER

UPPER
AUSTRIA

LINZ o
Steyr

SALZBURG

SALZBURG

VIENNA
Wiener-Neustadt

Sopron o

STYRIA

GRAZ o

Marburg o

Pettau o

Cilli o

Varazdin o

Zagreb o

LAIBACH

CARNIOLA

Fiume o

Komárom

Pécs o Bajao

ROVIGNO

ISTRIA

TRIESTE

GRADISCA

GÖRZ o

CARINTHIA

KLAGENFURT o

VORALBERG

INNSBRUCK o

TIROL

Bozen o

Trient o

Rovereto o

SWITZER-
LAND

ITALY

GERMANY

R O M A N I A

---- The border between Hungary and
     Austria and between Hungary and Bosnia

—·—·— The borders of the Austro-Hungarian Monarchy
     and other frontiers

body proceeded through the streets of the capital with flags and banners. In the newly-completed Parliament on the Danube embankment, Dezső Szilágyi spoke of the significance of King and Nation coming together. This in his view, served as an eternal guarantee of the ancient freedom and unity of the Hungarian people.

Later on, Francis Joseph, accompanied by the kings of Serbia and Romania, opened the newly-improved Iron Gate (the name given to the ravine which then marked the common border of Austria-Hungary, Serbia and Romania), through which the Danube flowed. (Navigation there was perilous before the Hungarian government improved conditions.) The Court and the diplomatic corps spent most of the year in Budapest, where the annual meeting of the delegations was also held. It did indeed appear as though the idyllic empire of King Matthias had been revived. However, the bright lights of the Millenary celebrations were switched off in the autumn and in the New Year everything continued where it left off. Eighteen ninety-six witnessed stormy parliamentary elections and political battles, along with the strengthening of the working-class movement. The next year witnessed strikes among the harvesters and growing agrarian socialist activity on the Great Plain and in the *Tiszántúl*. From this there emerged the first programme for the distribution of land among the impoverished peasantry. These developments did not go unheeded: the rural socialists were hauled off to prison by the gendarmes and the leaders of the industrial labour movement expelled from the capital by the police. The socialist press was banned and legislation enacted to prohibit strikes among the harvesters.

The poor, the workers, and the national minorities hated the strong-arm approach adopted by the Bánffy government, and they put up strong and resolute resistance to its oppressive measures. The parliamentary opposition also disliked Bánffy's brutal policy, and itself suffered harsh treatment at his hands. Parliament toppled Bánffy at the end of 1898.

Hungary entered the twentieth century with a whole host of unresolved social and nationality problems. By this time the entire Habsburg empire was undermined by contradictions which threatened its very existence.

Nations and national minorities under dualism

Ever since the Middle Ages seven peoples—Slovaks, Ruthenes, Romanians, Germans, Serbs, Croats, Magyars—and some scattered minorities had lived side by side in Hungary. We have already seen how the neighbourly co-existence of these peoples and their common alliance against the Turks came to an end with the spread of Habsburg power. The Habsburg empire was multinational and was dominated by a German ruling class centered in Austria. From the eighteenth century onwards, nationalism began to develop in Europe; the national consciousness of its peoples began to grow, and national culture began to flourish. With time even the small peoples wished to establish independent nation-states of their own, and these developments had serious implications for the Habsburg empire. Conflicts between these peoples sharpened in the period 1848–49—the time of the Revolution in Hungary. With the Austrian victory, the common adversities of the non-German ethnic groups brought some sense of community between them, although the problems remained unresolved even in the years of Austrian absolutist rule.

The Compromise of 1867 created a new situation. The main reason why the leading Hungarian circles entered into alliance with the Habsburgs and Austria's ruling circles was to preserve their territorial assets and political power intact. The Compromise also served to maintain their dominion over the non-Magyar minorities living in Hungary. During the negotiations which led to the Compromise, and even more so after its enactment, the political leaders of the non-Magyars protested against an agreement which only took account of Austrian and Hungarian interests. True, in 1868 the Hungarians passed the Nationalities Law designed to protect the non-Magyars of the country and in the same year reached agreement with the Croats, who were now to enjoy limited autonomy within Hungary. However, the Nationalities Law was for the most part a dead letter, and it was only many years afterwards that the Hungarian landlords and the Hungarian public accepted the slight concessions to Croatia. The other nationalities continued to express their discontent. Their main grievance was that the legislation enacted after the Compromise failed to recognize their separate national identities and to grant the autonomy and political rights which were warranted by these.

The question, said Mihajlo Polit, a Serb liberal, was not whether the nationalities should be entitled to draw up petitions in Serbo-Croat, Slovak, Romanian or German, but whether "on the basis of self-rule, the villages, towns, and counties should bear the stamp of individual nationalities". In other words, autonomy for the minorities should be the aim and no citizen should be "an alien in his own homeland". Under the consolidated dualist system, the political parties of the national minorities could achieve little success. Although the minorities were allowed to use their mother-tongue and were permitted to develop their economic and cultural associations, dominant Magyar nationalism was increasingly asserted in education. After several years of unsuccessful efforts, the parties representing the national minorities declined. The first to do so was the Romanian, and in the 1870s the others followed suit. These parties lapsed into passivity, confining their activities to cultural work and to keeping alive the national idea.

The last quarter of the nineteenth century, however, saw significant changes in the economic situation and social structure of the national minorities. Modern capitalist farming methods, along with modern transportation and banking facilities, reached the central and southern grain-producing regions of Hungary. At the same time, the concomitants of industrialization and civilization generally also arrived. By the turn of the century the mountainous eastern periphery and Transylvania had both been opened up. In the twenty-five years before 1914 even these outlying areas witnessed an expansion of their railway networks. Industrial concerns were established and banks increased three- or fourfold both with regard to number and to capital available. From the point of view of both economic and political development, special mention must be made of the Slovak *Tatra*, the Romanian *Albina* and *Victoria*, and the Serbian credit co-operative networks. New industrial settlements and industrial regions flourished in the Slovak-populated districts of Upper Hungary, as well as in the Banat and in Southern Transylvania.

As a result of economic progress, the middle class among the national minorities became stronger, and in the more backward areas a middle class came into being for the first time. The growth of this class brought with it the beginnings of embourgeoisment for the peasantry, and an industrial working class came into being. In spite of considerable development Romanian and Ruthene society remained overwhelmingly agrarian in character: the proportion of Romanians and Ruthenes employed in industry, commerce and transportation was below 8 and 5 per cent respectively. Only 4.5 per cent of Romanians and 1 per cent of Ruthenes lived in towns. Embourgeoisment in Slovak, Serb, and Croat society was more advanced. Only 70 to 75 per cent of these people worked in agriculture, while the proportion of those in industry, commerce and transportation rose to between 15 and 20 per cent. Literacy was higher among Serbs, Slovaks and Croats; the intelligentsias of these peoples played important roles. The Serbs had a sizeable landowning class and an affluent middle class, while the Slovaks had a comparatively developed middle class, and the Croats possessed a complete social structure. Since it lacked a large landed aristocracy and gentry, society among the nationalities was more democratic than Hungarian society. Their middle class was less inclined to adopt gentry values and stood closer to the lower middle class and the peasants. At the same time the bourgeoisie was not the chief enemy and oppressor of the peasantry and working-class elements in these ethnic groups: this distinction belonged to the big Austro-German landowners and capitalists in general, and to their Hungarian counterparts in particular. As a result, forging a democratic national unity to oppose the government and ruling circles was easier for the nationalities than for the Hungarians themselves.

The great economic changes, the structural transformation of society, and the deepening crisis of the dualist system created, around the turn of the century, favourable conditions for the national minorities' struggle. The so-called Memorandum Trial (1894) involving the leaders of the Romanian National Committee caused considerable controversy. This and the congress of the national minorities held in Budapest in 1895 indicated not just the revival, but also the strength of feeling among the non-Magyars. At the beginning of the twentieth century every nationality party cast off its passivity and once more became involved in political life. Behind this change of approach lay hidden a change of generation and the participation of new classes in politics: positions in the Churches and in the middle-class hierarchy were passing to more democratic and secular-minded elements. Above all, the nationality parties now strove to broaden the popular base of their support and to win over their own working people. Accordingly, in their new programmes they laid stress on economic and social reform, and on democratic political rights. The demand for national independence was not emphasized and, in any case, this seemed a remote goal in the early years of the twentieth century. The desire to transform the Austro-Hungarian empire into a federation lost prominence, and nowhere was there any open mention of secession.

In the Slovak movement, the staff of the journal *Hlas* represented orientation towards the Czechs—an ethnic group under Austrian, not Hungarian, rule. This journal supported Pavol Blaho and Vavro Šrobár, while Milan Hodža came forth with a Democratic Peasant Party programme and Andrej Hlinka a Catholic People's

Party alternative. At the time of its revival, the Romanian National Committee was led by Aurel Vlad, Alexandru Vaida-Voievod, and Teodor Mihali, although the writer and poet Octavian Goga and the outstanding politician Iuliu Maniu increasingly took over this role. The Radical Party, which was popular amongst the Serbs, followed Jaša Tomić's populist-peasant line. Of the parties, those of Hodža and Tomić co-operated with the forces of Hungarian democracy. Formed in autumn 1905, the Serbo-Croat coalition proposed an alliance with its Hungarian Opposition counterpart and maintained good relations with the latter. However, when the Opposition came to power in Hungary and continued the nationalist line of earlier governments, the situation changed. In 1908, Austria-Hungary annexed Bosnia-Herzegovina (an area populated by Serbs) and the new rulers in Hungary supported the move. Hungarian hostility to an autonomous South Slav state based on independent Serbia was therefore openly revealed.

Whilst the middle-class nationality parties were unable to reach even temporary agreement, there was close co-operation between the workers and peasants of the various groups. Slovak, Romanian, Serb and Magyar working people fought shoulder to shoulder in István Várkonyi's Agrarian Socialist Party against their common oppressors. Movements were organized to seize the land and to provoke strikes among the harvesters. In Hungary, unlike Austria, the unity between the Socialist Party and the trade union movement did not break down, even when separate Slovak, Romanian and Serb sections and agitation committees were formed within the framework of the Socialist Party in the early years of the twentieth century.

During this period national minority culture underwent great development. Above all, literacy and basic general education became more widespread. Cultural associations such as the *Matica Slovenska* performed important and progressive work. After the banning of the latter, local associations, e.g. the Romanian *Astra* and the Serb *Matica Srpská*, continued the fight. They successfully cultivated the languages and literatures of their respective peoples, studied their history and encouraged nationality folk arts. The national minority newspapers were similarly effective: before the First World War there were fifteen Romanian, fifteen Serbo-Croat and thirteen Slovak daily newspapers, as well as several literary and scientific journals, published within Hungary's borders. Thanks largely to this extensive cultural activity, the cultural level and national consciousness of the national minorities rose. They became prepared for the time when the First World War would create the preconditions for national independence and union.

The face of Hungary

The Millennium was largely the occasion of the Hungarian upper classes, and ordinary people played an almost negligible part in the celebrations. The society which entered the twentieth century in a festive an optimistic mood was, as regards fundamental social relations and employment structure, capitalistic. Hungarian society had acquired an essentially bourgeois character, although feudal remnants survived in the form of an aristocracy and gentry. In this society the main line of division lay between the upper class and the people, but here also existed a perceptible difference between the historic part of the upper class and the newcomers to this class.

At the apex of the social pyramid stood the aristocracy, composed of rich landowning magnates endowed with the title of prince, count, and baron. Through division and bestowal of aristocratic status the number of families bearing these titles increased considerably in the period between the Compromise and the First World War, although earlier three families had borne the title of prince, ninety-one the title of count, and 113 the title of baron. Six hundred families possessed estates of more than 600 hectares (roughly 1,500 acres). One hundred and eighty-four had estates of more than 6,000 hectares (roughly 15,000 acres), and these large estates were called *latifundia* at the time. The aristocracy still occupied a leading position in political life, the army, and the diplomatic corps, and provided many honorary directors of large firms. The aristocracy was isolated from the other social classes. Living in remote country houses or in town residences, it sought entertainment in its own clubs, married among its own members and, as a class, loyally supported the Habsburg dynasty. Situated nearest to it in the social hierarchy was the wealthy gentry class, possessing over 100–150 hectares (250–375 acres) of land per family and very much part and parcel of upper-class Hungarian society at both national and county level. These landed classes together enjoyed the greatest social prestige and their members filled the important positions in government and public administration.

However, many gentry families lost some, and even all, of their estates during this period. Those gentry members who were unable to keep abreast of capitalistic farming practices found it difficult to make their estates pay and left agriculture. Lagging behind in the process of embourgeoisment, they took jobs in public administration. In fact, gentry recruitment to these positions was so great that this class became the backbone of the bureaucratic apparatus required by capitalist Hungary at this time. The gentry was also prominently represented in the intelligentsia, and it determined the character and outlook of this body. The gentry world-view combined the conceit of the nobility with a powerful historical consciousness. Also present were patriotic feelings, which increasingly changed to nationalism, and the First Reform Generation's love of liberty, which was quickly changing to conservatism. The antidemocratic attitude of the landowners was also a feature, together with a value system which stressed the merits of landownership, agriculture, political activity, and public administration. Also favoured were intellectual careers. However, all forms of service to the public such as business and trade were out, and even more so was manual work.

A large section of the middle class and, later, the lower middle class was of German and other national minority origin. These people comprised the majority of white-collar workers and intellectuals at the beginning of the twentieth century and they aped the gentry's outlook and way of life. At the end of the period the numbers of earners in these occupations exceeded 300,000 and, with family members included, this milieu numbered 1 million. Not only its political influence, but also its very size made this grouping an important factor in Hungarian society.

It was during this period that the wealthiest and most influential part of the middle class (the small group of bankers, manufacturers and big entrepreneurs) caught

141

up with the large landowners at the top of the social pyramid. By origin most were not ethnic Magyars, for such an entrepreneurial middle class could never have emerged from the feudal society still existing in the backward and agrarian Magyar areas. Typically, the entrepreneurs came from the ranks of Jews who had settled in Hungary in the first half of the nineteenth century and from those German entrepreneurs and technical experts who came to Hungary between 1800 and 1900, although some were the Magyarized descendants of Greek, Serbian, and Armenian merchants who had emigrated to the country in the eighteenth century. The enormous wealth of these people was abundant compensation for their lowly origins. Under the reign of Francis Joseph, several hundred such families were ennobled and about fifty, among them twenty-eight Jewish families, acquired baronial rank. Most bought estates, palaces, and ancestors for themselves and their offspring. They therefore became genuine Hungarian aristocrats who donned Hungarian gala-dress and wore the sword of honour on festive occasions.

The upper middle class therefore assimilated with the traditional leading classes in public life and in upper-class society. However, in business activities it preserved its bourgeois virtues, of which ruthless acquisition and accumulation were just as much part as a rigorous work ethic, excellent business sense, and entrepreneurial risk-taking. Outstanding industrialists and bankers included Zsigmond Kornfeld, Leó Lánczy, Manfréd Weiss, Sándor Hatvany-Deutsch, Henrik Haggenmacher, Leó Goldberger, the Fellners, the Brülls, and their associates. These men contributed substantially to the modernization of the Hungarian economy, to the development of a modern banking system, and to the establishment of large-scale industry in Hungary.

The largest section of the middle class consisted of merchants, small manufacturers, actors, and university graduates. During this time the number, wealth, and landed property of this section increased also. This was true not only in Budapest but in the commercial and industrial centres in the countryside as well. These members of the middle class procured significant positions for themselves, although their power to influence important political and economic decisions remained limited.

What was it, then, which held together this "middle class", composed as it was of such vastly heterogeneous elements? One important trait uniting the various sections was their separation from the working people and from the middle strata of the non-Magyar nationalities. Consequently, they all had a vested interest in maintaining the dualist Hungarian state and social system. This, however, was insufficient in itself to unite them, and middle-class property and affluence were similarly unable to keep them together.

Some kind of rank, position, and a certificate of secondary-school education paving the way to an army career were the preconditions for admission into the Hungarian middle class. To these had to be added a particular outlook on life and an ostentatious manifestation of traditional patriotism. One element in middle-class cohesion was an increasingly uniform way of life which, according to the succinct contemporary description, featured a flat with three principal rooms, home-cooked and freshly-served midday meals, a free railway pass, and domestic servants. These, as well as a good education for the children, were the status symbols of middle-class society.

The bulk of lower middle-class earners, who numbered almost a million, also belonged to bourgeois society. Although they were still addressed in a deferential manner, they were no longer respected accordingly. The term "lower middle class" covered strata which differed widely in terms of occupation, income, and social status. This grouping ranged from the prosperous artisan working with assistants to the grocer and shoemaker, and from the poor junior clerk to the junior army officer. Within the lower middle class, a line of division was clearly discernible between the real petit-bourgeois with his own workshop, store, house and perhaps small plot of land or vineyard, and those declining from lower middle-class status who made a living by doing manual work. The rift widened between the assimilated retailer and small manufacturer strata on the one hand and the *déclassé* elements, the victims of capitalism, on the other. The remaining guild members and the bottom strata of the lower middle class constituted the rest of this particular social grouping, which was conservative in outlook. Lacking a consciousness and value system of their own, these latter elements were without structural cohesion.

Below the lower middle class were situated the workers and poor peasantry, the broad masses of the people many millions strong.

The life of the poor

Who were the poor of Hungary? Those who had no land, no wealth, nor secure livelihood, those who made a living out of other people's stubble—this is how Lajos Kiss, an expert on the life of these people, saw it. In 1900 the poor in Hungary comprised two million day-labourers and farm servants, as well as some 500,000 dwarf-holders whose tiny plots did not provide them with a proper means of subsistence. The hundreds of thousands of smallholders who owned bad-quality land and who possessed no livestock or machinery were also included in this category.

At the end of the nineteenth century, the time of the Great Agricultural Depression in Europe, the life of the poor was made extremely difficult by low grain prices and a growing tax burden. Some smallholders tried to improve their position by raising livestock, but this required the work of the whole family. Another alternative was sharefarming, on slowly deteriorating terms, with the younger son or daughter working as a day-labourer. In the course of the last quarter of the nineteenth century, there developed a pressure which drove the poor of the villages to labour day and night from early spring until late autumn. On the other hand, these people were without work in the winter, a state of affairs partly alleviated by fatty food if the larder was full and aggravated by hunger if it was empty.

The external conditions of the peasant way of life changed slowly and very gradually. In the more prosperous regions of Transdanubia and the Great Plain dried mud was slowly replaced by brick as a building material and tiles superseded thatch and reed for the roof. Otherwise the form of the peasant dwelling did not fundamentally change. The stove connected to the chimney constituted a major innovation. The kitchen thereby became free of smoke and, as a result, fit for habitation. Iron cooking stoves also came into common use in this period, transforming both the heating

143

and cooking situation. From this time on, the former living room, which had always been overcrowded, lost its ordinary function and became a room used only on special occasions. The kitchen took over as the centre of family life, serving all kinds of purposes from cooking to sleeping, and as the place for neighbourly chats.

Eating habits also changed. In addition to wheaten and rye bread, (both were consumed according to region and nationality) along with girdle-cake and polenta, potatoes became a staple food of the masses. Previously mutton was the meat most commonly eaten but with the soil now being allowed to lie fallow and with the decline of cotton production, pork took its place. This was because pigs could be raised on small plots of land, and although pigs yielded a good deal less meat, they did produce much lard, bacon and smoked sausage. At the turn of the century only the poorest did not slaughter pigs.

The monotony of work was eased by important holidays. On such occasions the village people put on their best clothing—their folk costume. In the nineteenth century loose white linen clothing was replaced by colourful folk garments, above all by the embroidered peasant cloak, embroidered shirts, jackets, skirts, and head-dress. Naturally, in the course of time items of commercially-produced clothing also found their way even to the remotest village; the cotton skirt, dungarees and the jacket-type coat were just a few examples. However, the objects and practices of more urban interior decoration and dress were characteristic of the ordinary working day. Festive occasions brought forth the "folk" dress and articles for personal use which so conspicuously indicated peasant status. The second half of the nineteenth century witnessed the emergence of the most beautiful regional folk cultures: the Matyó, Kalotaszeg, Kalocsa, and many others.

The sharp contrast between the more urbanized everyday existence of the peasant and his consciously-preserved folk culture was not merely an ethnographical curiosity, but was indicative of the duality of the peasant way of life, and of its growing stagnation and crisis. The majority of the smallholder peasants failed to become market-orientated farmers in the same way that the déclassé elements unable to find work in industry failed to integrate into the ranks of the workers.

The great mass of the rural proletariat was made up of seasonal workers, harvesters, navvies and farm servants. Their number topped the 2 million mark at the beginning of the twentieth century and, counting the members of their families, the figure exceeded 4.5 million. Farm servants were usually bound to estates by contracts valid for several years. In practice these often amounted to a life-long commitment: the estates had a regular work force and contracts could be renewed repeatedly if the farm servant's work and conduct found favour. The farm servant's remuneration consisted of some cash, payment in kind, and a small plot of land. Farm servants' duties were innumerable: the working day for these people lasted from sunrise to sunset, and the livestock had to be looked after on Sundays and holidays as well. The farm servant's wife was obliged to express gratitude to her husband's employer by performing several weeks of unpaid work, as well as various minor services. Farm servants were not allowed to leave the estate without permission, were not allowed to put up guests, and were under the supervision of the ispáns and the estate bailiffs. For the farm servant, work began in early childhood as assistant to the swineherd and ended, at best, as headman of the farm. Over the centuries there evolved a closed hierarchical society which was as conscious of, and as sensitive to, differences in position as was the high aristocracy itself. At the bottom of the hierarchy stood the day-labourers, followed by the drivers, first of the oxen, then of the horse-drawn carts. Above them came the liveried coachmen, the most prestigious of these three groups. The husbandmen came next, with the horseherds and the shepherds at the top. The artisans, blacksmiths, cartwrights and machine operators constituted a separate caste; they were addressed as "sir" and did not mix with the farm servants.

The "people of the puszta" lived in great poverty and backwardness—eating, working, and speaking frugally. They mostly lived in stable-like barracks and, from the early twentieth century on, in farm servants' quarters shared between two or four families. It was only after 1900 that servants' quarters of better quality were built. These contained a separate room for each family but the kitchen was shared. The furniture consisted of plank beds, straw mattresses, and a chest. The staple diet of farm servants was carrots, onions, bread, polenta and bacon, with lean meat and pastry on holidays.

Harvesting and threshing were done in teams, called harvester gangs, which were recruited especially for the summer. These were hired for two to three months and received one-tenth of the harvested crop in payment. By the early twentieth century, however, this had dropped to one-eleventh or one-twelfth. Crammed into a few months, the harvesters' work was extremely difficult. For the rest of the year they were lucky if they could get work for a few weeks as day-labourers, doing mowing, construction work, and wood-cutting. As a migrant worker, the harvester was not closely attached to the estate and the bailiff. His life was more insecure and more subject to hardships than that of the farm servant, but he was also freer. The harvester's thinking was less limited than that of the farm servant and his spirit of enterprise greater. It was primarily these rural day-labourers who went to find seasonal work in the towns; it was they who settled in the suburban factory districts, and they who set out to seek their fortune in other lands.

At the end of the nineteenth century, emigration from Hungary gathered momentum. In the twenty-five years prior to the First World War some two million people, mostly smallholders and agricultural labourers, left the country. Initially their purpose was merely to save up money to buy land in Hungary, and a quarter did in fact return to their homeland. Some acquired land, others purchased houses. But a million and a half people emigrated for good, mostly to the United States and Canada. However, only one-third of these people were Magyars; the rest were Slovaks, Ruthenes, Germans, and Croats. Emigrating Hungarians tended to settle in clusters, the majority in the vicinity of Ohio, Michigan, Cleveland, Detroit, and Pittsburgh, where they went to work in the mines.

A new world, a new homeland, a new language, a new culture, and a new way of life—all brought considerable afflictions for the first, pioneering, generation of Hungarian emigrants. Understandably, they tried to stay together, sought the community they had been accustomed to, cultivated their mother-tongue, and preserved a love of their homeland.

Earthquake

On October 8, 1905, express messengers from Vienna carried top secret orders to the army corps at Pozsony, Budapest, Kassa, Temesvár, Nagyszeben, and Zagreb. Troops were to occupy the Hungarian capital and key points in the provinces. But why did Francis Joseph want to wage war against the Hungarian half of his empire?

The crisis dated back to January 1905. Count István Tisza's Liberal government had lost the election and thirty years of Liberal rule had come to an end. The opposition parties gained a majority in Parliament and formed a bloc hostile to the prime minister. These parties demanded concessions which were unacceptable to the Crown, and from this there arose a cabinet crisis. Tisza no longer possessed a majority in Parliament and the emperor-king would not permit the victorious opposition parties to form an administration in which the Party of Independence was dominant. The constitutional machinery of dualism became paralyzed.

More remote causes of the crisis dated back to the end of the nineteenth century. As prime minister, wealthy landowner and bank president Kálmán Széll could ensure only a few years of calm (1899–1903). The crisis between the Crown and Hungary stemmed from the old question of the army. When the Széll government introduced its army bill early in 1903, the National Opposition issued a programme demanding that the language of command in all Hungarian units be Magyar and that the Hungarian national coat of arms be included in the insignia of the Imperial and Royal Army. When these demands were rejected, the opposition resorted to filibustering in Parliament, with the result that parliamentary business was obstructed. This tactic was so effective that the budget could not be passed and, in May 1903, the country entered a state of constitutional vacuum known as "ex lex". In autumn 1903 Francis Joseph in his Chlopy address warned the Hungarian Opposition in no uncertain terms, declaring that he would tolerate neither the undermining of the common army's unity nor the infringement of his own royal prerogative. When this resulted in the fall of yet another Hungarian cabinet, Francis Joseph asked Count István Tisza, known for his firmness, to form an administration.

The son of the powerful prime minister Kálmán Tisza, István Tisza had been brought up in a period when liberalism was already in decline and when power was there to be exercised, not fought for. From his father he had inherited political ability; from his uncle, Count Lajos Tisza, his title; and from his family his upper-class conceit. At the turn of the century the government party was in search of a leader and was determined to make István Tisza a politician. Tisza, a devout Calvinist who believed in his calling, regarded himself as a political Hercules who would restore law and order, and clean the Augean stables of decadent parliamentarism. From 1903 onwards Tisza dealt firmly with obstruction in Parliament. After temporary successes a minor parliamentary coup in November 1904 left him isolated. Most members of his own party opposed his coercive methods and throughout the country the Opposition, whom Tisza constantly provoked, demanded his dismissal.

It was in such a situation—made worse by the alarming news of the Russian revolution—that elections took place in January 1905. These brought a heavy defeat for the government party.

Things were made more difficult by the fact that, in the midst of the political turmoil, working people also launched a struggle. Their aim was to improve working conditions which had deteriorated during the economic depression of the previous few years. "The entire country is veritably shaken to the core ... The workers in workshops, factories, and on building sites are downing their tools," wrote *Népszava*. Discontent grew during the spring and summer of 1905. Huge strikes, one of them staged by over 20,000 workers in the capital, took place. Then, in the summer a harvesters' strike broke out and spread to southern Transdanubia. These developments, as well as demonstrations, helped to make the situation explosive.

Under these circumstances the country could not be left without a functioning government and consolidated political rule. For lack of anything better, in 1905 the emperor-king Francis Joseph appointed his favourite soldier, Géza Fejérváry, to be prime minister. Fejérváry had previously been minister of defence and was commander of the Royal Hungarian Lifeguard. The Lower House immediately protested and there was a public outcry throughout the whole country. After Fejérváry's unconstitutional government suffered defeat in a parliamentary vote of confidence, Parliament announced that the traditional form of national resistance dating from feudal times would be put into effect. This meant that the counties would not collect taxes, would not supply their annual complement of recruits, and would not comply with orders issued by the government. In the summer of 1905 another national resistance movement was launched by the conservative landowners, and the clergy, who had suffered under Liberal rule, supported this.

Hard pressed, the government accepted a proposal by József Kristóffy, the minister of the interior, that national resistance should be countered by introducing electoral and social welfare reforms. By doing this, the government could expect support from the Social Democratic Party, the organized worker masses which were several hundred thousand strong, the radical intelligentsia, and the national minority politicians. On September 15 a huge demonstration took place outside the Parliament in which 100,000 Budapest workers demanded the right to vote and the freedom to organize trade unions. In response, the Opposition planned to present its own demands on October 10, the day Parliament was to reconvene after its adjournment. It was out of fear of the consequences that the ministry of war in Vienna issued its military orders. Those had been prepared in advance and were to be executed in the event of insurrection.

But nothing happened on October 10, 1905. Although the leaders of the Opposition coalition remonstrated loudly, they also called on their supporters to preserve constitutionalism and to support peaceful efforts. They denounced excesses through which the radical popular elements had shown their fighting spirit. The upper-class Opposition ostensibly wished to negotiate a compromise solution, and its willingness to negotiate was increased by the events of the revolution in Russia, by the tsar's "October Manifesto" granting universal suffrage, and by the Moscow uprising in December. Also persuasive were the demonstrations which took place in Vienna at this time and which finally led to the introduction of further electoral reform in Austria. At first the leaders of the Coalition retreated from their earlier position and said that they would be satisfied with the acknowledgement in principle of the justice of Hungary's army demands. When, however, Francis Joseph dissolved Parliament by military means in February 1906 and threatened to introduce absolutist rule, the Opposition leaders came round to the view that the Crown's position would have to be accepted.

In April 1906 the Opposition concluded a secret pact with Francis Joseph in which it capitulated totally, undertaking to form a government on the basis of the 1867 Compromise agreement and relinquishing its demands for military and other national concessions to Hungary. It promised to renew the economic Compromise when it expired and in fact did so in 1907. The Opposition also undertook to introduce democratic electoral reform, but it never implemented this pledge.

The cabinet crisis of 1905–6 ended with apparently no results, for neither national concessions nor democratic reform were achieved. Yet there was a result of sorts, namely that the Opposition's real nature became clear. Its capitulation to Francis Joseph and its ensuing four years in power showed that the landowners and gentry middle-class members who belonged to it were no different from the old government party. They manipulated the people by means of traditional national slogans, and were just as undemocratic and chauvinistic. Neither the oppressed nor the national minorities of the country could expect anything from the Opposition. One positive consequence of the crisis was that the forces of democracy, the real national and social opposition of the system, became more organized, increased in strength, and achieved a certain degree of cohesion.

The beginnings of the labour movement in Hungary

The Hungarian working-class movement had become an organized force by the turn of the century. In its early days it survived intense persecution, especially under the ruthless Bánffy government (1895–99) when almost a hundred workers were killed, several hundred imprisoned or deported from the capital, and numerous trade associations and rural workers' circles dissolved. However, it was precisely during these years that the workers waged their most steadfast and most difficult struggle. In 1897 miners staged a huge strike in the industrial region of Resica and Anina, while 10,000 brick and construction workers did the same in Budapest. In 1897–98 there were harvesters' strikes and a wave of unrest in the *Nyírség*, in the *Tiszántúl*, and in the southern part of the Great Plain. April 1904 witnessed the first railway strike in Hungary: the entire network was paralyzed and the army had to be called in to deal with the situation. In 1905 a wave of strikes swept through the country and in 1906 extended as far as Miskolc, Temesvár, Fiume, and Nagyvárad.

The organizing of the workers into trade unions took place rapidly. Unions were formed in each occupation and trade, and a Trade Council was set up in 1899 to act as an umbrella organization. Both the Trade Council and the unions were under the leadership of the Social Democratic Party and this leadership became consolidated at around the turn of the century under its leaders Ernő Garami, Jakab Weltner, and Dezső Bokányi. From 1908 onwards the former teacher Zsigmond Kunfi emerged as the most influential leader in the party. The Social Democratic leadership steadfastly advocated revolution as the party's ultimate goal, together with the need for

148

a socialist society. But although the party leadership stressed the revolutionary character of the movement, in practice it wished to follow the path of reforms —adapting a centrist line between the right-wing revisionist and the left-wing revolutionary trends of the international working-class movement. The right to vote was the Social Democrats' chief demand. Others were civil rights; equality between the nationalities; the abolition of privileges; the nationalization of mines, forests and Church land; and the abolition of entailment.

This programme was geared to conditions in the advanced Western capitalist countries, and despite the fact that it succeeded in winning the support of the Hungarian workers, it failed adequately to grasp the two issues fundamental to Hungarian development, the agrarian question and the nationalities problem. Hungarian Social Democracy rejected the idea of distributing the land as it felt that this would run counter to the scientifically-confirmed tendency for the means of production to concentrate into larger units. The leadership of the party maintained its rigid position even when the movements among the peasantry openly demanded land for the millions of rural poor. "The people need bread, not land", was the party's slogan in the early years of the twentieth century, but this was more suited to self-justification than to winning over the destitute masses in the countryside.

The programme of the Social Democratic Party did not openly declare a position on whether Hungary should be a republic or on demands for greater concessions to the country from Vienna. Also left vague were the issues of self-determination for the nationalities and the plan to establish a federation, which had already been accepted in Austria. The programme did, however, mention "total autonomy", "the election of all bodies and officials", and "the abolition of all inherited offices and titles". The wording used had the effect of leaving a number of things unclear. It was not said whether Francis Joseph would be affected and whether "total autonomy" referred to independence for the Hungarian state or to self-determination for the national minorities. Not only did the programme ignore such fundamental issues of Hungarian political life, but in practice, too, the Social Democrats failed to grapple with these sensitive problems. In point of fact the party directed its entire effort towards achieving universal suffrage with a secret ballot. It subordinated all other goals, plans, desires, and even the economic struggles of the workers (which it organized and encouraged) to this end.

Although neither the Social Democrats' programme nor the labour movement took up the problems relating to the highly topical issues of democratic transformation and national self-determination, socialist ideas exerted considerable influence on the people, shaping their consciousness in the process. In opposition to the official liberal nationalist and right-wing conservative political and conceptual system, a socialist counter-culture was created. This was characterized by worker solidarity, new ideas, socialist literature and theatre, music, singing and a community spirit in socialist associations. The socialist counter-culture attracted hundreds of thousands of people, although membership of the organized movement did not exceed 200,000 even during its most successful period. The working-class movement exerted particularly great influence over the radical intelligentsia which emerged at the beginning of the twentieth century.

In 1900 young sociologists, lawyers, and political publicists founded the journal

Huszadik Század (Twentieth Century) and a year later the Social Science Society. Their aim was to investigate Hungarian society, to discover the causes of Hungary's backwardness, and to identify the direction leading to development. The Society organized in-depth discussions and launched the sociographic series *Magyarország felfedezése* (Discovering Hungary). It exposed, one after another, the grave consequences of the system of large estates and the rule of the landed aristocracy. These were shown to be poverty for the vast majority of the people, an anti-democratic political system, and the oppression of the national minorities. This radical group also founded the most radical group of freemasons, the Martinovics Lodge, and encouraged the formation of the Galilei Circle, which organized extra-mural education for the workers and tried to encourage a revival of intellectual life. Oszkár Jászi was one of its leading intellectual figures and alongside him stood erudite associates Pál Szende, Gyula Rácz, and Ervin Szabó, the last of whom broke with Social Democracy.

The group emerged in an organized form in June 1914, shortly before the outbreak of the First World War and under the name of National Civic Radical Party. Its programme included the abolition of feudal remnants, land reform, human rights, an independent tariff zone, the protection of the country's interests, and equality for the national minorities. As belated advocates of the Enlightenment, the Radicals accepted the socialist idea as their distant goal and co-operated with the working-class movement. Together they arrived at a new interpretation of patriotism: "Where there is justice, there is the Fatherland!" They believed that the idea of national autonomy, which had been hijacked and reduced to a slogan, should be linked to a programme of social revival. They re-formulated the idea of "country and progress", as known to the Age of Reform. By "country" they understood the country of the whole people and by "progress" they understood social advancement. This is why they came to be called "the Second Reform Generation".

At the end of the first decade of the twentieth century, leftists disappointed by the conservative nationalist leaders of the Party of Independence joined the Radical group. These people aspired neither to a political career nor to ministerial position, but genuinely represented the tradition of 1848. Their leader, Gyula Justh, was an old warrior for independence, and it was he who made the transition from the coalition of landowners, gentry officials, and clergy to the idea of popular patriotism and left-wing ideals. This change of direction was also effected by the young aristocrat Count Mihály Károlyi, who entered the political arena in the 1910s and soon became the leader of the independence politicians.

From the left-wing independence politicians, socialists, and radical intellectuals, Hungarian democracy slowly and belatedly emerged. This occurred too late to avert the First World War and its consequences, although it did appear in time to give a prospect for renewal to the sober and progress-minded elements of the nation.

"A peacock takes its perch"

Hungary was a colourful country at the turn of the century. It was open to foreigners and foreign influences alike, and therefore its culture was rich and varied. The Millennial Monument, the reconstructed Royal Palace, and the enormous neo-Gothic Parliament building all exuded the national tradition. In 1896 the first *art nouveau* palace, Ödön Lechner's Museum of Applied Arts, was inaugurated. At this time too, Simon Hollósy, together with his students, founded a new school of painting at Nagybánya, and the Comedy Theatre, a home of modern European acting, was opened. As Hungarian society restructured itself, with the process of embourgeoisment making substantial headway, so its scientific and artistic life became more complex. Alongside the traditional romantic and popular-national neo-classical culture of the nobility, there emerged new middle-class urban and populist trends. It was in the field of literature that the simultaneous stratification and ferment in cultural life were shown most clearly.

At the highest level, the national tradition was continued by the elderly writer Kálmán Mikszáth. However, in the novels he wrote during the first decade of the twentieth century—for example, *Különös házasság* (A Strange Marriage) and *A fekete város* (The Black City)—the anecdotal and cheerful tone of Mikszáth's narrative was increasingly replaced by a bitter and sharp criticism of society. The national tradition was diluted by Ferenc Herczeg to make it suitable for a lower middle-class readership, and it was he who invested the declining gentry with middle-class qualities, popularizing them in his short stories and plays in the journal *Új Idők*. The novelist Géza Gárdonyi brought the national tradition closer to the people, primarily in his fine historical novels.

Edited by József Kiss, the journal *A Hét* was the first publication for the middle class and the big city. The quiet break with the noble tradition became increasingly obvious in the works of writers who sympathized with the urban poor and the oppressed. This was especially so in the work of Sándor Bródy, a writer who paved the way for a new literature. Ferenc Molnár and Jenő Heltai, both good story-tellers and playwrights, stood closest to the spirit of Budapest's middle class.

Although Ferenc Molnár did not concern himself with the serious problems of Hungarian society and was not alarmed by the premonition of impending disaster, he did, with refined irony, shed a revealing light on the upper-class world of his day. In addition, he was a great master of the stage and his plays brimmed with sparkling wit. Although less talented perhaps, Jenő Heltai was a warmer personality than Molnár.

In poetry, traditionally the outstanding genre of Hungarian literature, neither the representatives of the popular-national tradition, nor those of the new urban taste produced anything of real quality. A revolutionary change in literature was brought about by the radical democratic intelligentsia, which made its mark with the appearance on the literary scene of Endre Ady. Ady was an outstanding poet of the twentieth century and his significance was not confined solely to literature. Not only did he renew the subject-matter and language of Hungarian poetry, but he also radically transformed its relationship to the people and the nation. Ady formulated the new national ideal of the radical reform generation. In his poetry, he exposed the hitherto hidden depths of ordinary Hungarians. In Ady's poems, the language, voice, suffering, and rebellion of the Protestant preacher can be heard, along with the bards of the castles, and the *kuruc* who lived in hiding.

Endre Ady was the poet of the Hungarian soul and at the same time the prophet of Hungarian destiny. By means of his work, faith, and actions, Ady soon rallied behind him friends and enemies alike. Ady represented a watershed in the Hungary of the Habsburg empire. Around him gathered the innovative, creative spirits and on him Ernő Osvát and Baron Lajos Hatvany built the literary journal *Nyugat* (West). *Nyugat* later attained great fame and the outstanding writers and poets of the period all belonged to its circle. They were joined by Zsigmond Móricz, a friend of Ady's, who revived popular narrative prose. Other members included the poet Mihály Babits, a master of form inclined to intellectual exclusiveness and whose art was remote from that of Ady. Mihály Babits carried on the legacy of János Arany. Another *Nyugat* writer was Dezső Kosztolányi, the poet so receptive to Western impressionism. Others included Árpád Tóth, a soft-spoken poet who sympathized with the people; Gyula Juhász, who united tradition with rebellion; and Frigyes Karinthy, a satirist with a philosophical frame of mind who also possessed a sense of the absurd and the grotesque. The *Nyugat* circle also attracted thinkers who were far removed from the materialism of the radical left. They included Dezső Szabó, Béla Balázs, and György Lukács, the greatest philosopher of the age. Lukács was initially an idealist and was won over by Ady to the concept of a new, progressive, Hungarian spirit.

The musical tradition of the Romantic era was continued at the beginning of the twentieth century by Jenő Hubay and was later modernized by the talented young musician Ernő Dohnányi. The activities of the Opera and the Philharmonic Society refined the musical taste of their educated audiences, which were drawn from a narrow section of society. The majority of the middle class and the lower middle class were ardent operetta goers. Their favourites included the Viennese waltzes of Johann Strauss, *Cigánybáró* (The Gypsy Baron), and later Ferenc Lehár and his witty and animated work *Víg özvegy* (The Merry Widow). Soon Victor Jacobi, Jenő Huszka, and Imre Kálmán produced indigenous Pest operetta and *Csárdáskirálynő* (The Queen of the *Csárdás*), which has reigned supreme ever since. The nobility, whose taste was becoming increasingly middle-class, preferred the Hungarian-style singing of popular tunes, the sentimentally composed songs of Lóránd Fráter and Pista Dankó, and the melancholic, sometimes lively, music of the gypsies which made it so easy to cry and to make merry. This soon gave rise to the creation of the so-called popular play based on peasant life in the nineteenth century and which contained songs composed for the purpose. Another work which resulted was *János Vitéz* (John the Hero) whose lyrics, written by Jenő Heltai, were set to music by Pongrác Kacsóh.

The distinction between a Western-style musical culture and the Hungarian custom of singing popular songs was lessened by the two young musicians and scholars Béla Bartók and Zoltán Kodály. These two Hungarian geniuses started out from national Romanticism but soon discovered a pure source, the genuine, ancient pentatonic folk song. The two men went on study trips to collect long-forgotten and neglected Hungarian, Slovak, and Romanian folk songs which they then adapted to the new forms of expression in modern European music. Bartók's opera *A kéksza-kállú herceg vára* (Bluebeard's Castle) and the ballets *A fából faragott királyfi* (The Wooden Prince) and *A csodálatos mandarin* (The Miraculous Mandarin) raised an archaic popular genre to the realm of subtly-composed music. Like Ady's poetry, Bartók's music gave expression to the complaints and humanism of the twentieth-century individual represented in the suffering Hungarian people. The works of Bartók and Kodály sparked off a huge offensive by artistic and political conservat-ism but nevertheless they became the foundation of a new Hungarian musical culture.

The turn of the century also marked the beginning of an entirely new epoch in the history of Hungarian fine art. Admittedly, the start of this new era was not accom-panied by the appearance of new geniuses but nevertheless work of considerable value was produced. As with literature, music, and the theatre, the fine arts also revealed a three-part division of culture and taste. The circles committed to tradition rejected innovation, including Pál Szinyei Merse's early Impressionism, and even great masters such as Gyula Benczúr and Bertalan Székely were not receptive to new developments. Innovation in a middle-class vein was represented by the Nagybánya School and above all by Károly Ferenczy in his pictures. These were inspired by French Impressionism and were imbued with a sense of light and air.

The *art nouveau* of the turn of the century inspired the painting of János Vaszary and especially József Rippl-Rónai, an outstanding artist brought up in Paris. From the circle of innovators a small avant-garde group known as "The Eight" broke away. This rallied painters who shared the markedly constructivist vision of Károly Kernstok. Many of its members eventually broke with traditional forms of expres-sion and moved on to abstract art.

There were, however, two exceptionally talented artists at this time—Tivadar Csontváry Kosztka and Lajos Gulácsy—who could not be placed in either of these categories. Both depicted a magical reality behind and beyond the visible world. Full of symbols, Csontváry's Biblical scenes sought lost community and identity, as did Gulácsy's dream world, Naconxypan, with its timeless and other-worldly in-habitants.

During this period Hungarian scientific life also enjoyed a revival. Having learnt from the achievements of German—and later French and British—scholarship, the social sciences developed rapidly. The same was true for legal and historical scholar-ship—both traditionally popular in Hungary—and also for linguistics and literary history. A new development occurred as the natural sciences took root. Loránd Eötvös became famous not only for his invention of the pendulum used in geological research, but also for his theories on the measurement of gravity and magnetism. Alongside Eötvös, and partly under his guidance, there emerged the first great school of Hungarian mathematicians, made famous through the names of Gyula Kőnig, József Kürschák, Lipót Fejér, and Frigyes Riesz. This school produced great scholars such as János Neumann, who made a substantial contribution to number and set theory; and Leó Szilárd and Jenő Wigner, who both performed out-standing work in nuclear physics. The period witnessed the emergence, alongside the world-famous medical school in Vienna, of the Budapest School of Medicine.

This followed in the wake of excellent doctors such as Frigyes Korányi, János Balassa, Endre Hőgyes, and others.

It appeared as though abundance of great talent in all fields of art and science was Nature's way of compensating for the centuries of mediocrity in Hungary. The early twentieth century witnessed the rallying of some of the finest writers, artists, and scholars of the country. "In the struggle waged with intellectual weapons the victory is already theirs," wrote Endre Ady in 1907. "The time will come when it will be theirs in the political struggle as well. That time will see the rebirth of Hungary."

And that time did come, although not in the way envisaged by Ady and his associates before the First World War. Many of Hungary's leading intellectuals, artists, and scholars were killed in the fighting and many crippled for life. The loss of the war and the failure of the two subsequent revolutions broke the spirit of most of the survivors, forcing them either into exile abroad or into oblivion at home.

The road to Sarajevo

The political crisis of 1905, which was accompanied by fierce class struggles and national resistance across the country, clarified the political situation to some extent. After thirty years the National Opposition finally gained power—but nothing changed. This was despite the fact that the Party of Independence which won the most seats in 1906, had for decades been the repository of national desires and hopes. The Constitution Party had promised national reforms and the Catholic People's Party social ones. These were not, however, forthcoming from the new Wekerle government, which was in power from 1906 to 1910 and which was supported by these parties. Admittedly, the landowners were granted the high agricultural tariffs they had been promised and the middle class received sizeable financial support for industry. Also, a new code of regulations was drafted for officials and their pay raised. Moreover, nationalist public opinion was placated by a new magyarizing education act. Nevertheless, important national reforms—the establishment of Hungarian as the language of command in the Hungarian army, the creation of an independent tariff zone, and the introduction of universal suffrage—were never implemented. Universal suffrage had even been agreed with Francis Joseph in 1906 but this made no difference. In the autumn of 1907 the Wekerle government renewed the economic Compromise with Austria for the last time, although the terms negotiated were unfavourable for Hungary.

The cabinet was studded with big names. Its members included Count Gyula Andrássy the Younger, a scholar, writer and party leader; Count Albert Apponyi, a talented speaker; Ignác Darányi, an expert on agriculture; Count Aladár Zichy, son of the founder of the Catholic People's Party; and Ferenc Kossuth, the son of Lajos Kossuth but disappointing in comparison with his famous father. The Opposition's period in office shed true light on the nature of Hungarian politics. The real alternative to the traditional liberalism was not the conservative nationalism which the Opposition represented, but radical democracy.

The peasantry and the lower middle class now began to realize this. In 1906

András Áchim formed his Peasant Party at Békéscsaba and for the first time a political party linked the issue of political democracy to the demand for land distribution. It was in vain that Áchim was stripped of his seat in Parliament, and it was in vain that he was harrassed with libel suits and personal attacks. The popularity of his party spread rapidly among the countryfolk in the "Stormy Corner" and on the Great Plain. In 1908, 400 settlements sent their representatives, who included a number of non-Magyars, to the party's congress in Cegléd. This congress, which witnessed the unveiling of a statue of the great peasant leader György Dózsa, adopted a programme demanding the distribution of landed estates more than 1,000 hectares in size. Finally, upper-class Hungarian society could tolerate Áchim no more: in May 1911 the two sons of Endre Zsilinszky murdered Áchim on the grounds that he had insulted their family.

In Transdanubia István Nagyatádi Szabó founded the *Országos Függetlenségi 48-as Gazdapárt* (National Independence and '48 Smallholders' Party), often referred to as the *Kisgazdapárt* (Smallholders' Party). This party adopted a more moderate platform than Áchim's Peasant Party. It did not entirely reject the system of big landed estates, but it did call for the abolition of entailment, for a more equal distribution of land, and for the suffrage. Although Nagyatádi Szabó's party was less radical than Áchim's, it also tended towards support for democratic transformation.

Within the Party of Independence, Gyula Justh and his left-wing supporters gave voice to their disappointment in the leadership. Backed by that segment of the lower middle class which supported the ideals of 1848, as well as by peasants and intellectuals, Justh broke with the leadership of Ferenc Kossuth and Count Albert Apponyi in 1909 and founded a new party. This demanded universal suffrage and gradually recognized that both alliance with the radicals and land reform were inevitable. These developments constituted a great step forward. Justh's party, wrote Oszkár Jászi, had always been the party of the peasants, artisans and poor intellectuals, but it was thanks to Justh's efforts that it returned to Lajos Kossuth's original 1848 programme.

From the very beginning the Coalition government stood on shaky and precarious ground. In 1909 its internal unity disintegrated and, after a not very successful period in office, it fell in 1910. It was replaced in that year by the old Liberal group led by Count Károly Khuen-Héderváry and László Lukács, both István Tisza supporters, and now re-organized as the *Nemzeti Munkapárt* (National Party of Work). After his defeat in 1905, Tisza had retired from public life to reconsider the political and social situation in the country. When antagonism towards him began to wane, he returned to the political scene with a new approach. Tisza now realized that the true enemy of the existing socio-political order was not the parliamentary Opposition, but the growing democratic and socialist popular movements. Accordingly, the most important task of the ruling class was to keep its power and property intact. This was Tisza's primary objective, not the proper working of the parliamentary system.

In the 1910s Tisza made great efforts to rally the propertied classes and the forces of conservatism. He did not rule out negotiations with Croat and Romanian national minority leaders and had no qualms about using force to break parliamentary obstruction. In May 1912 Tisza was elected president of the Lower House, a development highly unpopular with every shade of opposition thinking. On May 23 a huge mass demonstration swept the Hungarian capital, and demonstrators built barricades against the mounted police and gendarmes sent to deal with them. Trams were overturned and finally the army had to be called in to restore order. The government ruthlessly suppressed this wave of unrest, which swept not only Budapest but also the countryside. Tisza used coercion to silence parliamentary opponents and forced through a long-disputed army bill, together with draft legislation preparing for war.

By this time, though, conflict involving the Habsburg empire was not far off. In 1912 the members of the Balkan League (Greece, Bulgaria, Serbia, and Montenegro) waged war on the Ottoman empire to shake off the Turkish yoke once and for all. The Balkan League enjoyed rapid and remarkable success; the Turkish army was defeated and Turkey driven out of Europe almost entirely. Austria-Hungary looked on helplessly as hostilities engulfed the region to the south of her, and was unable to intervene. But the First Balkan War did not bring peace to the region. In a squabble over the spoils, the other states turned on Bulgaria and the fighting started again. Bulgaria was considered to be friendly to Austria-Hungary but received no assistance from it. The Second Balkan War ended in crushing defeat for the Bulgarians and was a heavy blow to Austria-Hungary's prestige.

The Treaty of Bucharest (August 1913), which ended the Second Balkan War, stripped Bulgaria of the fruits of her previous victories and substantially added to the size and standing of Serbia. Moreover, it also strengthened Romania, which had also joined in the hostilities, and accentuated the Monarchy's serious loss of face. Powerful and self-conscious states had emerged on the southern and eastern frontiers of Austria-Hungary which, with Turkey already defeated, could soon turn against the empire itself. The small Balkan states could also expect backing from France and Russia, both major powers. By contrast, the Triple Alliance, to which Austria-Hungary belonged, began to lose cohesion. Italy drifted away somewhat and Germany was not prepared to give full-hearted support to Austro-Hungarian expansionism in the Balkans.

Thus, the situation of Austria-Hungary became potentially very grave. The Balkans could explode at any time and nationalism among the peoples there threatened the very existence of the multinational empire. The Serbians, Romanians, and Italians all wished to recover areas of the Monarchy in order to achieve full national unity. At home the struggle was still for suffrage and parliamentary control when the shadow of world war fell across Hungary and the whole of Europe.

The outbreak of war

The inevitable was finally brought to pass by revolver shots. On June 28, 1914, Gavrilo Princip, a Serbian student, assassinated Archduke Franz Ferdinand—the next in line to the Habsburg throne—in Sarajevo, and also his wife. The events following Franz Ferdinand's visit to the Bosnian capital, from the ceremonial procession there to the assassination, from the commencement of sabre-rattling to the outbreak of war itself, are known to almost everyone. Yet many still continue to regard these as chance happenings. The truth is, however, that fate was neither blind nor anonymous in Sarajevo. It sprang from imperialism, the bonds of which the Great Powers had been loosening for years.

At first, news of the assassination caused sensation rather than anger. In his summer residence at Ischl the emperor-king, Francis Joseph, received the news with resignation and as the will of a just God. So did the Hungarian prime minister, Count István Tisza, on his Geszt estate. However, the war party, and especially the aggressive Chief of General Staff Conrad von Hötzendorf, wanted to exploit the sympathy generated by the assassinations to settle scores with Serbia. As soon as Vienna received the go-ahead from Berlin, preparations for war began.

Although the events themselves are well known, the same cannot be said of the causes, their relatedness, and the secret motives behind the overt actions. One can legitimately ask why, once the military and diplomatic leaders of Austria-Hungary had decided on war and obtained Germany's support, the attack did not begin right away. The answer lies in the opposition they encountered from István Tisza, the same politician who afterwards so zealously committed himself and his country to the struggle. Initially, Tisza regarded the international balance of power as extremely unfavourable from the point of view of Austria-Hungary, believing that Bulgaria, the Monarchy's only reliable ally to the south, had been utterly exhausted as a result of the Balkan Wars. He also took the view that Germany had shown definite signs of sympathy towards Romania which, the Hungarian leadership feared, would eventually break into Transylvania. Tisza resisted for almost a fortnight. In spite of this, though, Austrian and German politicians, together with the military leaders, finally convinced him that the time was now ripe for the Central Powers to go to war. Any delay would serve the interests of the Entente—made up of the "enemies", France, Britain, and Russia. Furthermore, they also convinced him that Romania would remain neutral in any conflict.

But what was the Austrian case against Serbia? On what grounds did Vienna send its ultimatum? Austria claimed that Serbia was responsible for agitation against the empire and, in addition, for a whole host of terrorist acts within its borders. Were these accusations true? Could the Serbian government have known about the plans for the assassination of the archduke?

Pasic, the Serbian prime minister, denied throughout that it did. In 1924, however, one of his fellow ministers admitted—and his admission seems to be substantiated by a number of documents—that the Serbian government had in fact known of the assassination plan, had disapproved of it, but had been unable to prevent its implementation. Moreover, owing to a tense domestic situation, it had not dared to notify Vienna.

It does indeed appear as though the Serbian government was to some extent responsible for having failed to give a warning. However, in July 1914 the Viennese government was entirely unaware of this. In fact, a special commissioner of inquiry dispatched to Sarajevo reported that there was no evidence to substantiate allegations of the Serbian government's complicity. In short, the leading politicians of Austria-Hungary, among them Tisza, drafted and dispatched the unacceptable ultimatum of July 23 in the belief that the Serbian government was innocent.

But it was not on grounds of innocence that the Pasic cabinet rejected the important demands of the ultimatum just two days later. The real reason was that Russia and France encouraged and prompted it to do so. When President Poincaré visited St Petersburg on July 20, 1914, both France and Russia—counting on the support of their British friends—believed that the balance of power at the time would favour the Entente should a war with Germany and its allies break out. As a result, the assassination in Sarajevo soon assumed an importance extending well beyond narrow dynastic interests. The relationship between tiny Serbia and a decaying Austro-Hungarian empire became a crucial issue between power blocs of world importance. The assassination of Franz Ferdinand was only the spark which set off a powder-keg long in existence.

Neither the volatility of the international situation nor the mutual antagonism of the Great Powers can, however, overshadow the responsibility of individuals for events. The war was, after all, planned and started by human beings. What is certain is that this responsibility rests chiefly with the Monarchy's war party, including Francis Joseph who, as he put it in his general order to the army, had "weighed everything and thought over everything" but who in reality had yielded to pressure from his own soldiers and from the German General Staff. In this sense, part of the blame must rest with István Tisza, who, despite having realistically assessed the balance of power and the likely consequences of aggression, did not vote against the declaration of war and did not resign when it was approved. The German military and political leaders (including Emperor William II) who pledged their support during this critical time must also take some responsibility.

Naturally, seventy years afterwards it is not really the assessment of blame which should be the task of historians. More important by far is the clear presentation of the causes and consequences of the conflict and the thorough understanding of a system in which expansionism and war were inherent.

The Austro-Hungarian empire declared war on Serbia on July 28, 1914 and that same night the Monarchy's Danube flotilla began to bombard Belgrade. On July 30, Russia and Austria-Hungary simultaneously began mobilization against each other. On August 1, Germany ordered mobilization and declared war first on Russia and then, two days later, on France. On August 5, Austria-Hungary declared war on Russia and on the same day Britain declared war on Germany. A week later a state of war was declared between the Anglo-French alliance and the Austro-Hungarian empire.

By this time the report of Princip's revolver was entirely drowned in the clamour of marching armies, the sound of guns, and the explosion of empires.

Problems at the front—and at home

News of the declaration of war was received in Hungary with a sudden outburst of patriotic enthusiasm. Everywhere colourful and noisy ceremonies were staged to see the soldiers off to the war—which everyone believed would be short. However, the rapturous enthusiasm of the early days was soon eroded by the humiliating and catastrophic defeats of the first few months. The inadequately-prepared and poorly-commanded armies of the empire suffered defeat in every theatre of war. The Monarchy's offensive ground to a halt in Serbia and on the Eastern Front advance gave way to retreat as the Russian army pressed forward across the Carpathian Mountains. It was only with German military assistance that Austria-Hungary was able to halt Russia's winter offensive of 1914–15, to break through on the Russian front in May 1915, and to advance into Serbia. However, Italy's entry into the war in 1915 on the side of the Entente reduced the value of these military successes. This was because Austria-Hungary now had to divert resources to yet another front, as the Italians attempted to advance into the mountainous southwestern areas of the Monarchy.

In 1915, the Central Powers (Germany, Austria-Hungary, Turkey, and, in October, Bulgaria) scored considerable successes on the Eastern Front and in the Balkans. However, they were unable to turn these to good account.

The following year another enormous Russian offensive pushed the front line back inside Austro-Hungarian territory, and this advance prompted Romania to enter the war against the Central Powers. In August 1916 Romanian troops invaded Transylvania—only to be repelled by an Austro-Hungarian army assisted by German troops. This force afterwards occupied most of Romania.

In 1917 the growing plight of the Central Powers was alleviated by the Russian revolutions and by Russia's subsequent withdrawal from the war. This advantage was, however, soon offset by the entry into the conflict of the United States on the side of the Entente. Thereafter, despite Germany's tactical victories on the Western Front and Austria-Hungary's in the war against Italy, the enemy's superiority, both *matériel* and military, gradually became overwhelming. By the end of 1917 the empire, which had sustained serious losses and had suffered a heavy death toll since the very beginning of war, became utterly exhausted. Disaffection, desertions, and mutiny also began to affect the army.

The civilian population behind the lines also experienced hardship. The most important factories were turned over to war production and placed under military supervision, with attendant military discipline. In the first year of the war there was already a shortage of basic commodities and the black market flourished. In 1916 the production of cereals used for bread fell back to two-thirds of its prewar level and in 1918 it was down to half. The government soon introduced the compulsory handing in of produce, livestock, and horses—and resorted to requisitioning. While this hit the peasantry very hard, it did not, even with rationing, solve the problem of keeping the urban population supplied.

The living conditions of the workers had seriously deteriorated by 1915–16. Throughout the country people had to go without food and fuel. Moreover, heads of families, the normal breadwinners, were usually absent on military service. Everywhere the dead were mourned and the captured and crippled lamented. Those with fixed incomes suffered most. The volume of paper money in circulation increased fifteenfold during the hostilities, and sharply accelerating inflation was aggravated by the raising, on eight separate occasions, of war loans. War-widows, orphans, and disabled servicemen received just enough aid to keep them from starving. According to contemporary estimates, the real earnings of skilled workers dropped to half of their pre-war levels while those of white-collar workers and day-labourers fell to 40 per cent of their 1913 value.

The growing discontent of the masses gave considerable encouragement to the anti-war activities of the Social Democrats and radical leftists. In turn, these men and women imparted a growing consciousness to the anti-militarist sentiments of the workers, and Mihály Károlyi's anti-war move in Parliament at the end of 1916 was received with sympathy by them. Despite military discipline, strikes erupted in many places, and in 1917, for the first time during the war, May Day was celebrated. The yearning for peace which was filling every stratum of the population at home spread irresistibly under the influence of the Russian revolutions of February and October 1917—and as a result of increasingly confident socialist agitation. This longing even began to reach rank-and-file soldiers at the front, and encouraged belligerent governments to put forward peace initiatives.

On November 21, 1916 Francis Joseph died. In keeping with his life, his funeral was cold and almost bureaucratic. The monarch's death marked the approaching end of an empire and of an entire epoch. His successor Emperor Charles (King Charles IV of Hungary) reigned for just two years and was a weak and gullible character. Although Charles realized that only extensive reforms and the immediate conclusion of a peace treaty could save his empire in its desperate situation, mere good will was inadequate at such a decisive stage. Reforms remained at the level of promises, and Charles's feeble and half-hearted peace attempts were doomed to failure. His greatest act in the eyes of the masses was his dismissal of the intensely hated Tisza, who had stubbornly rejected any change in direction. Although they were more flexible, Tisza's successors continued his war policy and, in the final analysis, no changes of any substance were introduced in Austria-Hungary right up to the final collapse.

The fighting dragged on—despite powerful mass protests. During the winter of 1917–18 soldiers at the front and their families back home were going hungry. As before, strikes, mutinies, and protest movements were suppressed. The continuation of the war was the chief means of procuring domestic calm—aided by the gendarmerie and police. In 1918, however, these traditional methods became increasingly ineffective. Letters confiscated by military censors bear witness to widespread destitution, bitterness, and a powerful desire for peace. "This is no life", wrote a peasant woman from Mezőgyán to her prisoner-of-war husband in autumn 1917, "we the poor cry ourselves to sleep, wake up crying, eat crying, thinking over our lives and why the ground does not open beneath our feet to swallow us up." As for the rich, "Would the Good Lord send a war on those of them who have not had enough of this bloodshed, and make them homeless, too."

The situation became even more unstable during the long, hot summer of 1918.

HUNGARY SINCE 1918

The Revolutions of 1918 and 1919

Military collapse and the revolution of 1918

Each event of the last year of the war brought nearer the inevitable demise of the Austro-Hungarian empire. The military situation, internal decay, and the policy of the Entente all served to precipitate this.

On January 8, 1918 President Woodrow Wilson of the United States delivered an address to Congress in which he outlined his famous "Fourteen Points". Referring to "the peoples of Austria-Hungary", he stated that they "should be accorded the freest opportunity for autonomous development". Vienna and Budapest would have liked to secure the empire's survival and a favourable peace on the basis of the Wilson plan. For their part, the politicians representing the non-Magyar peoples used the "Fourteen Points" as a pretext for secession and territorial expansion for the new states which were to emerge later on. These states were already guaranteed by secret treaties and promises made during the war which involved the meeting of Italian, Czechoslovak, Romanian, and South Slav demands.

In Soviet Russia, Lenin's Bolshevik government concluded a separate peace treaty with the Germans at Brest-Litovsk (March 3). As a result of this, Germany was able to redeploy substantial forces to the Western Front. Tens of thousands of captured Hungarian soldiers fought in the Russian Civil War on the side of the Bolsheviks and also helped oppose the interventionist armies. In March, Béla Kun formed the Hungarian section of the Russian Communist (Bolshevik) Party.

At home not a day passed without strikes and demonstrations calling for an end to the war, universal suffrage with secret ballot, and democratization. In line with an initiative in Vienna, a three-day general strike was organized in January. In February, sailors of the Imperial and Royal Navy staged a mutiny in the Adriatic port of Kotor (Cattaro). This was suppressed on orders from Rear-Admiral Miklós Horthy.

On May 20, 1918 a major mutiny of troops broke out in Hungary which the authorities were only able to put down after a day of heavy fighting. Desertion rates grew higher and higher. The minister of interior dissolved the Galilei Circle, an organization of intellectuals and young leftists, and put its leaders—among them Ilona Duczynska—on trial. The government of Sándor Wekerle attempted to resign, first in January and subsequently on several occasions in the course of the year. However, Charles IV and his advisers refused to concede political leadership to the Opposition, then rallying around Count Mihály Károlyi.

163

On April 8 the empire's national minority leaders declared in a joint resolution in Rome that those they claimed to represent no longer wished to remain within an Austro-Hungarian empire. This contributed to the final decision of the Entente Powers to accept the French idea of a *cordon sanitaire*. What this meant in practice was that crumbling Austria-Hungary would be replaced by independent liberal states, the purpose of which was to isolate revolutionary Russia by creating a "protective band" along its western border, as well as to close off the path of possible future German expansionism. In February 1916 émigré Czech and Slovak politicians had formed the Czechoslovak National Council, and from September 1918 onwards the other national minorities formed similar bodies of their own.

Meanwhile the Hungarian units of the Imperial and Royal Army suffered devastating defeat on the Italian front, with the names Piave, Isonzo, and Doberdo leaving indelible marks on the memories of that generation. On June 20 workers of the MÁV Engineering Works in Budapest demonstrated against the futile destruction and bloodshed of the war, and against the methods employed by the factory's military commanders. The law-enforcement detachments ordered to the scene opened fire on them, and in response a wave of strikes once again engulfed the country. In many places, workers' councils, organizations hitherto unknown in the Hungarian working-class movement, were formed.

Early in August 1918 the Entente armies broke through and pressed victoriously ahead on the Western and Balkan fronts. In September Bulgaria capitulated, followed in mid-October by Turkey. Under its commander, Franchet d'Esperey, the French Eastern Army pressed forward in the direction of Hungary.

Vienna now made a last desperate effort to retrieve the situation. On October 16 Charles IV proclaimed Austria to be a federal state. On October 17, István Tisza, having survived an assassination attempt the previous day, made a statement to the Hungarian Parliament, declaring simply: "We have lost the war." Coming from him, this was a bombshell.

On October 25—much later than the national minorities—Mihály Károlyi formed the Hungarian National Council in Budapest. Oszkár Jászi then drafted its twelve-point programme for the establishment of Hungary's own independence, an immediate and separate peace treaty, universal suffrage with secret ballot, land reform, and recognition of the rights of the national minorities. It was taken for granted that the king would appoint Károlyi to replace Prime Minister Wekerle, who had again tendered his resignation, especially as by now quite a few politicians and organizations—among them the Budapest police force—had gone over to the National Council. However, Count János Hadik became the new premier. In protest, on October 28 the people marched from the Inner City to Buda Castle to demand Károlyi's appointment. A battle broke out between demonstators and law-enforcement detachments on the Chain Bridge.

On the very same day the Czechoslovak Republic was proclaimed in Prague. On October 29 Croatia joined newly-emerging Yugoslavia and the day after that the Provisional National Assembly in Vienna proclaimed Austria to be an independent state. Although the Austro-Hungarian army was still fighting against the Italians, the empire itself had almost completely collapsed.

During the night of October 30–31, 1918 Budapest's streets were crowded with soldiers and civilians who initially cheered the National Council based in the Astoria Hotel. Later, however, the people occupied public buildings, prevented the movement to the countryside of troops loyal to Károlyi, and captured Budapest's military governor. As in March 1848, they freed political prisoners. Asters and rosettes replaced the torn-off insignia on soldiers' uniforms, and also appeared in the buttonholes of civilians' jackets. Although asters are generally considered to represent death, in autumn 1918 they greeted a new spring.

"We did not want to take over power yet, we wanted to organize our forces," wrote Károlyi in his 1923 memoirs, "but in the meantime the entire revolution developed." At this point Charles himself was forced to retreat: on October 31 he asked Károlyi to form a new government.

During the afternoon of the same day a few armed soldiers and workers forced their way into Count István Tisza's town house in Hermina utca where, after a brief verbal exchange, they assassinated the former prime minister. In the minds of the people Tisza had come to represent the entire dualist system and its pro-war policy. Popular wrath had long been fermenting against him, and in his death contemporaries saw the administration of justice by History.

Revolution triumphed and, for the first time since 1848, an independent Hungarian government was formed. It seemed that the collapse of the dualist system was paving the way to the democratization of Hungary and the more harmonious coexistence of the various peoples of the Danubian Basin. However, the legacy of the past obstructed this path and no one at the time estimated correctly the enormous effort that would be required to clear it.

Towards a liberal democracy

The appointment of Mihály Károlyi as prime minister in autumn 1918 was received with unprecedented enthusiasm and general approbation. Never before had a Hungarian statesman been obliged to lead the nation under such tragically difficult conditions. Everyone expected Károlyi to secure for Hungary favourable treatment and fair peace terms. This general hope stemmed from the fact that in Hungary Károlyi had always been regarded as having not just sympathy for the Entente but also contacts with it.

The Great Powers, however, treated Hungary as a vanquished nation, and considered the new government to be no more than the legal successor to the old. They appreciated neither its liberal democratic nature, nor its pro-Entente orientation. It was under Károlyi that the country's territorial disintegration took place, and under conditions which caused profound disturbance to the whole of Hungarian society. The acceptance of this therefore became even more difficult.

On November 3, 1918, a week before the Germans, the Austro-Hungarian army and the Italians facing them signed an armistice in Padua. However, Franchet d'Esperey, the overall commander of the Entente forces in the Balkans, did not recognize the validity of this agreement for his own section of the front. Accordingly, the Károlyi government signed, on November 13, a military convention with Franchet in Belgrade. This was the first occasion the victors acknowledged the existence of an independent Hungary and its new government. Unlike the armistice agreement of November 3, the military convention established a demarcation line between Hungary and her enemies within the borders of the historic state.

This was not the only development which undermined confidence in the government. Adding insult to injury, Romania and the new Czechoslovak and Yugoslav states ignored this agreement entirely. Even before the signature of the Belgrade convention, first Czechoslovak and later Romanian forces crossed the line—with full authorization from Paris. In spite of vigorous protests from the Károlyi government accompanied by limited resistance, they halted only in mid-January 1919. The limits of their advance corresponded roughly to what eventually became the new Hungarian frontier in these areas. In the meantime, however, Romanian and Yugoslav units clashed over possession of the Banat. French troops were forced to intervene and occupied Szeged in the process.

At home, consolidation was rather slow, and the failure of the negotiations with the Entente was an important reason for this. The Károlyi government now regarded the revolution as complete and subsequently wished only to introduce constitutional reforms. For their part, however, the industrial workers, the smallholders, the poor peasants and the many prisoners of war who had returned from Soviet Russia regarded it as only a beginning. For them it was merely the prelude to another revolution—a revolution along Soviet lines. Although law and order were successfully maintained in Budapest, in the countryside public buildings were attacked, some of the officials and gendarmes driven out and even lynched, and shops looted. Very often armed clashes occurred. Only the introduction of martial law could stem the tide of revolt.

This spontaneous discontent soon acquired both purpose and direction. On November 24, 1918, the *Kommunisták Magyarországi Pártja* (Hungarian Party of Communists) was formed under the leadership of Béla Kun. The Communist Party had a political programme and an organizational framework; its popularity grew rapidly among the workers, demobilized soldiers, and the unemployed. The Communists aimed at the transformation of the bourgeois democracy into a dictatorship of the proletariat.

Within the Social Democratic Party, the principal party supporting the coalition government, a pro-Communist left-wing group was becoming increasingly influential. Inside Károlyi's own Party of Independence and even within the government itself opinions differed as not just over policy, but also over the way it should be implemented. A group of Károlyi's supporters left the Party of Independence because they thought the government too weak in the face of the revolutionary left wing. At the same time right-wing groups supported by members of the former ruling circle, the middle class, and especially army officers wanted to do away with bourgeois democracy and bring back the former conservative system. Under the leadership of Count István Bethlen, a Transylvanian aristocrat, and Gyula Gömbös, a career army officer, they began to organize against the Károlyi regime.

It was therefore under very difficult conditions that the government implemented its programme. On November 16, amid great ceremony, Hungary's independence was proclaimed and a republican state form adopted. On January 11, 1919 Mihály

166

Károlyi became Hungary's first president. Legislation was enacted to introduce universal suffrage with the secret ballot, and to guarantee freedom of the press, assembly, and association. The democratization of the public administration was begun, and, at the suggestion of Jenő Varga, in March 1919 it was decided to set up a separate ministry to commence nationalization. Oszkár Jászi, Oszkár Asbóth, Gyula Szekfű, Marcell Benedek, and others were all appointed university and college professors. The *Nyugat* circle of writers and intellectuals established the Vörösmarty Academy with Endre Ady as its first president. Following Ady's death on January 27, 1919, Zsigmond Móricz took over the post. Members of the National Council's committee of artists included József Rippl-Rónai, Ödön Márffy, Károly Lyka, Mihály Babits, György Lukács, Gyula Krúdy, Lajos Kassák, Ferenc Molnár, Béla Bartók, Zoltán Kodály, Ernő Dohnányi, and Jenő Hubay—among others.

However, neither higher wages nor unemployment benefit enabled ordinary people to make ends meet. In addition to shortages of food and other basic commodities, there was also a shortage of fuel. Industry was paralysed and unable to offer much work. Families fleeing inland from areas under foreign occupation needed groceries and accommodation, and providing these was a serious burden. To make matters worse still, the influenza epidemic of the time was also taking its toll.

On February 16 the government's land reform law was passed. This was a piece of legislation justly described by Zsigmond Móricz as historically significant. However, the distribution of land it was supported to bring about commenced only on one of Károlyi's estates. The reaction of the land-hungry peasants was to take possession of the large estates unilaterally. On the whole these peasants regarded collective possession of the land as the first step to its distribution among individuals, despite the fact that the Social Democrats and the Communists had both advocated collective farming.

The government was unable to prevent these developments, just as it was unable to prevent the expulsion from office of the newly-appointed government commissioners. The administration of a number of towns (for example, Székesfehérvár and Szekszárd) and a number of counties (for example, Hajdú-Békés and Barcs) passed into the hands of so-called directories.

The Károlyi government failed to reach agreement with the country's non-Magyar peoples. Oszkár Jászi had earlier developed the concept of a "Danubian United States" or an "Eastern Switzerland". This offered a federation of democratic states and, within it, self-government for the national minorities. The Hungarian nationalists rejected the idea, as did the leaders of the neighbouring countries. Since the leaders were hostile and since Budapest had lost its authority over the minorities, negotiations for the implementation of this scheme proved impossible.

At the beginning of 1919 the Károlyi government struck at its left-wing and right-wing critics. Attempts were made to curtail the right-wing opposition and to liquidate the Communist movement. On February 21, 1919, Béla Kun himself and fifty-four Communist leaders were imprisoned on the pretext of a street demonstration and a shooting incident. Shortly afterwards, demonstrations were staged demanding their release. Károlyi, however, ensured for them such generous conditions (for example, a separate building and unrestricted visiting) that Béla Kun and his colleagues were able to control their movement from jail. They planned to topple the government on March 23, although in the event this was done by the Paris Peace Conference.

To assist French and British military intervention against Soviet Russia, the Peace Conference decided to create a neutral zone along the Hungarian-Romanian border. A note to this effect was handed to Károlyi on March 20, 1919 by Lieutenant-Colonel Vix of France, the Allies' representative in Budapest. Under the terms of the Vix Note, as it became known, the Hungarian government was to pull its troops back some fifty kilometres from their forward positions in the east. As it did not wish to comply with this demand and since it was in no position to offer armed resistance, the Károlyi government resigned.

The Social Democratic and Communist leaders, having negotiated for some days, now quickly added the finishing touches to an agreement. The two parties were to merge and assume power. Károlyi would have been ready to join the new government but his services were not requested.

The Republic of Councils

On March 21, 1919 the Revolutionary Governing Council took office and Hungary was proclaimed a Republic of Councils. Béla Kun became the people's commissar (minister) for foreign affairs and was in effect the leader of the new government. Hungary now entered into an alliance with Soviet Russia and at the same time called on the workers of the neighbouring countries, urging them to join the common struggle against the imperialist powers and the bourgeoisie.

The young Communist movement, under Lenin's direction, had counted on a wave of revolution in Central Europe which would then have spread to the victorious Western countries. "We have based the revolution on the international revolution," said Béla Kun on March 27, 1919. For a short time it appeared that his expectations were justified; on April 13 council power was—temporarily—established in Bavaria as well.

The dictatorship of the proletariat in Hungary was accepted without resistance, even by those who did not agree with its domestic programme. The reason for this was its rejection of the humiliating Vix Note.

At both central and local level, public administration came under the control of workers' councils. Industrial, mining, and transportation companies employing more than twenty people were taken into public ownership. Also nationalized were the banks, other financial institutions, and even retail and wholesale businesses. The Red Guard was responsible for maintaining law and order at home and plans were drafted for a Red Army. Schools were nationalized in order to complete the process of separating Church and state. Wide-ranging schemes were launched in the field of public education. Hungarian intellectuals of European renown participated in the cultural work of the Republic of Councils: György Alexics; Lajos Fülep; Károly Mannheim; Irén Dienesné Götz, who had studied under Madame Curie; Béla Balázs; Lajos Kassák; Tibor Déry; Milán Füst; Géza Gárdonyi; Frigyes Karinthy; Dezső Kosztolányi; Anna Lesznai; Alexander Korda; Béni Ferenczy, and many others all contributed. Initially, Zsigmond Kunfi was responsible for cultural and scientific affairs but later György Lukács took over this role.

On April 4, 1919 every medium-sized and large estate passed into "the possession of the proletarian state". No compensation was paid. The distribution of the land was, however, prohibited: as the government saw it, this was the only way of guaranteeing the production of sufficient food and of preventing the "expansion" of the rural petite bourgeoisie. The nationalized estates were organized for the most part along the lines of the state farms of the 1980s. Eventually, where this was unavoidable, small building plots were allocated for houses. This, however, did not alleviate the profound disappointment and discontent of those in agriculture. Once again the landless were not given land and the landed peasants feared that their property would soon also be taken. One serious consequence of this was that later on the peasants refused to sell their produce for so-called "white money", the banknotes issued by the Republic of Councils. The counter-revolution was afterwards able to exploit this to its advantage.

The delegates at the Paris Peace Conference were shocked by the developments in Hungary, and heated arguments took place between the politicians and the military on the reasons for them. The Anglo-American position was that much of the blame lay with France's attempts to extend the influence of its client states. Finally, General Smuts was despatched to Budapest to assess the situation on the spot, and to persuade the Hungarian government to accept a slightly modified neutral zone. In the meantime, however, the French military leadership, with the active co-operation of Prague and Bucharest, was already organizing a military offensive against Hungary.

Although Smuts lent a sympathetic ear to Béla Kun's proposal for the calling together of an international conference on the economic future of the Danube Basin, he was not authorized to sign an agreement. For their part, Kun and his colleagues, hoping that their intransigence would bring about further negotiations, rejected the new suggestion for a neutral zone.

It is unlikely that any negotiation could have led to more favourable frontiers for Hungary and could have ensured the survival of the Republic of Councils. The existence of a proletarian dictatorship was entirely contrary to the wishes of the victors, which included the fullest possible satisfaction of the territorial claims put forward by Hungary's neighbours as well as the isolation of Soviet Russia. To put the matter briefly, in the long run the Allies could not permit the Republic of Councils to survive. Subsequent events confirmed that the victors were only manoeuvring for position. The possibility of actually deciding events did not rest with the Hungarian government.

On April 16 the Romanians launched their offensive and this was followed on the 27th by a Czechoslovak incursion. Now only partially organized, the Hungarian Red Army was driven back. On May 1 the Romanian troops halted at Szolnok and the Czechoslovak forces at Miskolc but in spite of this the situation appeared catastrophic.

In the meantime Budapest and other areas not under occupation celebrated May Day. The government and the Central Workers' Council remained constantly in session, and Béla Kun attempted various diplomatic initiatives. Finally the crisis was resolved. The government remained in office and started to organize the country's defences. Under the command of such outstanding leaders as Vilmos Böhm, Aurél Stromfeld, Jenő Landler, and others, the Hungarian Red Army launched its counter-offensive as early as May 20. The Red Army hoped that a breakthrough on the northern front would enable it to link up with the Soviet troops.

Success attended the Red Army's endeavours. On June 6 Hungarian troops entered Kassa (now Košice, Czechoslovakia) and ten days later the Slovak Council Republic was proclaimed at Eperjes (now Prešov).

The prosecution of the war placed a great burden on the organized workers serving in the Red Army. It also put a great strain on the country as a whole. The various counter-revolutionary groups could easily exploit the growing economic and political difficulties which resulted. These groups provoked strikes and insurrections in almost every part of the country and on June 24 they even felt bold enough to make a bid for power in Budapest. However, central and local forces defeated every counter-revolutionary move. The result was that the government faced no serious challenge in July.

Meanwhile the representatives of conservative, upper-class Hungary rallied around Count István Bethlen in Vienna. In Szeged, now under French occupation, Major Gyula Gömbös organized the so-called National Army with Admiral Miklós Horthy as its supreme commander. The National Army contained officers commissioned in the days of the empire and exhibiting a reactionary disposition. Showing both chauvinism and anti-Semitic feeling, these men represented the extreme right wing of the counter-revolutionary elements.

It was extremely embarrassing for France that the attack mounted by its small allies had failed to overthrow the Republic of Councils. Shelving military measures for the time being, French prime minister Clemenceau now launched a diplomatic offensive. His most successful effort was a note which reached Budapest from the Peace Conference on June 13. The new frontiers in Central Europe had now been decided and the note gave details of them, also calling on the parties concerned to withdraw their forces accordingly. After an extremely heated debate, the Revolutionary Governing Council decided to comply with the order, and the Red Army immediately pulled back from its advance positions in the north. However, the neighbouring countries ignored the note completely, refusing to withdraw in turn. By conforming with the Paris instruction, Hungary made a tactical error and early in July the Peace Conference began preparations for decisive military intervention. These progressed only slowly, though, and the Hungarian government could have used the note as a basis for negotiation, enabling it to play for time. The withdrawal of the army led to general demoralization and put the Governing Council in a hopeless situation. During the course of July the trade-unions, the workers generally, and other sections of the population were coming round to the view that Hungary should settle its differences with the Entente.

Since their advance of earlier in the year, Romanian troops had occupied the region east of the Tisza river. The Peace Conference acknowledged this area as Hungarian in its note of June 13 but no Romanian evacuation took place. After several unsuccessful protests, the Governing Council ordered the launching of its Tisza offensive to expel the Romanians. This was a decision which undoubtedly hastened the fall of the Republic of Councils. Taking full advantage of its relative strength, the Romanian army drove the advancing Hungarian troops back. This time the Romanians did not stop at the line of the Tisza but pressed on towards Budapest.

On August 1, 1919 the resignation of the Revolutionary Governing Council was announced at the final, dramatic session of the Budapest Central Workers' Council. The trade-union leader Gyula Peidl was nominated to form a new government. Between August 3 and August 4 the Romanian army entered Budapest: the dictatorship of the proletariat in Hungary was over.

Hopes for a rapid spread of the revolution had remained unfulfilled. It had been demonstrated that in the small country that Hungary had become, an isolated dictatorship of the proletariat could not survive a concerted foreign onslaught.

The attempts of 1918 and 1919 to resolve the social and political problems of Hungary within a bourgeois democratic and then a socialist framework failed. However, memories of the two revolutions lived on in Hungary throughout the interwar years, so did recollections of the territories lost at the end of the war.

Hopes, realities, consequences

From this distance in time it is not easy to assess the attitudes of Hungarian writers, artists, and intellectuals towards the Republic of Councils, following as it did the failure of the Károlyi government and widespread disillusionment with the policy of the Allies. For the most part, their view reflected the idealistic expectation and almost messianic sense of mission typical of the age, not a realistic assessment of what the possibilities actually were. Also rather lacking was a conscious acceptance of what proletarian dictatorship would really mean. In March 1919, however, few thought of the difficulties and conflicts likely to occur.

On April 16, 1919 Gyula Krúdy wrote: "There is no need to fear the future, a new Hungary, a flowering of human aspirations and ideals thrown up by revolutionary fervour. Let the old world be destroyed, crumble, and disappear." Zsigmond Móricz shared Krúdy's enthusiasm: "Communism, which naive dreamers feared because they saw in it the prison or the phalanstery, will bring about a splendid era of the genuine flourishing of the individual . . . Now begins true, happy, really human, life."

Freedom of creative work and participation in public life were not merely the privileges of Lajos Kassák and his circle, and of socialist writers, activists and artists. Zsigmond Kunfi's and György Lukács's policy in the area of culture and science was liberal even by the standards of the mid-1980s.

The experience of the years 1918–19 left its mark not only on the works and careers of mature, established intellectuals, but also on the minds of Gyula Illyés and László Németh—grammar-school pupils at the time and future writers. Also influenced was Péter Veres, a member of the Workers' Council and another writer. Even those who did not necessarily identify with either of the two revolutions were affected by the events.

The valiant efforts of the country as a whole to put up some form of resistance to the hostile world surrounding it impressed a wide circle. Oszkár Jászi, a consistent

171

supporter or bourgeois democracy who never regarded Communism as a possible solution, did not criticize the Republic of Councils openly—although he expected it to result in military intervention, counter-revolution, and the loss of the bourgeois democratic achievements. (Indeed, it was fear of counter-revolutionary terror which caused Jászi to leave Hungary on May 1, 1919.) Mihály Károlyi remained in the country until the July crisis, and even attempted to assist the government. From exile, Károlyi was more than willing to co-operate with Béla Kun and the Communists. Staff officer Aurél Stromfeld not only served bourgeois democracy but also masterminded the great military successes of the Red Army. Rudolf Andorka, Géza Lakatos, Ferenc Szombathelyi, Döme Sztójay, and Henrik Werth, all prominent under Horthy, did not refuse to serve either.

Of the Social Democratic leaders, only Ernő Garami emigrated. Jenő Hamburger, Jenő Landler, and the other prominent left-wingers declared for the Communists before March 21. Péter Ágoston, Vilmos Böhm, and Zsigmond Kunfi also accepted the dictatorship of the proletariat.

The Republic of Councils' sense of mission also extended to the idea that Hungary should play a mediating role between East and West, and that it should attempt to spread the revolution. "Today, we Hungarian proletarians are the vanguard of the liberation struggle originating from Russia," wrote the *Tata-Tóváros Kurir* on March 30, 1919.

Were conditions, then, ideal? By no means. The confident expectations of spring 1919 were not fulfilled, in the same way that the high hopes of autumn 1918 turned to disillusionment. The revolution did not spread further and was unable to establish direct contact with Soviet Russia. The country had to contend with foreign invasion in April, and living conditions deteriorated rather than improved. It turned out that the dictatorship of the proletariat was exactly what its name implied and that it did not shrink from the use of terror when it considered this necessary. Károlyi and his colleagues would also have liked to preserve the bloodless character of their revolution but in November, they resorted to force in an effort to maintain law and order. From the very beginning the Republic of Councils was determined to use coercion, and when deemed appropriate, this also included the taking of hostages. It did not hesitate to send Tibor Szamuely, Ottó Korvin, and the feared security detachment (the "Lenin Boys") to suppress strikes and uprisings.

The Communists believed that the Soviet system could be established much more quickly in Hungary than in Russia. The fact that Hungary was economically and socially more developed than Russia meant, so they thought, that presumed steps such as the distribution of the land to the peasants could be missed out. They also thought that nationality problems in Hungary and in the Danube Basin would disappear with the establishment of internationalist, and therefore allied, proletarian dictatorships.

Aiming to preserve Hungary's territorial integrity, Károlyi and his colleagues were unable to counter the occupying forces either by diplomatic or by military means. The council government, however, which in a note addressed to the neighbouring countries stated: "We acknowledge without reservation the territorial-national claims you have announced," sent the Red Army as far as Kassa (Košice) and Eperjes (Prešov) in the hope of spreading the revolution.

Political conflicts unresolved by the merger of the Social Democratic and Communist parties also began to emerge more sharply. The situation was further complicated by the fact that the line of division did not necessarily lie between the two parties themselves. The Communist József Révai pressed for the abolition of the trade-unions; Tibor Szamuely, Ottó Korvin, and Mátyás Rákosi advocated firm application of dictatorship; while Ervin Sinkó and Jenő Landler had doubts as to the latter's expediency. Jenő Hamburger was just as much against the idea of distributing the land as were his fellow Communist people's commissars.

It fell to Béla Kun to mediate between the various shades of Social Democracy and Communism. He was sufficiently flexible to reach a compromise even in the most critical of situations and to prevent the split which would have endangered power itself.

The Revolutionary Governing Council was compelled to acknowledge that by July its support in the country had fallen off considerably. The landless had not been given land, the peasantry had been hit by requisitioning, and the livelihoods of shopkeepers and artisans had been shaken. Moreover, the abolition of the land tax had produced an unfavourable effect, as had the prohibition of alcoholic beverages in force throughout the country. The abolition of religious education in schools was also unpopular. The trade-union leaders strengthened the conviction among workers that "the dictatorship should be lessened" and that Hungary "should come to an agreement with the Entente". However, worker power which excluded the Communists was unlikely to last. After the end of May, the enthusiasm of the majority of writers and artists supporting the regime began to wane and disillusionment spread in their ranks. Despite doubts and reservations, however, they did not turn against the Republic of Councils.

The impact of the events of 1918 and 1919 was wide-ranging and contradictory. Several outstanding Social Democratic leaders, such as Jenő Landler and Jenő Varga, became Communists, and after the collapse of the Republic of Councils Stromfeld joined left wing of the working-class movement. After August 1919 differences emerged between the Hungarian Communists and Social Democrats over the causes of their joint failure. Controversy over correct strategy and tactics became even more heated than before, and became incorporated into the fierce exchanges within the Communist International. The Communists split into factions (the Kun and the Landler factions), with Kun and his entourage advocating an extreme brand of Communism condemned by Lenin as an infantile disorder.

The international Communist movement attached great significance to the fact that in Hungary the Republic of Councils had come into existence without the need for armed struggle. In Hungary, however, a sizeable segment of the bourgeoisie and the intelligentsia later turned away even from bourgeois democracy, because the events of 1918–19 led many to conclude that the dictatorship of the proletariat was merely its corollary. Thus, not only were the dictatorship of the proletariat and the entire Communist movement discredited, but also liberalism. During the 1930s ideas for the reformation of Hungarian society and the improvement of Hungary's status in Europe in some ways bore the mark of this. Supporters of radical change sought a "third way" between East and West, between Communism and bourgeois democracy. Even the counter-revolution, which later emerged victorious, could not free itself from this legacy: an existence based on the negation of both ideologies. Its authority was initially asserted by means of unrestricted terror and then legislative and administrative methods, propaganda, and such like. Not only were Communists, left-wing Social Democrats, and moderate socialists forced into exile, but prominent representatives of bourgeois liberalism and radicalism as well. Those fighting for democracy at home thereby suffered an irretrievable loss. Hungarian society paid a high price for the abortive experiment of 1919, which inevitably weakened the political opposition within Hungary to the Horthy regime.

In spite of this though, it was under the counter-revolutionary regime that such an opposition succeeded in achieving what had been impossible in the day of the empire: representation in Parliament and local government. The opportunity for this was a concession the regime had to make in order to endure. The Communist movement was, however, outlawed and forced underground. In spite of these unfavourable conditions the party and movement not only survived the twenty-five years of the Horthy regime, but also kept alive the memory of the Republic of Councils.

Recollections of what happened in 1918 and 1919 persisted in the period that followed. However, domestic and international developments during the interwar period proved to be significant to the evaluation of those events. When the advocates of radical change began to draw up plans for a new Hungary in the early 1940s, very few of them regarded Károlyi's bourgeois democracy as a model to copy. On the other hand, supporters of socialism regarded the Republic of Councils as an inspiring historical precedent rather than as the blueprint for the future.

Between two World Wars

The rise to power of the Horthy regime

Although the counter-revolution proved to be victorious and enjoyed the support of the Allies, its consolidation was slower and more difficult than anyone had expected.

After Peidl's so-called trade-union government had been forced to resign, István Friedrich established a new administration in Budapest on August 7, 1919. Nevertheless, the counter-revolutionary government formed in Szeged at the time of the Republic of Councils continued to function and demanded its share of power. The counter-revolutionary high command soon transferred its headquarters from Szeged to Siófok in Transdanubia, and shortly afterwards, its leader, Miklós Horthy, became the most important figure in the counter-revolutionary group. The rival government launched a massive and brutal campaign of reprisals in the areas it controlled. This was directed against those involved in both revolutions, and the detachments headed by Pál Prónay, Gyula Ostenburg-Moravek, Iván Héjjas, and others in places staged pogroms against the Jews. For the first time in Hungarian history, internment camps were set up in which men and women were held without trial for years. In the region under their control, the Romanian authorities staged similar reprisals.

Owing to unfavourable international reaction the "white terror", as it became known, created difficulties for the counter-revolution. Count István Bethlen, his colleagues, and later Count Albert Apponyi, head of the Hungarian peace delegation in Paris, pressed for the restoration of legality.

It was only after intervention by the Great Powers that an official government acceptable to the Entente was formed in the Hungarian capital. Following the visit to Budapest by British diplomat Sir George Clerk, Károly Huszár became prime minister on November 4, 1919. An alliance of the so-called Christian-national parties gave the Huszár government its majority in Parliament, although the Social Democrats and the liberal opposition were also represented there. After seizing much property (which was then sent to Romania) the Romanian troops evacuated Budapest and eventually, in March 1920, the *Tiszántúl*. In accordance with the wishes of the Entente, the new Hungarian political system had to be based on parliamentary democracy, and legality for the Social Democrats and the liberal opposition. In line with these stipulations a more liberal system could have been created than actually was but the Allies were not particularly interested in promoting this.

On November 16, 1919 Miklós Horthy and his army marched into Budapest. In January 1920, in accordance with Clerk's wishes, a general election was held on the basis of a wide suffrage and the secret ballot. The Social Demoratic Party was, however, browbeaten into inactivity, and the Social Democrat journalist Béla Somogyi and his colleague Béla Bacsó were killed by the Ostenburg-Moravek detachment. The investigation led by Minister of the Interior Ödön Beniczky revealed the responsibility of the high command, but no further action was taken. Under the leadership of István Nagyatádi Szabó, the Smallholders' Party became the largest political party in Parliament. In spite of unfavourable conditions, Vilmos Vázsonyi's National Democratic Party, representing the bourgeois opposition, also won seats in the new Parliament.

The Allies and Hungary's neighbours insisted that the Hungarian throne remain unoccupied. Either the return of Charles IV or the election of another Hungarian king would, as they saw it, have constituted a move towards the restoration of the Austro-Hungarian empire. This did not mean, though, that Hungary was to remain a republic.

The new Parliament now restored the monarchy as an institution. There were two reasons for this. The monarchy not only ensured legal continuity, but also justified any future claims to the lost royal territories. But there was to be no king, and office of regent was reinstituted.

On March 1, 1920, with armed officers inside the building, Parliament elected the fifty-two year-old Miklós Horthy as regent. Although the voting was overwhelmingly in his favour, neither Horthy's education nor his previous career made him suited for the office. His political views were characterized by staunch conservatism, anti-Soviet sentiment, and a powerful desire to regain the lost territories. Initially, Horthy's chief support came from his army and the officers' detachments, but after a short while he was able to accept the political consolidation advocated by Count István Bethlen. Horthy was the figure who balanced the conflicting elements in the regime, as well as serving as its symbol.

By now the Peace Treaty was nearing completion and its acceptance would inevitably be a prerequisite for the international acceptance of Horthy's rule. Ironically, the regime which was forced to sign the treaty was the same one which regarded revision of the latter as the cornerstone of its policy.

Headed by Count Albert Apponyi, the Hungarian peace delegation in Paris requested modifications to the treaty and the holding of plebiscites in the disputed areas. The Allies, however, refused to make any concessions, and June 4, 1920 the document was signed in the Trianon Palace at Versailles.

Under the Treaty of Trianon only 30 per cent of Hungary's territory and 40 per cent of the old Kingdom of Hungary remained to the new state. One in three Hungarians now found themselves under foreign rule, about half of them in compact ethnic blocs immediately across the new frontiers. The treaty limited Hungary's army to a long-service force of 35,000 men (no air force was allowed) and regulated the use of ports, waterways, and railways. In addition, the building of new railways was to be controlled and Hungary obliged to pay reparations. An important part of the Peace Treaty was the so-called minority clause, under which all ethnic minorities in the new states were entitled to the same rights as the majority. However, the governments concerned did not observe this clause and the rights of the Hungarian minorities were everywhere violated. The strong opposition to the Treaty of Trianon stemmed from the forced partition of the Hungarian nation and from the serious situation of ethnic Hungarians. Every section of society and every political party—including the workers' parties—joined in rejecting Trianon. Public opinion, however, was divided over the extent and form of the revision to aim at. Unlike the nationalists, who wanted to recover everything, the Social Democrats and the liberal left-wing demanded only the return of predominantly Magyar areas. For their part, the Communists looked to the proletarian revolution to sweep away the Trianon treaty.

On July 19, Count Pál Teleki became prime minister. Wishing to strengthen the position of the traditional ruling classes which included the big landowners and industrialists, he promoted political consolidation on the basis of conservatism. Teleki introduced firm measures to suppress the extremist army officers who were still pursuing suspected revolutionaries. To provide an outlet for anti-Semitism and partly to alleviate the problems of the middle class, Teleki introduced the so-called *numerus clausus*, a measure which restricted the proportion of Jews among university students. He also began talks with the Social Democratic leaders with a view to pacifying the working-class movement. He introduced limited land reform in order to mollify discontent among the peasants, and this succeeded in conferring on about another two million people the security and status deriving from land ownership. Teleki's scheme did not affect the pattern of land distribution significantly, and only 7 per cent of the land in Hungary was involved—far less than in the neighbouring countries, which introduced their own land reform programmes after the First World War, programmes which were based on the distribution of large estates formerly in Austrian and Hungarian hands. The greatest mistake of the Hungarian land reform was that it failed to increase significantly the number of viable small and medium-sized peasant farms and did not curtail the oppressive predominance of the *latifundia*. Under the land reform, members of the *Vitézi Rend* (Order of the Brave) also received land. This was by Horthy and comprised of officers and soldiers who had rendered valuable military service. Each *vitéz* received a "*vitéz* plot" and owed allegiance to Horthy himself.

Despite his achievements Teleki was unable to bridge the gulf between the pro-Habsburg legitimists and the "free electors" advocating the election of a national monarch. On March 26, 1921 Charles IV staged an unsuccessful bid to recover his throne, but the issue of who was to be king remained unresolved. Other urgent tasks included setting up a political party of the ruling élite, the effective and lasting curtailment of the extreme right wing, and the normalization of the situation of the trade unions and the Social Democratic Party. Other priorities were the creation of a post-Trianon national economy and the formulation of an independent Hungarian foreign policy. The size and complexity of these tasks stemmed from the greatly-changed political and economic situation which now prevailed in the country.

Political consolidation under István Bethlen

Count István Bethlen served as prime minister of Hungary from April 14, 1921 until August 19, 1931. Although his political career began as early as 1901, Bethlen did not occupy any government post before the collapse of the empire. Bethlen became the key figure of the counter-revolutionary era. He was not only an excellent tactician, but also a statesman of vision and the most eminent politician to emerge during the Horthy years.

István Bethlen successfully tackled a whole host of problems of crucial importance to the consolidation and stabilization of the regime. On October 20, 1921 Charles IV again arrived in Hungary and attempted for a second time to win back his crown. Exploiting the commotion caused by this, and the threatening moves in the neighbouring countries, Bethlen passed a law dethroning the House of Habsburg. This was a decisive victory over legitimism. By means of skilful diplomacy, he secured the return to Hungary of the Pécs area occupied by Yugoslavia despite the Treaty of Trianon. Sopron and its surrounding district were returned by Austria as a result of the plebiscite of December 1921.

Bethlen created a political alliance embracing not just the large landowners, financiers, and industrialists but also the gentry, and army officer and civil servant elements of the middle class. Therefore, compared to the situation before 1918, the ruling group was both larger and broader. In 1923 Bethlen forced Gömbös and his fellow racists out of the government party. From this time until 1944, the extreme right wing was—for the most part—an opposition grouping.

In 1922 Bethlen brought together a number of political groups in Parliament to form a single government bloc. The Unity Party thus created absorbed and thereby eliminated the Smallholders' Party, which had held out for more extensive political rights and a more radical land reform. While in the neighbouring countries peasant parties similar to the Smallholders' played an important role at this time, in Hungary the peasantry was to lack an independent political party of its own until 1930. Bethlen also reached agreement with the Social Democratic Party. In return for concessions, the Social Democrats were given greater freedom of action and were allotted a place in the constitutional structure. Law III of 1921 banned the Communist Party, the activity of which was subject to official persecution for the rest of the period.

Bethlen introduced an electoral system which restricted the size of the electorate. Budapest and twelve other towns now enjoyed the secret ballot, but in the rest of the country open voting, with all its opportunities for intimidation and other abuse, was restored. Throughout the period the Unity Party had an absolute majority in Parliament and showed obedience to the prime minister. The international trend at this time towards the strengthening of executive power at the expense of the legislature's monitoring role showed itself in Hungary, too, and this was well suited to Bethlen's purpose.

In company with the new states established at Trianon, Hungary also had to rely on foreign credit to stabilize its economy, to establish a separate national bank, and to introduce its own currency. This was necessary to eliminate inflation and to effect economic recovery. At the beginning of March 1924, Bethlen, with support primarily from Britain and Italy, procured a loan guaranteed by the League of Nations. In May the same year the National Bank of Hungary was established. On January 1, 1927 the old unit of currency, the crown, was replaced by the new and stable *pengő*, with one gold crown being worth 1.16 *pengő*s. Bethlen and his finance minister, Tibor Kállay, also pressed for the development of industry together with the active participation of leading—predominantly Jewish—financial and business circles.

During the second part of the decade Bethlen built on his achievements. He restored the previously-abolished Upper House of Parliament in order to counterbalance the popularly-elected Lower House should the latter exhibit signs of extremism. Bethlen went on to restrict the areas of competence already allocated to local government at county and municipal levels. His measures in this area greatly limited the autonomy of Budapest, the stronghold of a powerful opposition. To fill the gaps, the power of central government was extended, as were the functions and responsibilities of the centrally-controlled civil service.

At the same time the government's social security legislation brought benefits to almost a million people. Between 80 and 90 per cent of the urban workforce profited by it. Obligatory retirement, disability, and other insurance schemes were introduced, but these did not extend to the agricultural proletariat. In 1928 the government modified the anti-Jewish *numerus clausus* legislation restricting the admission of Jews to Hungarian universities and similar institutions.

Count Kunó Klebelsberg, minister of religion and education, implemented Bethlen's general policy in his own area of responsibility. With a view to proving the superiority of Hungarian culture, he devised a scholarship scheme for the training of Hungarian scholars in foreign countries. He established Hungarian institutes abroad (for example, the Collegia Hungarica in Vienna and Berlin and the Accademia Reale d'Ungheria in Rome) which still function today, and also set up the Biological Institute at Tihany. As well as developing the secondary-school network, the Bethlen government spent 48 million *pengő*s from the state budget on the building of elementary schools up to 1930, more than the total spent for this purpose by all Hungarian governments between 1869 and 1918 (the equivalent of 46 million *pengő*s). By 1930 five thousand elementary school classrooms had been built, along with many new houses for the teachers.

After becoming prime minister, Bethlen won the confidence of the Great Powers, and especially of the British, by appearing to accept the provisions of the Peace Treaties. At the close of the decade, however, when consolidation was complete, Bethlen was openly declaring revision of Hungary's Trianon frontiers to be the aim of the country's foreign policy. This coincided with much criticism of Trianon in the West; Lord Rothermere's *Daily Mail* even launched a "Justice for Hungary" campaign. In 1925 the Bethlen government's opposition to Trianon involved it in a big scandal. It was discovered that several million French francs had been forged in Hungary to finance revisionist propaganda. Commitment to a revisionist policy drove Bethlen to conclude a treaty of friendship with Mussolini's Fascist Italy in 1927, and he wanted to develop this into a Hungarian–Italian–German alliance.

The Wall Street Crash of October 1929, however, caused a chain of events which was to bring down the prime minister. The collapse of the American stock market resulted in such a profound economic crisis that on August 19, 1931 Bethlen and his government resigned. At this time no one seriously thought that Bethlen's departure from office would be permanent.

It is not easy to sum up in a single word or phrase the system created by Bethlen, a system which remained unchanged until the German occupation of Hungary in 1944. Bethlen's structure rested on the balance between the three groups within the ruling élite, a balance which altered during the years of the Horthy regime. These alterations showed themselves in the differences between the policies of the various governments; the balance made it possible for the Social Democrats and left-wing middle class to be represented in Parliament and at local government level right up to 1944—an impossibility in any other country under Nazi domination. But in spite of this, the functioning of the political system in Hungary precluded the possibility of a shift to the left. Although it ensured more favourable conditions for a shift to the right throughout the period, the Bethlen order made it impossible for the extreme right to take power unaided. Moreover, when with German assistance the extreme right did actually take power, the whole system collapsed.

Bethlen created a rigid and conservative political structure. His was a regime which not only utilized traditional constitutional forms and governmental practices, but which also curtailed their normal workings from the very beginning. In addition, Bethlen did not baulk at employing new authoritarian and dictatorial methods. On the other hand, the Bethlen regime left ample scope for the self-organization of society and for the expression of opinion. In early 1930s there were over 14,000 associations in Hungary, and hundreds of daily and weekly papers and journals were published.

The Great Powers and the member states of the Little Entente not only found Bethlen's political system acceptable, but helped it in difficult situations. To the Great Powers the Bethlen regime constituted a guarantee against both revolution and a Habsburg restoration. Moreover, seen from the neighbouring states the Bethlen regime was preferable to democracy. For these countries revisionist demands made by a democratically-elected Hungarian government would have been more difficult to counter.

This was why the Social Democratic and middle-class liberal opposition was unable to procure support either from the Great Powers or from the Little Entente for the liberalization of the system and for Bethlen's dismissal. Removal of the prime minister was attempted on several occasions during the loan negotiations and at the time of the forged francs affair.

At the time the principal complaint of the left-wing opposition was that, although Bethlen had introduced a multi-party system, the government party was too powerful and prevented its proper working. Furthermore, it was impossible for the government to be changed through the ballot-box in the British manner. After 1933, however, owing to international and domestic changes, efforts centred on the preservation of the Bethlen structure and the prevention of its replacement by a Nazi-type dictatorship.

The Great Depression and the shift to the right

As well as economic consequences, the Great Depression brought in its wake long-term political ramifications. In response to growing unemployment and falling production on both sides of the Atlantic, new governmental methods appeared. State intervention became more extensive. Under Franklin D. Roosevelt's New Deal, America also adopted measures which curtailed some traditional liberties.

The Depression hit Hungary in 1930–31, slightly later than some other countries, and the problems it brought were also resolved later. There were two main reasons for this delay. Firstly, the initial results of the economic stabilization had appeared only two to three years before the Depression. Secondly, agricultural exports, of decisive importance to the Hungarian economy, ground to a virtual halt.

The peasantry became indebted, production flagged, and some 600,000 people became redundant on the land. Industrial output dropped by between 40 and 80 per cent, and in industry employment was 30 per cent lower in 1932 than in 1928. The general decline in middle-class living standards was accompanied by a new phenomenon, the "overproduction" of intellectuals and white-collar workers. This gave rise to a sizeable group of unemployed graduates, who were reduced to seeking casual labour. It was not uncommon to find them clearing away snow from the streets and they featured among the regular customers of the soup kitchens. It was only during the economic boom preceding the Second World War that Hungary's economy and society were able to recover from the tribulations and disruptions of the Great Depression.

Naturally, unemployment gave an impetus to the working-class movement and intensified Communist activity. On September 1, 1930 a huge demonstration was staged in Budapest and several hunger marches were organized in the countryside. The socialist working-class movement enjoyed almost no contact with the impoverished elements of the agricultural population, while the various right-wing organizations exerted considerable and increasing influence. Once again the various religious sects offering consolation for the sorrows of this world became extremely popular.

The developments of the 1930s increasingly attracted attention to the state of the Hungarian village and the plight of the poor peasantry. The so-called Reform Generation, made up of young intellectuals and populist writers, turned to the hopelessly backward conditions in rural settlements—conditions unlikely to improve. The year 1930 witnessed the foundation of the Independent Smallholders' Party. This party was led by politicians of standing—Tibor Eckhardt, and, later, Zoltán Tildy and Endre Bajcsy-Zsilinszky.

The Depression, with its attendant unemployment and mass poverty, created conditions conducive to the rise of new, national socialist, parties in Hungary. These found support among the middle classes, the officer corps, and the bottom groups of the lower middle class. Also attracted to them were the unskilled, politically-uneducated workers flocking to the towns from the countryside.

Indicative of the confusion reigning in the ruling circles was the appointment of Count Gyula Károlyi to succeed Bethlen as prime minister. Károlyi, the old Szeged leader and distant relation of Hungary's first president, formed a new government

THE ADMINISTRATIVE DIVISION OF HUNGARY, 1921–1938

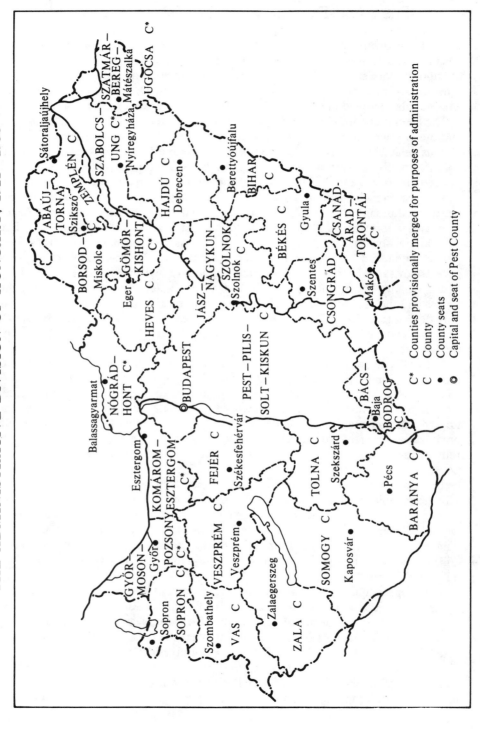

C* Counties provisionally merged for purposes of administration
C   County
●   County seats
◎   Capital and seat of Pest County

on August 24, 1931. At first Károlyi was willing to include members of the middle-class liberal opposition in the government, but this was not done. As regards the mass movements, Károlyi introduced summary justice following the Biatorbágy viaduct explosion, which caused the Vienna express to plunge into the valley below, and two Communist leaders, Imre Sallai and Sándor Fürst, were executed. In spite of these steps, Károlyi was unable to stem the tide of discontent and on September 29, 1932, Gyula Gömbös succeeded him as premier. From Gömbös the ruling élite expected strong government and the restoration of law and order.

On January 29, 1933, Hitler came to power in Germany. From now on, the international climate in Central Europe was radically changed, and the extreme right in Hungary now received foreign support. All this imparted an ominous quality to Gömbös's appointment as head of the government. Admittedly, as prime minister Gömbös was unable to pursue his earlier extremist race-protection policy but although he did not enact anti-Jewish legislation, he did attempt to bring about a transformation of society similar to that in Mussolini's Italy. This was promoted by drafting a ninety-five point National Work Plan, by developing the prime minister's role as controller of the machinery of state, by encouraging a spirit of militarism, and by trying to organize a corporate system.

In economic affairs Gömbös achieved unquestionable results. (Foreign exchange restrictions were part of his policy in this field.) However, when he began to extend intervention to the realm of politics and society, Gömbös encountered powerful resistance. His attempt to abolish Budapest's self-government rights gave rise to the "Alliance for the Protection of the Constitution" comprising not only the parties of the left-wing opposition, but also the majority of Christian-national groupings. Under collective pressure from some members of the government, conservative political circles, and the left-wing opposition, Gömbös was forced to abandon his plan to transform the hitherto club-like Unity Party into a fascist-type mass organization, which, with its suggestions of totalitarianism, would have subordinated to itself the state and public administration apparatus. Gömbös's reform policy was advantageous in some respects and brought about a slight social advance for certain groups in the middle strata. Gömbös introduced social welfare measures and initiated major construction projects. During his prime ministership the slum area of Tabán—near Budapest's Royal Palace—was demolished and the National Sport Swimming Pool built. On the whole, however, the Gömbös period was less than satisfactory. It triggered off changes in the membership and political orientation of the officer corps and public administration apparatus which led to a strengthening of pro-German sentiment, which was to have serious consequences during the Second World War. It was also under the Gömbös government that the *Levente*, a para-military youth organization, turned into a serious movement, and the activities of the various veterans' and rifle associations began to grow. Gömbös dealt firmly with the working-class movement and the year 1933 witnessed the arrest of János Kádár, among others.

In 1934 the government found itself at the centre of a serious international scandal. It turned out that Italy had sponsored the assassination of King Alexander of Yugoslavia in Marseilles and that members of the Croatian *Ustase* movement responsible for his murder had, with Gömbös's connivance, been partly trained in Hungary.

Gömbös was the first foreign leader to visit Hitler after the latter's accession to power and throughout his period in office he strove to strengthen Hungarian-German links. At the same time, however, he tried to ensure a role for Budapest as mediator between Berlin and Rome, and to exploit the benefit of this to serve his policy of territorial revision. Since the proposed German annexation of Austria aroused concern in Hungary and was at this stage opposed by Mussolini himself, the Hungarian government played an active part in forging an Italian–Austrian–Hungarian alliance.

Gömbös's attempt to create a totalitarian state failed, and his death in 1936 made it easier for the ruling circles, afraid of an excessive shift to the right, to set a new course for government policy. On October 10, 1936, Horthy appointed the conservative Kálmán Darányi as prime minister.

After the Bethlen years, a fluctuation can be observed in the policy of successive Hungarian governments. Whenever involvement with Germany and leniency towards the Arrow-Cross and other extreme right-wing parties reached dangerous proportions, a change of government took place and a certain amount of backtracking occurred. In actual fact, however, it was impossible to prevent the general drift of government policy towards alliance with Germany abroad and a shift to the right at home.

The course and difficulties of foreign policy

The opportunities for, and goals of, an independent Hungarian foreign policy were influenced by many factors. One major determinant was that the small countries emerging from the ruins of Austria–Hungary did not individually, or even collectively, possess the strength and international standing formerly enjoyed by the Habsburg empire. In the economic and political sphere these states were under the influence of their larger and more powerful neighbours. Consequently, their fate became inextricably linked to the balance of power between the larger nations of Europe.

After the revolutions of 1918–19 and the subsequent signature of the Trianon Peace Treaty, Hungarian foreign policy was motivated by the desire to bring about territorial revision. However, because Hungary was too weak to effect this by itself, suitable foreign allies were needed. At the same time, the function of foreign policy was to ensure the survival of the counter-revolutionary system at home. Hungary could gain admission to the international arena not merely by signing the Treaty of Trianon. Also required was the dethronement of the House of Habsburg and admission to the League of Nations. France and Hungary's neighbouring states were opposed to Hungary's joining the League, but, despite of the difficulties they raised, Hungary became a member in September 1922.

From 1920 on, Czechoslovakia, Romania and Yugoslavia concluded bilateral agreements giving rise to the "Little Entente" alliance. This was dedicated to the preservation of the *status quo* in Central Europe and the isolation of Hungary, with the consequent frustration of Hungarian revisionist hopes. Initially inspired by Rome, the alliance eventually came under France's patronage and became an instrument of French foreign policy. This circumstance, together with the fact that Britain had given its full backing to the counter-revolutionary regime as early as 1919, had a curious effect on British-Hungarian relations. In its own way Britain supported Horthy's Hungary and helped Budapest in its various difficulties. The liberal politician Rusztem Vámbéry pointed aptly to one of the reasons for this. In his view, Hungary was for Britain "a naval base offsetting French influence in Central Europe".

Although close Franco-Hungarian co-operation was made impossible by Trianon and the existence of the Little Entente, links between the two countries were not completely absent in the 1930s. The bourgeois left especially advocated the strengthening of ties to offset Hungary's pro-Italian and pro-German orientation. French loans played an important part in the reconstruction of the Hungarian economy after the Depression.

Relations with most of the neighbouring countries remained tense and, in the twenties, when Social Democracy had considerable influence over Austrian policy, they were not very close with Vienna either. On the other hand, Hungary made several attempts to improve relations with Yugoslavia. The main purpose of these efforts was Hungary's wish to break up the Little Entente. Historical traditions, lack of disputes, and similarities between the two regimes all contributed to the maintenance of good relations between Hungary and Poland.

David Lloyd George, head of the British delegation at the Paris Peace Conference, had pointed out to other representatives the likely consequences of their decisions in 1919. For him, in its existing form the settlement would lay the foundations of an eventual alliance of dissatisfied states desiring revision which would include, among others, Germany and Hungary. The foreign policy of the Horthy regime was oriented precisely in this direction, although not to the exclusion of all other directions and not from the very outset.

The Hungarian government did not aim at close links with Weimar Germany and when Bethlen eventually tried to improve relations he achieved fairly little. The road to Berlin passed through Rome. From the economic point of view there were good reasons for this and, in the meantime, the illusion of Hungary's mediating role between Italy and Germany had to be forgotten.

It was only towards the end of the 1920s—after completion of political consolidation and the stabilization of the economy—that the Horthy regime had an opportunity to launch an independent foreign policy initiative. There was only one path open to the Hungarian government: in 1927 Bethlen concluded a treaty of friendship with Mussolini's Italy and this also constituted the first major diplomatic move of the Horthy years.

Hitler's appointment as chancellor quickly altered the international balance of power, and with it the course of Hungarian foreign policy. The rapid build-up of the Reich's military strength after 1933 was accompanied by a powerful drive to overthrow the Treaty of Versailles, Germany's "Trianon" signed reluctantly in 1919. Germany now aimed at territorial expansion and although this strengthened the pro-German faction in Hungary, it also increased concern in more moderate circles as to whether Hungary would be able to preserve independence in its domestic and foreign policy. While official policy aimed at the realization of Hungarian revisionist goals by joining forces with the Germans, the socialist and bourgeois opposition strongly opposed this.

At first Britain and France rejected the German aspirations for territorial aggrandizement and as long as Italy constituted a significant counter-balance to Berlin, Hungarian governments strove to base their policy on Italy. From 1938 onwards, however, all this changed. Germany's international position was becoming stronger, as was its influence in the Danube Basin, and Hungarian foreign policy now rallied behind Germany lest the opportunity for revision be missed. The appeasement policy of Britain and France also played a part in this, making it clear that Germany would encounter no resistance from the Western democracies—in the immediate future at least. Hungarian foreign policy decisions were also motivated by the fact that Hungarian agricultural exports found adequate markets in Germany and not in Italy.

In March 1938, with Italy's acquiescence, Hitler annexed Austria and gave Germany a common frontier with Hungary—causing justified concern to the latter. The *Anschluss* was followed later in the year by the Munich Agreement, which sanctioned German annexation of Czech territory vitally important to the security of the Czechoslovak state. Britain and France had discarded the entire post-1918 Peace Settlement as well as their own previous policies. The Horthy regime owed the success of the majority of its revisionist demands to the Munich Agreement, albeit only indirectly, and the impact of this success, which was considerably exaggerated by a massive propaganda campaign, was undoubtedly increased by the fact that the frontier adjustments, which for the most part followed the ethnic principle, were achieved by peaceful means. The regime was able to add to its revisionist triumphs even after the outbreak of the Second World War; for the time being though, Hungary did not become Germany's comrade-in-arms.

Often, Hungarian foreign policy moves were initiated by Rome or Berlin. A case in point was the establishment of Hungarian–Soviet diplomatic relations, the way for which had been prepared by Bethlen during the first half of the 1920s, but which had been vetoed by Horthy at the time. Later, in 1934, it was on advice from Mussolini that the Gömbös government established diplomatic links with the Soviet Union. These were strengthened, at Hitler's suggestion, after the signing of the Nazi-Soviet pact of August 1939. Because it fitted in with German war preparations, Berlin approved of the conclusion of the Treaty of Eternal Friendship between Yugoslavia and Hungary in 1940.

Count Pál Teleki, who took over as prime minister in February 1939, strove to maintain Hungary's "non-belligerence" when the Second World War broke out in September. In the same year, however, his government signed the Anti-Comintern Pact directed against the Soviet Union and originally concluded by Germany and Japan in 1936. On November 20, 1940 Hungary signed the Tripartite Pact—the formal alliance of Germany, Italy and Japan made some two months earlier. In short, Hungary's bonds to Germany and the Axis Powers were becoming closer and closer.

The efforts to keep Hungary out of the war failed, as indeed they were bound to fail. Teleki's suicide on April 3, 1941 was unable to deflect the government from the revisionist path which it had chosen and which chained Hungary to German policy. The Hungarian army participated in the German attack against Yugoslavia (April

11, 1941), and the senior military leaders, especially Henrik Werth, the Chief of the General Staff, pressed for Hungary's voluntary participation in Hitler's war against the Soviet Union. It was in vain that Soviet diplomacy tried, through József Kristóffy, Hungary's ambassador to Moscow, to dissuade the Bárdossy government from taking this fateful step and even offered support for Hungary's claim to Transylvania. In spite of all this though, on June 27, 1941 Hungarian troops crossed the Soviet border, just days after the initial German assault.

Entry into the war against the Soviet Union followed inevitably from the course Hungarian foreign policy had set for itself and led the country to disaster. Hungary became subordinated to the German war machine, and the loss of the entire Second Hungarian Army at the river Don (January–February 1943) was a futile sacrifice of human life. Based on revisionism and the bolstering of the counter-revolutionary system, Hungarian foreign policy was by its nature unsuited to the normalization of relations with the neighbouring countries. The alliance with Italy inevitably brought commitments to the Germans, war against the Soviet Union and, consequently, the hostility of Britain and the United States. All this was in spite of the fact—realized by Teleki himself—that when the war was over Hungary would not be permitted to retain territories it had recovered.

J. F. Montgomery, United States ambassador to Budapest, described Hungary's relations with Germany as those of a "reluctant ally". This, however, was only part of the truth. From the very nature of Hungarian foreign policy it followed that it was not merely with reluctance that successive Hungarian governments adjusted to German wishes. Hungary's revisionist claims were not completely satisfied by the two Vienna Awards and hopes of further territorial acquisitions gave it an interest in keeping Hitler happy. Indeed, Germany's overall satisfaction with the various Hungarian governments explains why Hitler did not, up to March 19, 1944, consider it necessary to occupy the country.

Competition between Hungary and Romania for Hitler's favours was an important element in Hungarian-German relations. Budapest strove to procure additional territory from the Romanians while Bucharest wanted to recover the areas already lost to Hungary. This served Germany's purposes and Hitler did not hesitate to play the two countries off against each other. On the personal level though, the Führer's preference was much more for Romania's Marshal Antonescu than for Admiral Horthy.

On some issues Hungary did indeed show reluctance to fall in with the Germans. In 1939 the Teleki government opened the borders to about 100,000 Polish refugees, among them Polish troops bearing arms. These new arrivals were given work in Hungary and even had their own schools—certificates from which were afterwards officially recognized in postwar Poland. Hungary also gave sanctuary to French prisoners of war escaping across the border from Germany. Despite strongly-worded and repeated demands, right up to the German occupation Hungarian governments refused either to confine the Jews to ghettoes, or to deport them. After the annihilation of the Hungarian Second Army on the Don, the Kállay government refused to send significant new forces to the front. Finally, it was this reluctance and the attempt to salvage the regime for the postwar period that gave rise to a peace initiative in 1943 when—under the Kállay government—secret negotiations were started with representatives of the Allies.

The left-wing opposition to the Horthy regime

From the earliest days of the counter-revolutionary regime there existed an increasingly strong left-wing opposition to those in power. This opposition criticized government policy from a democratic standpoint and sought a democratic course for change, although it lacked social, ideological and organizational homogeneity. Hitler's accession to power, however, brought some moves towards unity and later, in the search for a way out of the Second World War, these received greater impetus.

The most significant and most radical element of the left-wing opposition to the Horthy regime was, understandably, the working-class movement. This was divided. After the overthrow of the Republic of Councils, the alliance between the Communists and the Social Democrats was ended and the two parties once again became separate entities, although in the Horthy period only the Social Democrats could operate legally. The top Communist leaders (Béla Kun, Jenő Landler etc.) were forced into exile, along with centrist and left-wing Social Democrats prominent during the revolutions. The Communist Party was hard hit by its illegal status and brutal persecution by the public administration and police. Severe losses were caused by repeated arrests, imprisonments, and even executions. Put to death during this period were such prominent Communist leaders as Imre Sallai, Sándor Fürst, and Zoltán Schönherz. In spite of all these difficulties though, the Communist Party was able to reorganize its ranks time and again, although its numerical strength remained extremely low throughout the period. Besides a few cells, it had no real organizational structure. The setting aside of international differences, the easing of dogmatism within the international working-class movement, the need to fight Nazism, and the Popular Front policy emerging from this enabled the Communists to work out a programme more in harmony with the domestic situation. Although this continued to regard the overthrow of the Horthy regime as its main aim, it no longer included the establishment of the dictatorship of the proletariat as a short-term goal, and attributed appropriate importance to the distribution of the land.

From the mid-1930s onwards the leading Communists in Hungary strove to join, or even initiate, those chiefly left-wing moves which aimed to establish a broad national platform against Nazism and the Hungarian right. Towards the end of the period, when the Soviet Union's future role in the Danube Basin was becoming obvious, the governing circles also tried to treat the Communist Party as a serious political force. The leadership of the party formed into two groups: those in the Soviet Union (Béla Kun, Ernő Gerő, György Lukács, Mátyás Rákosi, and József Révai), and those at home, accepting all the risks that underground work entailed (Ferenc Donáth, Lajos Fehér, János Kádár, Gyula Kállai, Gábor Péter, László Rajk, István Szirmai, and Sándor Zöld). In accordance with Comintern principles, the party's political line was determined by the Moscow group.

The Social Democratic Party constituted the left wing of the legal opposition, although the leading positions in it were filled by persons of lower ability than those forced into exile. The policy of the party was, however, determined by a realistic assessment of the situation. It took into account the need for co-existence with the Horthy regime on a longer-term basis, and recognized the fact that in the foreseeable

188

future at least it would be impossible to topple the system by relying solely on internal forces. In the interwar period, the Social Democratic Party played an outstanding role in organizing (mostly skilled) industrial workers and white-collar employees. The legality of the party and its extensive network of organizations allowed scope for underground Communist activity; in fact, the Communists used these organizations to establish contact with the workers. The strength of the Social Democratic Party derived throughout the period from its close relationship with the trade-unions, whose membership fluctuated between 100,000 and 150,000 in the interwar years, and no other political party or organization could boast mass backing to this degree. The socialist trade-unions and, to some extent, the Social Democratic Party were the chief areas of the Communist Party's illegal activity. Although aiming at radical change in the political system, the Social Democratic Party did not desire revolution and dissociated itself from the Communists. The Communists, for their part, up to the mid-1930s generally regarded the Social Democrats as "Social Fascists". It was only slowly and with delay that the Communist leaders were able to follow the Comintern's binding tactical guideline.

The Social Democratic Party's legality did not protect it from harassment by officialdom and the police, nor did it safeguard the organizers of strikes from arrest. The Social Democrats continued their cultural activity among the workers and ran a very active sports movement. Despite innumerable libel suits and other forms of persecution, the party paper *Népszava* came out until March 1944. During the Second World War cultural programmes organized on trade-union premises effectively counted as political meetings.

From the 1930s onwards, the younger generation within the Social Democratic Party became increasingly influential. Men such as Árpád Szakasits, who became secretary-general of the party in 1939, and György Marosán represented the more consistent, or left-wing, section of the organization and took their place alongside Károly Peyer and the moderate leadership. Two other notable figures in the party were Illés Mónus and Anna Kéthly.

For a long time ideological, tactical, and personal differences between the two workers's parties militated against their co-operation. However, the Nazi occupation of Hungary in 1944 brought the former antagonists closer together and led to the conclusion of a formal alliance between them. After the liberation of Hungary from the Germans, this alliance became the foundation on which central political authority was based.

Despite the numerical weakness of the left-wing opposition to the Horthy regime, the proponents of liberal democracy constituted an important counterbalance to the system. Their attitude reflected the political outlook of the Hungarian bourgeoisie and its interpretation of the two revolutions. Their opportunities were, however, limited by the fact that their most able and prominent leaders had been forced into exile. Another big handicap was that right-wing and extreme right-wing propaganda blamed not only the working-class movements for the revolutions and Trianon, but liberalism and democracy as well. Because the liberal opposition contained many Jews, the anti-Semitic feeling in the country constituted a further disability.

The aim of the National Democratic Party, headed by Vilmos Vázsonyi and, after the latter's death, by his son János, was not the abolition of private ownership, but

189

rather the transformation of the capitalist order in Hungary along the lines followed in Western Europe. The same held true for the Kossuth Party, led by Vince Nagy, Rusztem Vámbéry, and Rezső Rupert, as well as for Károly Rassay's party. The latter was known by several names and was the most important of the three from the 1930s onwards. As the Civil Liberty Party it established close ties first with Bethlen and then with Miklós Kállay.

Credit must go to these parties for their consistent struggle for greater equality, for their resistance to dictatorial moves, and to any withdrawal of rights. Their political position was voiced on the pages of *Esti Kurir, Újság, Világ,* and *Magyar Hírlap.*

During the 1930s the left wing became more powerful and associated itself with new political trends—primarily those showing concern for the interests of the agrarian population and a solution to nationality problems. In addition to the Independent Smallhorders' Party formed in 1930, a National Peasant Party was set up in 1939. The latter had many members who sympathized with the working-class movement and the Communist Party. Leading members of these two parties were in the forefront of public life during the Second World War, and in some cases even afterwards. Examples were Endre Bajcsy-Zsilinszky, Tibor Eckhardt, Ferenc Nagy, Zoltán Tildy, István Dobi, Imre Kovács, and Béla Varga.

A substantial contribution to the shaping of public opinion and to the strengthening of opposition to the regime was made by sociologists and populist writers interested in rural life. These included Ferenc Erdei, Géza Féja, Gyula Illyés, János Kodolányi, László Németh, Zoltán Szabó, Péter Veres, and others. Their influence was so profound that it can still be felt today. The sensitivity of contemporary writers to social problems and the illusory nature of Gömbös's reforms prompted Lajos Zilahy in April 1936 to launch the *Új Szellemi Front.* Soon the majority of populist writers who backed the Gömbös reforms realized that the prime minister's goals were completely different from their own.

On March 15, 1937 the new left, which was partly made up of young Communist intellectuals, organized the March Front, summing up its demands in twelve points, as a reminder of the 1848 Revolution. Essentially, these points constituted a reformulation of the demands of the traditional left-wing opposition to the system. Whereas the liberal democratic middle class and the Social Democrats put more stress on the achievement of political rights, the March Front and the populist writers allocated the main role to national goals and the requirements of peasant society.

In the Christmas 1941 issue of *Népszava* the writings of anti-fascists, Social Democrats, and Communists such as Marcell Benedek, Gyula Szekfü, Árpád Szakasits, and Gyula Kállai appeared side by side. This bore witness to the growing unity within the opposition, and it was this more general collaboration which in 1942 gave rise to the anti-government Historical Monuments Committee.

During the Second World War, and more especially towards its end, the role of the left-wing opposition became increasingly important. It protested against Hungary's entry into the war and later pressed hard for a break with Germany. In 1943 the Independent Smallholders' Party allied itself with the Social Democrats, and the Communists formed the legal "Peace Party". In 1944 an alliance between the Social Democrats and the Communists was also established. The left-wing opposition organized resistance to the German occupation forces and, after Horthy was deposed, to the rule of the puppet Hungarian Nazis, the Arrow-Cross. In May 1944 it formed the Hungarian Front and later the Hungarian National Liberation Committee. In these organizations Endre Bajcsy-Zsilinszky, Vilmos Tarcsay, János Kiss, György Pálffy, László Sólyom, Lajos Fehér, György Markos, and others risked their lives to organize resistance. The Nobel Prize winner Albert Szent-Györgyi and the middle-class groups rallying around him also joined the resistance movement. In 1944–45 armed Hungarian resistance units helped expel the Germans and their Arrow-Cross allies from the country.

The struggles and sacrifices of the resistance movement, which fought for the establishment of a new Hungary, bears witness to the fact that inside the country there were still men and women with a genuine desire for democratization.

Yet the anti-fascist left-wing opposition was unable to achieve a breakthrough, and to mobilize and rally behind itself a majority of Hungarian citizens. The opposition was still divided as late as 1944. In the campaign for political democracy the conditions in the countryside were not given the attention they deserved. The populist movement's opposition programme stressed national independence, and this inevitably associated it with right-wing nationalism—with its connotations of Magyar supremacy in the Danube Basin. At the root of the differences within the left-wing opposition lay conflicting ideas on the future of postwar Hungary. The entire left-wing opposition wanted a change of regime, but only a minority wished to go beyond this to the abolition of private property and the putting into effect of a socialist transformation. As elsewhere in Europe, armed resistance emerged in Hungary only when the country was occupied by the Germans. In Hungary there was very little time to establish this armed resistance and the Soviet army crossed the border as early as September 1944. A divided left, almost the entire leadership of which had been arrested, was unable to combat the Horthy regime, its pro-German military leadership, and the German army. The left was just not strong enough to prevent the Arrow-Cross takeover of power on October 16, 1944.

Economy and society during the interwar years

Hungary's territorial losses in 1918 had serious economic consequences. Many of the country's existing natural resources were lost and its industrial structure became even more distorted than it had been under the empire. The Hungarian economy became much more dependent on the world economy and, because of this, foreign trade acquired crucial importance. Under Habsburg rule, Central Europe had been an integrated economic unit, the various areas of which were mutually interdependent. Trianon contained no provisions for the establishment of economic ties between the new Hungary and its neighbours and later on political factors militated against such links. Hungary's export capacity was overwhelmingly agricultural and Germany was the most promising market for its farm products. Germany gradually became the greatest buyer of Hungarian agricultural produce, and accounted for half of Hungary's foreign trade in 1938. After Trianon, protectionism and isolationism were general in Central Europe, as the various states all attempted to strengthen and consolidate their new economies. Hungary was no exception and the conditions of the time demanded substantial government support for industry. Because of this the role and influence of big capital became greater within the ruling groups than they had previously been. The National Association of Manufacturers, the Association of Banks and Savings-Banks and the National Hungarian Agricultural Association all played a decisive part in the shaping economic policy. By the end of the 1920s, industrial production reached its 1913 level, having in one period actually exceeded it by 12 per cent. The average of growth rates for Europe as a whole was, however, more than double this figure.

Light industry developed the most dynamically. The number of workers in the textile industry increased fivefold and the canning industry became competitive even on the world market. New branches of industry were created and old ones were modernized. As early as the 1920s, production of crude oil and bauxite began in the western half of the country. The aluminium industry was launched with German assistance and output of electricity trebled. Hungary's new diesel railway locos and rail-cars were marketable even in the United States. The chemical industry (for example, the Pét Nitrogen Works) was one of the most modern and rapidly developing in the country, as was the pharmaceutical industry (for example, Chinoin and the Gedeon Richter Works). There were outstanding achievements in the electrical industry. Good examples include Ottó Bláthy's voltmeter, the United Incandescent Lamp Factory's krypton bulbs, and the Orion Company's radio sets. Owing to the general level of Hungarian industry and technology, Oszkár Asbóth's helicopter and György Jendrassik's turbine could not be manufactured in Hungary.

During the interwar period Hungary became a slightly more industrialized country but the output of Hungarian industry still reached only 43 per cent of the European average. What is more, small workshop production accounted for a quarter of all industrial output in the country.

In agriculture, arable land accounted for 60 per cent of the total land area. Although yields per hectare improved, lack of capital and credit made serious development impossible.

In 1938 there were only 7,000 tractors in the whole country and—in the aftermath of the Depression—the farm animal stock in 1938 was still below its 1925 level. The development of agriculture elsewhere in Central and Eastern Europe was greater than in Hungary. Owing to a number of reasons (for example, the economic crisis after the First World War, the Great Depression, and low demand resulting from the population's poor average living standard), the domestic market did not expand at the necessary rate.

As regards the density of its railway network, Hungary ranked seventh in Europe. During the interwar period, electric locomotives were put into service on the main line from Budapest to the Austrian border. Civil aviation was introduced and Budapest's Ferihegy Airport counted as one of the largest in Europe.

Generally speaking, the pace of economic development between the wars was slower than during the period from 1867 to 1918. Nevertheless, between 1920 and 1941, industry's share of national income rose from 30 to 36 per cent. In Austria during the same period, this figure exceeded 50 per cent but in the Balkan countries it was only 20–25 per cent. On the whole, Hungary's agricultural character was slightly lessened. Even in 1937–38, however, per capita national income was only 120 US dollars. This was only half the European average and between a third and a quarter of that enjoyed by the Western European countries. All of this put Hungary in the ranks of the moderately-developed states.

The Treaty of Trianon also brought about a change in the country's social structure, a change that was strengthened by the developments of the following twenty-five years. The proportion of those employed in industry, commerce, and transport grew, while the proportion in agriculture declined. Nevertheless, those working the land still accounted for almost half of the population. White-collar workers grew in number, partly as a result of large-scale middle-class immigration from the lost territories, and partly because of the proliferation of the bureaucracy. About one-third of white-collar workers were employed in the public administration.

Hungary's social structure at this time resembled a pyramid at the apex of which there were two groups. The first was made up of over 500 aristocratic and big land-owning families (for example, the Zichy, Pallavicini, Festetics, and Esterházy families), and by about fifty finance-capitalist families (for example, the Chorin, Kornfeld, Perényi, Vida, and Weiss families).

The character of the middle class was determined by its inclusion of slightly more than 12,000 gentry, senior civil-servant, and senior military officer families. Their financial position was weaker than that of the big landowners but this was offset by their predominance in the state apparatus and in county administration. They occupied key positions in the army and most politicians of the period came from among their ranks. Civil servants and officers of gentry background, together with those of more plebeian origin, rigidly preserved the forms and trappings of the upper-class way of life. Many advocated racism, sympathized with the extreme right, and pressed for a pro-German policy.

The number of middle-ranking urban business families in the upper middle class was roughly the same as the number of gentry and senior civil servant families. These families were much better off financially than they were in terms of social prestige and political influence. Although they basically supported the system, the fact that many were Jews led to their rejection of extreme right-wing sentiments. At the same time, the liberal opposition parties could count on them to some extent.

In the heterogeneous mass of the urban lower middle class, between 300,000 and 350,000 artisans, shopkeepers, and traders made up the self-employed groups. Over 60 per cent worked without even one assistant and their much-vaunted independence was therefore no more than an illusion. The living standard of this section was not as good as many thought. Junior white-collar workers and junior officers for the most part lived rather modestly, but at least they had a regular salary, and a state pension on retirement.

The rapid rise in the numbers of qualified professionals and freelance intellectuals was a new phenomenon during the interwar years. Developments in technology, education, and health policy triggered off an ever-growing demand for teachers, engineers, and doctors of medicine. The sharpening of social tensions within the intelligentsia's ranks was another characteristic feature of the era. At the beginning of the 1930s, the dramatic increase in the number of unemployed professionals became a serious problem. Lack of job prospects made some professionals receptive to right-wing radicalism, which ran high within their ranks. Owing to the characteristic features of Hungarian bourgeois development and the policy of the Horthy regime, the majority of Jewish intellectuals were in the free professions, indeed there were virtually no other opportunities open to them. The "Changing of the Guard" was demanded not only by the Christian intelligentsia, but by the entire Christian middle class as well. This aimed at removing Jews from important positions and became one of the demands of the political movements and parties of the extreme right.

Even at the top of society dual stratification existed, and this was present to a greater extent within the middle classes. There were two groups—the "historic" or "traditional" elements and, distinct from them, those circles associated with capitalist development. Throughout the Horthy period the simultaneous coexistence and segregation of these groups became increasingly conspicuous. The fairly high proportion of Jews in the latter group was an important reason for this segregation. Similarly, a prosperous artisan, businessman, or shopkeeper could not compete with a landowner or civil servant in terms of social prestige, even if the landowner or civil servant were poorer financially. Birth and social standing were esteemed more highly than wealth derived from industrial or commercial activity. Before 1918 a grammar-school certificate and an officer's commission were the two most important requirements for entry into upper-class Hungarian society. After 1918, however, grammar-school qualifications became more common and the social origins of those attaining them became more diverse. Accordingly, the prestige of the grammar-school certificate declined and became insufficient in itself for admission. At the same time the circle of those finding their way into the officer corps also slightly expanded. As a result, the narrowness of upper-class Hungarian society was—very slowly and slightly—reduced.

At the bottom of the pyramid were the urban proletariat and the peasantry. The urban proletariat numbered over a million and largely comprised miners and industrial workers. Within the peasantry the most affluent segment section numbered some 50,000, and was made up of those with substantial farms. 300,000 were smallholders with land adequate for a living. Another 200,000 were dwarfholders—occupying land normally insufficient to sustain themselves. In addition, there were some 780,000 farmhands and labourers. These had no land and were the poorest group within the peasantry.

Some remnants of feudalism continued to persist in Hungary even between the world wars. The social prestige of the aristocracy surpassed that of every other stratum and the growth of a middle-class mentality progressed slowly—very slowly in the peasantry. Birth, titles, and rank were far more important than individual achievement and success. Caste-like discrimination existed in forms of greeting, address, and in social life generally. After the two revolutions, the state, educational institutions, and the Churches all fought to strengthen the principle of authority.

All societies depend for their existence on stability but Hungarian society in the interwar period approached petrification. Opportunity to rise on the social ladder was lacking and social mobility remained restricted. The sons of the more prosperous peasants could enter the public administration and could study at an agricultural college or even the university. The sons of small peasants could rise socially as teachers or priests. For the poorer strata, jobs in the postal service, on the railways, and in the gendarmerie and police offered not just opportunities for advancement but also state retirement pensions. Impoverished agricultural labourers flocked to the towns to find semi-skilled industrial work and to do unskilled jobs—for example, as caretakers, domestic servants, and messengers. Within the intelligentsia, however, there emerged a highly important, though not very large, group which had risen from the ranks of the peasantry.

Accordingly, it was only slowly, and chiefly from the 1930s onwards, that the narrow possibilities of upward social mobility began to loosen the fabric of society, thus broadening the base for bourgeois development. The natural development of this process was halted by the Second World War, and to some extent distorted by the anti-Jewish legislation preceding it.

Changes in lifestyle

The living conditions of the various social classes were invariably determined by the kind of work they engaged in, by the amount of income they derived from it, and indeed by whether there was any available work at all. Unemployment hit not only the industrial workforce but the middle-class intellectual and white-collar strata as well. Full employment was achieved only during the economic boom created by the Second World War. The problem of unemployment in the middle class was "solved" by the need for civil servants to administer the returned territories, by the introduction of conscription, and by legislation which removed Jews from the professions and certain other occupations.

In industry the working day varied between eight and twelve hours. Mechanization and the introduction of electricity improved working conditions, especially in big industry. In agriculture, however, threshing was almost the only mechanized process, and work mostly filled the hours of daylight. Salaried staff in ministries and offices worked between nine and noon, and sometimes stood by for duty during the afternoon hours as well.

In 1941 almost 40 per cent of Hungary's population lived in towns, and 71 per cent lived in settlements with electricity.

Urbanization remained rather patchy. Whilst the population of Budapest rose to over a million, that of other major Hungarian towns remained around the 100,000 mark. Forty-six thousand new homes were built in Budapest between 1930 and 1941, among them a host of "small urban flats", as they were known. A number of big industrial concerns, among them the Hungarian State Railways and Ganz-Mávag, built accommodation for their workers. Consisting of a single main room and lacking even such basic amenities as a bathroom, these were hardly luxurious. In Budapest some good middle-class homes were to be found in buildings bearing the stylistic characteristics of *Bauhaus* architecture. The value of these was determined not so much by the large number of rooms as by the level of comfort and convenience they offered. The miserable slum-like housing estates of the post-1918 years, which, incidentally, had all been named after Habsburg archduchesses (Augusta, Zita, and Maria-Valeria), still existed in Budapest at the time of the Second World War.

The 200–400 *pengő* monthly salary of the non-senior civil servant was considered adequate for a comfortable life during the 1930s. This was shown by the light-hearted song of the time "With 200 every month/ One can take it easy". During the 1930s, a minimum wage was fixed for industrial workers and the forty-eight hour working week was introduced—provisions which, however, remained in force only until the Second World War. The average monthly wage of factory workers, however, was around 100 *pengő*s, with skilled workers earning as much as 200 *pengő*s a month. In agriculture, in the wake of the Great Depression, one *pengő* was paid for a day's labour, and payment in kind was the general practice.

In 1930 social security provisions covered a million people and new hospitals were built in the county towns and in Budapest. Compared to the size of the country's population, the number of doctors in Hungary was high even by European standards. Quality of health care, especially in the villages, showed an improvement.

As a result of increased attention to education and to school-building, illiteracy dropped to between one-half and one-third of its 1914 level and the number of university students doubled. All this was undoubtedly connected with the unquestionable, albeit uneven, general improvement in living conditions. The quality of everyday life was much more favourable in the towns than in the villages. There was running water in only twenty-five towns and in these, with the exception of Budapest, it was mainly limited to the inner districts. Tram services operated in Budapest, Miskolc, Debrecen, and Pécs. There was an expanding bus service in Budapest and the first traffic lights in the capital were installed in 1928. Although the number of taxis rose rapidly (especially in Budapest), the hansom-cab and the fiacre could still be seen on the streets. Private cars were considered a luxury and in 1930 their numbers barely exceeded 13,000 in the whole country. On the other hand, the number of people who owned bicycles and motorcycles, indispensable in rural areas, rose quickly. The motorcycle and sidecar was tremendously popular at this time and was the equivalent of today's small family saloon.

Changes in dress and fashion altered the outward appearance of people. Men were less affected than women but important changes for them included the eclipse of the starched shirt-collar. The traditional suit remained but there emerged also a vogue for sports clothes. Women's fashions had, of necessity, to take account of the fact that thousands of women now worked in factories, shops, and offices. Although the traditional garb persisted in the village, women in the towns no longer wore long skirts and girdles. Dress lines became simpler and one reason for this was that initially even clothing material was scarce. The ready-to-wear clothing industry, although still very small, also contributed to the standardization of women's clothes. Long hair went out with the long skirt; it was replaced at first by the boyish "Eton" style and later by a style utilizing the newly-invented "perm". A lady would never be seen in the street without hat and gloves, although she would wear ankle-length trousers for sport—something previously unimaginable.

In the towns, goods were increasingly sold in specialized shops. By the second half of the 1930s the Meinl delicatessen chain—which had thirty-three branches in

Budapest—operated in twenty-two towns and villages. There were Del-Ka shoe shops in Budapest and in fourteen provincial towns. In 1926 the first truly big and modern department store, the Corvin, was opened in Budapest. Inside, escalators carried shoppers from the ground floor to the upper stories. Budapest's shops stood comparison with those of Berlin, Munich and Vienna. Nevertheless, in the provinces the general store remained the chief source of supply and in Budapest the small shop retained great importance. It was in the thirties that specialized shops began to appear in rural areas.

New types of entertainment and recreation came in, while the old ones increased their appeal among the general public. Christmas 1922 witnessed the opening of the Operetta Theatre in Budapest, and Hungarian Radio began to broadcast on December 1, 1925. At this time there were only twenty-one radio sets per 10,000 head of population, a number which had risen to 462 by 1938. From 1931 onwards the Hunnia Film Studio produced talkie motion pictures, and cinemas were opened in the towns and larger villages. The gramophone became very popular—but was beyond an ordinary family's means. Sports and hiking, on the other hand, became pastimes of the masses between the two World Wars. Tennis, fencing and sailing (the so-called "white sports") remained the preserves of the rich, while swimming, hiking, and soccer were accessible to everybody. Competitive sports also offered the poor a chance of rising on the social ladder. In addition, the flourishing sports clubs reflected and promoted social and, to some extent, political segregation. The groups of enthusiastic fans rallying around the more famous football teams differed from each other in character. The various university sports clubs had an exclusive Christian middle-class character while the Ferencváros Sports Club (FTC) attracted lower middle-class and semi-proletarian followers—some of whom sympathized with extreme right-wing views. The Hungarian Sports Club (MTK) drew the support of middle-class and Jewish circles—until it was banned. Between the two world wars the Social Democratic Party created its own sports network which drew participation of factory and office workers, as well as intellectuals. Sport and hiking also provided useful cover for the working-class movement, and especially for illegal meetings. The Nature Lovers Tourist Association contained many Social Democrats, Communists, and Freemasons. Walks and excursions through deserted countryside would often turn into political rallies.

It was during the interwar period that Budapest became a "City of Spas". The Palatinus Baths on the Margaret Island, the Széchenyi Baths in the City Park, and the Gellért Baths at the Gellért Hotel were all built in the capital before the Second World War. The Gellért Baths, with their wave machine, were especially famous.

Going away on holiday was a new custom which spread chiefly among the middle class. Holidays spent within Hungary were just as popular as those taken abroad. In the 1920s a great amount of land around Lake Balaton was divided into lots, and many spas were built which soon became enormously fashionable. This development of Lake Balaton boosted the development of local trade and provided employment opportunities. However, Siófok, Balatonföldvár, Balatonlelle, Balatonfüred, and Tihany became holiday resorts for different social groups. During the early 1920s the annual number of holidaymakers was 50,000 but by the end of the 1930s this number had risen to 200,000.

197

The café was an integral part of town life and cafés were often the centres of literary life and political discussion. In addition to the upper-class clubs, there were artisans' circles and associations, and the workers' cultural centres and village reading circles, together with boys' and girls' clubs, made for a lively social and community life.

It was also during this period that newspapers began to be read on a mass scale. Up to 1938 hundreds of daily newspapers, illustrated magazines, and journals were published. These included *8 Órai Ujság, Friss Ujság, Esti Kurir, Tolnai Világlapja*, etc. The pictures and news items in *Szinházi Élet* (which covered the world of the theatre) were popular amongst all social classes, while *Magyar Uri Asszonyok Lapja* was read by middle-class women.

From the beginning of the 1930s there appeared indisputable signs of an improvement in living standards and evidence of modernization. The value of these developments was limited however, and further progress in these areas became impossible with Hungary's entry into the Second World War, which brought wide-ranging economic consequences, including rapid inflation and growing food and commodity shortages. With the standardizing effects of fashion, along with the impact of radio, cinema, and the reduction of differences in living standards, the lines of division between various strata began to fade, but did not disappear.

Waves of emigration

Between the two world wars there were several waves of emigration from Hungary. These resulted in the loss to Hungarian science and intellectual life generally of some of the country's finest minds. Those who publicly advocated democracy or socialism were also forced to leave.

The suppression of the two revolutions, the white terror which followed it, and the consolidation of a conservative and right-wing political regime caused many Hungarians to emigrate. Another reason was the fact that many contemporaries felt that Hungary was in a hopeless situation, and this helped to make their own situation appear hopeless, too. The economic disruption, galloping inflation, and continuing mass unemployment of the early 1920s did indeed make future prospects seem bleak. Accordingly, not only those who took part in the revolutions and those committed to bourgeois democracy or socialism decided to leave. Young professional people and intellectuals also felt that foreign countries would be more agreeable for them, as did skilled workers, smallholders, and landless peasants. Many peasants left for economic reasons: they could not make ends meet at home.

Mines in Belgium and France (for example, those in Lens and the Pas-de-Calais) and the big industrial plants in the suburbs of Paris (for example, in Billancourt and Boulogne-sur-Seine) provided jobs for several thousand Hungarian miners and industrial workers. At the beginning of the 1920s, difficulties of adjustment, the need to protect their interests, and democratic convictions led the émigrés to establish in Paris the Hungarian section of the Human Rights League which for many years was directed by Mihály Károlyi and his wife Katinka Andrássy. Ernő Bóta was

198

one of those forced to emigrate when the counter-revolution triumphed in the autumn of 1919, and he played an important part in the setting up of this section.

In contrast with the period of dualism, emigration from Hungary in the years after 1919 occurred primarily for political, and not economic, reasons. Those leaving included not just leading political figures, but large numbers of lesser-known Communists, Social Democrats, and liberals. Before 1918 most emigrants from Hungary had headed for America, but between 1918 and 1938 the overwhelming majority of those leaving for political reasons remained in Europe. During the 1920s some 30,000 economic migrants from Hungary were taken in by the United States.

Not everyone leaving the country at this time travelled westwards. To Communists and those who had served as officials under the Republic of Councils the Soviet Union offered sanctuary and relief from persecution. It was there that the economist Jenő Varga achieved international recognition. Béla Kun, György Lukács, Máté Zalka, and others occupied various posts in the international Communist movement within the framework of the Third International. Hungarian Communist exiles in the Soviet Union, among them Mátyás Rákosi, Imre Nagy, József Révai, and Zoltán Vas, played an important role in promoting anti-fascist consciousness among Hungarian servicemen captured by the Soviets on the Eastern Front. These men subsequently rose to prominence after the liberation of Hungary in 1945.

Political conditions in Hungary and the bleak prospects for creative work drove many Hungarian social and natural scientists to other lands in the years after 1919. Sociologists Karl Mannheim and Karl Polányi, aesthetician and art theorist Arnold Hauser, and the mathematician Pál Dienes all sought opportunities abroad. Other emigrants were John von Neumann, an expert in number theory and computer science; and the physicists Edward Teller, Leó Szilárd, Eugene Wigner and Theodore von Kármán. All made outstanding contributions in their fields. The history of British and even world cinema could not be written without mention of the Korda brothers, especially Alexander. Béla Balázs made an important contribution to motion picture aesthetics. Outstanding Hungarian artists such as Marcell Breuer and László Moholy-Nagy joined the *Bauhaus* group in Germany. Béni Ferenczy, Sándor Bortnyik, Károly Kernstok, József Nemes Lampérth, Béla Uitz, and other prominent Hungarian artists were also forced to go into exile for various periods. The same fate befell Ferenc Molnár, the immensely popular playwright.

For those who emigrated, Vienna was the initial destination. It was there that many began their studies. From Vienna most went on to universities in Germany to complete their education. During the Weimar period in Germany, cultural activity flourished and Hungarian artists took full advantage of the congenial atmosphere there. Some, however, went further afield, to France and to Italy. Hitler's rise to power in 1933, however, caused Hungarian exiles to move on from Germany, and with the spread of Nazi control to other countries (for example, Austria and Czechoslovakia) Hungarian émigrés left these states as well. A number moved on to Great Britain and the United States. Some were actually invited on the basis of their professional accomplishments.

In 1938 Austria was annexed to Germany and after this the Hungarian government enacted anti-Jewish legislation more stringent than any previously seen in the country. This triggered off another wave of emigration. This time Britain, the

United States, and South America were the destinations, with the latter two more popular on account of the greater security they seemed to afford. In 1940 Béla Bartók and his family emigrated to New York. Bartók's exacting artistic and moral standards made it impossible for him to remain even as an onlooker in the country and thereby condone a system which had fostered the decline and destruction of humane values. Those who earned an international reputation abroad included the conductors Antal Doráti and György Solti. Those artists whose work was in the Hungarian language led a hand-to-mouth existence during their time in foreign lands. A good example was the actor Gyula Kabos, a popular star of the Hungarian screen.

From Oberlin, Ohio, Oszkár Jászi made tremendous efforts on behalf of his fellow countrymen. Using his reputation and his extensive contacts in the United States, he did much to procure American entry permits for Hungarian political exiles—despite the fact that strict immigration quotas were then in force.

During the interwar period, there was much emigration from the countries of Central and Eastern Europe to more affluent states. These offered a better livelihood and, later, a refuge from Nazism. Hungary, however, was the only country with a sizeable group of political exiles from 1919 onwards, and from the very beginning Mihály Károlyi was their acknowledged leader. First in France and then in Britain, Károlyi rallied these democratic refugees and set up the Hungarian Council in England, the aim of which was to work for the establishment of a democratic Hungary. Károlyi was ready to form a government-in-exile during the Second World War and attempted to organize Hungarian military units to fight alongside the Allies; the intention was that these would be recruited from Hungarian troops captured on the Eastern Front. However, for political and military reasons the Allies vetoed both courses of action, and Hungarians opposed to their country's pro-Nazi orientation were not given the opportunity afforded to Czechoslovak and Polish émigrés in Britain and the Soviet Union.

Although Hungarian political refugees were divided on many issues, on one they were agreed—namely their duty to proclaim the anti-democratic character of the Horthy regime to the world. During the Second World War they made a collective effort to bring Hungary out of the conflict, to create a new, democratic Hungary, and to promote harmonious relations among the peoples of the Danube Basin. Many actually took up arms against the Nazis. Hungarians fought not only in the Soviet Red Army and alongside Soviet partisans, but also in the American army, in De Gaulle's Free French, and in the French Resistance.

The overwhelming majority of Hungarian exiles, regardless of age, social status, and political beliefs, preserved their cultural identity while abroad and retained their ties with Hungary even when they opposed its political system.

Culture and the arts

In spite of highly unfavourable conditions and the drain on intellectual and artistic talent caused by emigration, Hungarian cultural life was extremely rich and colourful during the interwar period. Different generations worked alongside each other and diverse artistic trends co-existed peacefully. The varying social bonds and experiences of the leading cultural figures influenced art and the views artists had concerning their role in society. Within individual fields of art a wide range of genres were cultivated. Contact with intellectual trends in the rest of Europe remained unbroken, and these were enriched by Hungarian contributions. At the same time the official line on culture and scholarship was determined by conservatism and academicism. Consequently, most creative intellectual work was forced outside the official framework, although it was able to reach the public.

Within the boundaries of the new state, Budapest's role in cultural life increased considerably. However, minor intellectual centres also grew up in Debrecen, Szeged and Pécs.

The aspirations of progressive middle-class elements in the early years of the twentieth century, as well as the experiences of the two revolutions and their aftermath, left an imprint on the work of Hungarian writers and artists. In many countries there was growing interest in the subject of society, and in Hungary this acquired special significance in literature and the arts. Questions of vital importance to Hungary, the future of the Hungarians and interpretations of Hungarian and European identity, occupied every creative thinker. The special intellectual and ideological role of literature was not confined to Hungary, although conditions there gave it added importance between the two world wars. This explains the enormous impact of Gyula Szekfü's *Három nemzedék* (Three Generations), a historical analysis. Szekfü's later inquiry as to where Hungary had gone wrong and, for example, the work of Dezső Szabó were similarly influential. Szabó's *Az elsodort falu* (A Village Swept Away) was particularly noteworthy. The special role of literature explains the influence of the populist writers, although their ideas were by no means homogeneous. László Németh and others spoke of a middle course for Hungary somewhere between the Soviet system and the capitalist model. This conception of Hungary's role and a so-called "third way" between East and West has triggered off heated debate ever since.

The period between the two world wars was an important one in the history of Hungarian literature. It was then that the generation associated with *Nyugat* was at the height of its creative ability, and which included Mihály Babits and Zsigmond Móricz, who were not only authors, but also editors of the journal. Other writers were Dezső Kosztolányi, Gyula Krúdy, Frigyes Karinthy, and Lajos Nagy—to name just a few. A new generation emerged at the end of the 1920s: Attila József, László Németh, Gyula Illyés, Lőrinc Szabó, Tibor Déry, Péter Veres, and many others. Others appeared during the 1930s: Miklós Radnóti, Zoltán Jékely, Zoltán Zelk, István Vas, and Sándor Weöres. During the 1920s the "avant-garde" in literature was declining everywhere: when Lajos Kassák returned to Hungary from exile in 1926, this type of writing was already out of fashion.

As a result of the growing interest in society and politics, literature became partly sociological in character. Lajos Nagy wrote powerfully about the town, and sociologists and populist writers expert in rural life revealed, in a moving way, the destitution of the village. *Puszták népe* (People of the Puszta) by Gyula Illyés, *Falusi krónika* (Village Chronicle) by Péter Veres, *Viharsarok* (Stormy Corner) by Géza Féja, *Futóhomok* (Wind-Blown Sand) by Ferenc Erdei, *Cifra nyomorúság* (Tawdry Poverty) by Zoltán Szabó, and *Néma forradalom* (Silent Revolution) by Imre Kovács all spoke of what was happening in the countryside.

A large majority of the younger writers considered even *Nyugat* to be conservative and launched their own journals. These included *Szép Szó*, started by Attila József, Pál Ignotus, Ferenc Fejtő, and Zoltán Gáspár; *Válasz*, established by Pál Gulyás, Imre Németh, György Sárközi, Lajos Fülep, and László Németh; and *Tanú* launched by László Németh. As a successor to *Nyugat*, *Magyar Csillag* was launched by Gyula Illyés and Aladár Schöpflin. The writings of Sándor Márai and Lajos Zilahy delineated the bourgeois and his mentality. Ferenc Herczeg, the official doyen of writers at the time, fuelled gentry nostalgia.

In the interwar period, the traditionally high standards of Hungarian musical life were upheld by Béla Bartók and Zoltán Kodály. Further important contributions were made by Leó Weiner, Lajos Bárdos, Ernő Dohnányi, János Ferencsik, Ede Zathureczky, Mihály Székely, Endre Rösler, and Mária Basilides.

Official cultural policy towards the fine arts supported conservative-nationalist academicism and neo-baroque eclecticism. In spite of this, achievements in these fields were very diverse during these years. In painting, József Rippl-Rónai, Béla Czóbel, and Adolf Fényes followed the early Postimpressionist School. The Szentendre Group comprised Jenő Barcsay, Lajos Vajda, and Dezső Korniss. The most prominent figures of the Alföld School were Gyula Rudnay, József Koszta, István Nagy, and János Tornyai. István Szőnyi, Aurél Bernáth, Róbert Berény, and Ödön Márffy harked back to the traditions of the Nagybánya School, while József Egry followed in the footsteps of The Eight. Vilmos Aba-Novák and Pál Molnár C. belonged to the so-called Roman School. In sculpture Béni Ferenczy, Ferenc Medgyessy (who had an affinity for folk themes), and others produced outstanding work. Noémi Ferenczy created an entirely new style in the art of tapestry weaving. Gyula Derkovits was the outstanding representative of socialist expressionism and of the neo-realism which evolved from this. In the mid-1930s the Socialist Fine Arts Group was formed. Around this rallied painters and sculptors representing various artistic trends and ranging from István Dési Huber to Endre Szöllősi and Tibor Vilt. The avant-garde architects Farkas Molnár, József Fischer, and Lajos Kozma exerted profound influence over the younger members of their profession.

Artists who were socially and politically committed often clashed with the regime. Libel actions were brought against populist writers and sociologists, and the exhibition of the Socialist Fine Arts Group was banned in 1942.

The theatre enjoyed a boom in the interwar years. In addition to Hungarian plays, classics of the foreign stage and modern works were put on in Hungarian theatres. Margit Ladomerszky, Mária Lázár, Margit Makay, Mária Mezei, Anna Tőkés, Irén Varsányi, Andor Ajtay, Gyula Csortos, Gyula Hegedüs, Zoltán Makláry, Imre Ráday, and Artúr Somlay all performed during this period and became legendary figures in the history of Hungarian theatre.

Owing to the one-sidedness of state support and lack of patrons, a sizeable proportion of artists lived in difficult financial circumstances, with many writers and poets unable to make a living from their profession. Although after the mid-1930s there was greater popular interest in books, paintings, concerts, and the theatre, interest in the arts was confined to a minority. The intelligentsia and the educated middle classes provided the market for artistic work, but the tastes and demands of this section of the public coincided only marginally with the aspirations of the outstanding artists of the day: Béla Bartók's *The Miraculous Mandarin* won international renown outside Hungary. The general reading public preferred Zsolt Harsányi, Ferenc Herczeg, Sándor Márai, and Lajos Zilahy to sociological studies of the village.

It was not in every field and not even uniformly that élite and mass culture interacted. The different strata in society had different means of access to culture. Works, authors, institutions, and initiatives which attempted bridge the gap between art and the public acquired special importance. In the 1930s Hungarian writers and poets—including the populist writers and the poet Attila József—often spoke on Hungarian Radio. Géza Supka, the editor and publisher of the journal *Literatura* but also an archaeologist and well-known radical writer, organized the first Hungarian Book Day in 1929. The János Vajda Society organized performances in which Mária Basilides, Vilma Medgyaszay, Erzsi Palotai, Tamás Major, and Hilda Gobbi all participated. Many of these figures performed regularly to trade-union audiences. The socialist labour movement also played a role in the bringing of art to ordinary people. Indicative of this is the fact that Attila József held seminars.

The years between the two world wars witnessed outstanding achievements in cultural and intellectual life. The greatest problem was, as the artists themselves were all too painfully aware, that the number of people receptive to the arts remained smaller than they would have liked.

On the threshold of war

The period 1938–40 in Hungarian history was a time of strangely mixed developments and feelings. Lavish ceremonies were organized in the midst of ominous international events, and revisionist jubilation existed alongside grave anxiety for the future.

The year 1938 was the 900th anniversary of the death of King Stephen, the founder of the Hungarian state who was afterwards canonized. Nineteen thirty-eight was accordingly declared the year of Saint Stephen, and the Roman Catholic Church's Thirty-Fourth Eucharistic Congress was held in Budapest during May. Afterwards, certain ceremonies were arranged. There was a special gala meeting of the Parliament in Székesfehérvár, Stephen's capital. On St Stephen's Day (August 20) the "Holy Dexter" procession took place in Budapest and was attended by the leading figures in the state. (The "Holy Dexter" is the embalmed right hand of St Stephen.) This was followed by a colourful fireworks display in the evening. All these celebrations were given a special, and partly political, significance.

While Hungary commemorated St Stephen, the prospects for peace in Europe looked far from reassuring. Encouraged by the appeasement policy of Britain and France, Hitler annexed Austria to the German Reich in March 1938. The *Anschluss* gave Germany a common border with Hungary. While the Arrow-Cross declared that "1938 is Ours!", most Hungarians feared that the German army would not stop at the frontier. In a radio address Regent Horthy tried to calm the population and stated that any disturbances would be firmly dealt with.

In March 1938 Prime Minister Kálmán Darányi gave a subtle indication of what might come. In a speech delivered in Győr, he announced that his government was launching a five-year development programme (the so-called Győr Programme) involving the expenditure of 1 milliard *pengős* on the army and industry. At the time few realized the true significance of this. Indeed, for a while positive developments resulted from the increased expenditure: unemployment disappeared and living conditions improved perceptibly.

In September 1938 Britain, France, Italy and Germany concluded the Munich Agreement. By its terms the mountainous Sudetenland areas of Czechoslovakia were annexed to Germany. The incorporation of these regions, which contained three million ethnic Germans and the Czech army's main fortifications, was a grave blow to Czechoslovakia and made the rest of the country indefensible. But Hitler was not satisfied with these limited gains: in March 1939 the Germans occupied Bohemia and Moravia and set up a fascist puppet state in Slovakia. Munich opened the way for the Third Reich's expansion into Eastern Europe.

The peace settlement imposed on Europe after the First World War now collapsed completely. This had a profound effect on the whole of Hungarian society. Memories of the disintegration of historic Hungary were still vivid and the Horthy regime's propaganda was also effective. The fact that the Western Powers had capitulated to Nazi demands caused shock and confusion in liberal and socialist opposition circles alike.

Hungarian foreign policy, based as it was on the desire to overthrow Trianon, was ready to support the Axis Powers. The map of Europe was being redrawn and Hungary stood to gain if the architects of the new order were well disposed towards its aspirations. In domestic policy, too, the government was prepared to make concessions to Berlin to foster good relations and to advance the cause of territorial revision. Between 1938 and 1941 some of the lost territories were indeed recovered—and without the need for large-scale military action. After the Munich Agreement, the First Vienna Award (November 2, 1938) returned the southern border areas of Slovakia. These areas had an ethnic Magyar majority and contained the towns of Komárom, Érsekujvár, Losonc, Kassa, Ungvár and Munkács. The First Vienna Award represented a major success for the government and added 11,927 sq.km to Hungary's size. Another territorial gain was soon to follow. After the Germans occupied Bohemia and Moravia in March 1939, the Hungarian army marched into Sub-Carpathian Ruthenia. Hungary thus acquired control over the upper reaches of the river Tisza and established a common border with Poland.

Under pressure from Germany and the Arrow-Cross Party, the curtailment of the rights of Jewish citizens now began. In May 1938 sixty Christian Hungarian writers, artists, scholars, and public figures protested against this. Their appeal—"To the

Conscience of the Nation!"—was signed by Béla Bartók, Imre Csécsy, József Darvas, Noémi Ferenczy, Zsigmond Móricz, Aladár Schöpflin, Géza Supka, Árpád Szakasits, and Lajos Zilahy.

Legislation was enacted to restrict the number of Jews in employment as well as to limit their voting and marrying rights. Jews were excluded from the armed services and instead could be conscripted into labour service units. Jewish members of autonomous bodies were stripped of their seats. Since from 1939 onwards race and not religion determined one's status, the proportion of the population affected by anti-Jewish legislation exceeded 6.2 per cent—higher than the percentage classified in 1941 as Jewish by religion. Although the Hungarian race laws were not as severe as the Nazi Nuremberg Laws, they nevertheless seriously undermined Hungarian constitutionalism.

The Hungarian government granted special privileges for the ethnic Germans living in Hungary. Later on it enabled the German authorities to organize these people into the *Volksbund* and to recruit them into the SS.

On September 1, 1939 the German army invaded Poland and the Second World War began. Absence of pressure from Berlin to join in the attack made it easier for the Hungarian government to keep Hungary out of the hostilities. Count Pál Teleki, now prime minister for a second time, refused to give assistance to Germany and the Hungarian railways were not used for the transportation of German troops or supplies. At the same time Teleki opened the border to Polish refugees; Hungary preserved its non-belligerence.

The fact that the country now recovered even more territory seemed to vindicate the policy of Teleki and the governing circles. Since the Soviet Union had reoccupied Romanian-held Bessarabia and since Teleki was prepared to use military means to recover Transylvania, Germany and Italy—to avoid a conflict—made the Second Vienna Award (August 30, 1940). By the terms of this, Northern Transylvania (a total of 43,591 sq.km) was returned to Hungary. The area included the towns of Nagyvárad and Kolozsvár, together with the *Székelyföld* to the east. The population of the new territory was 51.4 per cent Magyar, which meant a total of 1,123,216 Hungarians. These were swelled by the 60,000 who moved up from Southern Transylvania. In the same time 200,000 Romanians left the areas annexed to Hungary and settled in the remaining parts of their state. On the Hungarian side the change of regime was accompanied by atrocities, to which the Romanian Maniu Guard promptly responded with great brutality south of the dividing line. All this dampened the spirits of the Transylvanian Hungarians, who had been overjoyed by union with the mother-country. The Hungarian authorities persecuted the left-wing socialist movement and applied the race laws in the newly-recovered area. As had previously been the case when Hungary annexed the Slovak border region, positions of authority in Northern Transylvania were filled by officials from within the Trianon frontiers. In spite of all this, though, the Magyar population of Transylvania considered the change to be favourable from the national standpoint.

The Second Vienna Award poisoned still further the already-bad relations between Hungary and Romania. It also helped Hitler to subordinate both countries to the German war machine by playing them off against each other.

The general shift to the right, revisionist successes, and the unrestrained propaganda of the Arrow-Cross produced their effects at the 1939 elections. The left-wing opposition had secured use of the secret ballot for the entire country by forcing a change in the electoral law, but in the political climate existing at the time it was the government party, the Arrow-Cross, and the national socialists who could best exploit this. The extreme right gained far more seats than the Social Democrats or the Independent Smallholders' Party ever had before. Now the Arrow-Cross consti-tuted the most powerful opposition group in Parliament.

The shift to the right and the German alliance notwithstanding, conditions in Hungary differed vastly from the parts of Europe under Nazi occupation. The admission to Hungary of Polish and French refugees is indicative of this. Also, in spite of the anti-Jewish legislation, the lives of Hungarian Jews were not directly threatened before the German occupation of the country (March 19, 1944). Indeed, many Jews fled to Hungary from neighbouring countries, where their deportation and liquidation had already begun. At first the reality of the war and the suffering it caused seemed remote. For the time being only the advantages of the German alliance and the success of the revisionist policy were apparent. In the spring of 1941, however, the situation changed.

Under considerable pressure from Hitler, Horthy and his General Staff decided to participate in the projected German attack on Yugoslavia—despite the "Treaty of Eternal Friendship" which Hungary had concluded with Belgrade on December 12, 1940. Teleki regarded this as a fatal step, and one he was not prepared to endorse. During the night of April 2–3, 1941 Teleki committed suicide, thereby acknowledg-ing the failure of his own policy along with the responsibility of revisionism for Hun-gary's entry into the fighting. "We have become breakers of our word," he wrote to Horthy in his letter of farewell. "We have sided with scoundrels. ... We shall be robbers of corpses! The worst of nations."

Teleki intended his suicide as a gesture, and anti-Nazi circles understood it as such. News of it caused a considerable international sensation, and was noted by a number of leading statesmen, including Winston Churchill. Teleki's death was, however, unable to alter the underlying course of Hungarian policy.

Hungary enters the Second World War

Teleki was succeeded as prime minister by László Bárdossy. On instructions from his government, the Hungarian army crossed the Yugoslav border on April 11, 1941 and occupied the *Bácska*, the triangle of territory between the Danube and the Drava rivers. Also occupied were the *Muraköz* and the *Muravidék*. By these actions Hungary acquired a further 11,417 sq. km of territory and more than a million new inhabitants, among them 370,000 Magyars. About 150,000 non-Magyars who had settled in these areas after 1918 were expelled. There could no longer be talk of peaceful territorial expansion, and it was clear even to the governing circles that a great price would have to be paid for the joint action with Germany.

Great Britain now broke off diplomatic relations with Hungary. To the departing Hungarian ambassador, György Barcza, Foreign Secretary Eden stated: "If a country is not master of its fate and voluntarily gives up its independence, then at least it does not conclude a treaty of friendship which it afterwards breaks. Tell them at home that Britain will remember this when peace is concluded."

By 1941 Hitler was already preparing his offensive against the Soviet Union. Several gestures were made by the Soviet Union to dissuade Hungary from entering the war on the German side. The Soviets returned Hungarian standards captured in the 1849 War of Independence and in return for Hungary's neutrality they were even ready to support Hungarian claims to Transylvania.

On June 22, 1941, the German attack on the Soviet Union commenced. Slovakia and Romania immediately offered to join the assault voluntarily. For its part, the Hungarian government was still waiting for a suitable pretext. The opportunity came when, as the official statement put it, Soviet aircraft carried out bombing raids on Kassa, Munkács, and Rahó. The anti-Soviet stance inherent in the Horthy regime and the vain hope of keeping the territories already returned led to Hungary's entry into the war on the Soviet Union just five days after the German offensive began. This critical step was not debated in Parliament and the decision was merely announced to the members. On June 27 the Hungarian army crossed the frontier.

Despite its initial successes on the Eastern Front, the German army demanded active support from its allies. Italian and Romanian armies advanced to the Don and in January 1942 the Hungarian government committed itself to despatch the Second Hungarian Army to Russia. This force—a total of some 200,000 soldiers and labour service members—arrived in position during the course of the summer and was placed under the command of the German military leadership.

In early January 1942, German and Hungarian army units killed around 5,000 Hungarians and South Slavs (mostly of Jewish extraction) in retaliation for alleged partisan activities. The perpetrators of this massacre escaped punishment at the time, but after the war Ferenc Szombathelyi, the then Chief of General Staff, was extradited to Yugoslavia, where he was executed.

By undertaking the attack on Yugoslavia and by declaring war on the Soviet Union, László Bárdossy fulfilled his fateful role, and on March 9, 1942 Miklós Kállay replaced him as prime minister. Initially Kállay continued the policy of his predecessor but soon he began some very delicate manœuvring. Kállay aimed to break with Germany at a suitable time and in a suitable way, to reach agreement with the Western Allies, and to ensure the survival of the Horthy system for the postwar period.

During the war, state intervention in the economy assumed unprecedented proportions, and industrial and agricultural production was made over for military purposes. Most factories were declared "war factories", the purchasing of agricultural produce was made a state monopoly, and a new system of compulsory delivery was introduced. Nevertheless, shortages of food and commodities grew constantly and remained even after the introduction of rationing. The black market flourished.

The Hungarian economy was subordinated to German interests and demands. In 1942, 90 per cent of Hungary's bauxite production went to Germany, as did 50 per cent of its oil production. Certain industries produced more for the German than for the Hungarian army. The situation was similar with agricultural produce. In

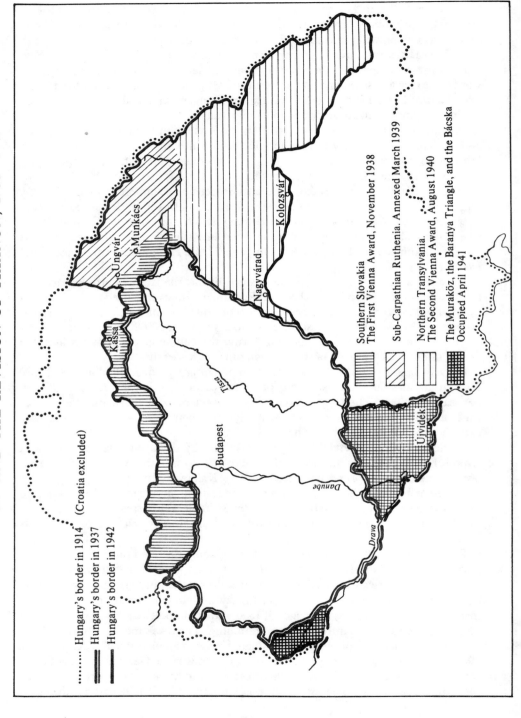

HUNGARY AND THE REVISION OF TRIANON, 1938–1941

.... Hungary's border in 1914 (Croatia excluded)

──── Hungary's border in 1937

──── Hungary's border in 1942

Southern Slovakia
The First Vienna Award, November 1938

Sub-Carpathian Ruthenia. Annexed March 1939

Northern Transylvania.
The Second Vienna Award, August 1940

The Muraköz, the Baranya Triangle, and the Bácska
Occupied April 1941

Ungvár
Munkács
Kassa
Kolozsvár
Nagyvárad
Budapest
Tisza
Danube
Drava
Újvidék

addition to the entire food surplus of the *Bácska*, most of Hungary's maize, wheat, and oil-seed went to Germany. Moreover, Germany failed to pay for what it received. Germany's debt to Hungary rose from 326 million *pengős* in 1941 to 550 million *pengős* in 1942. In short, Hitler's war was partly financed by Hungary.

After Hungary's entry into the war, special measures were introduced at home. These banned political rallies, inaugurated censorship of the press, and rigourously punished the practice of listening to enemy radio stations. Communist activity was dealt with under summary jurisdiction and a number of prominent Communist leaders were given long prison terms. The Communist Zoltán Schönherz was executed in 1942, and members of the presidium of the Historical Monuments Committee were arrested.

In spite of all this, from 1941 onwards people opposing the regime rallied around various opposition organizations, denounced the war, called for an end to the German alliance, and demanded Hungary's withdrawal from the hostilities. These men and women received encouragement in autumn 1942. The Allied Powers now halted the hitherto unchecked advance of the German armies and began to counterattack. In November 1942 the British defeated Rommel's army at El Alamein and American units landed in North Africa. Shortly afterwards the Red Army surrounded and annihilated the German Sixth Army at Stalingrad. This Soviet victory was a decisive event in the war.

In January 1943 Soviet troops launched a successful offensive along the river Don, and in the course of the fighting the Hungarian Second Army, stationed in the Voronezh region, was destroyed. In combat-readiness and fighting ability the Hungarian troops lagged far behind the Red Army. Owing to hostile behaviour on the part the Germans, the defeated Hungarian units, retreating in a disorganized way, lost more than 150,000 men. The Hungarian government tried to keep silent about the Voronezh catastrophe and to play down its dimensions. Only those who listened to Moscow-based Radio Kossuth or to the BBC learned the truth.

After the annihilation of the Hungarian Second Army, the Kállay government refused to send another army to the Eastern Front—in spite of German pressure to do so. With the end of the war in sight, Kállay wanted to build up combat-ready forces in Hungary, and his government put out diplomatic feelers in the West in an attempt to pave the way for an armistice and the country's withdrawal from the war.

The attempt to arrange an armistice, and to pull out of the hostilities

In 1943 the plans of the ruling circles and the ideas of the politically-aware public were influenced by Hungary's experiences in the First World War. Many expected that the Western Allies would once again land in the Balkans and that they would quickly reach the Hungarian frontier, enabling the country to go over to them. They did not wish to see Hungary on the side of the losers for a second time, and did not want the country to be militarily exhausted by the time an armistice was signed; effective armed forces at home would prevent a repetition of 1918–19. With the exception of the Communists, the anti-Nazi and anti-German opposition did not want revolution.

The Horthy–Kállay–Bethlen group and most of the liberal political parties, which included such well-known opposition figures as Károly Rassay, wished to take Hungary out of the war and to preserve, as far as possible, the existing political structure. But although every anti-Nazi group supported and approved of Kállay's negotiations and the proposed break with Germany, the majority wanted more than just this. The workers' parties, most of the Smallholders, the National Peasant Party, and the liberal radicals and democrats all called for fundamental reforms—including distribution of the land, the curtailment of big capital, and a thorough-going democratization of political life.

From January 1943 onward, several representatives of the Kállay government conducted negotiations with the Western Allies in Istanbul, Stockholm, and Switzerland. In Budapest a special bureau was opened with Horthy's younger son, Miklós Horthy Jr., at its head. For the period of transition, Horthy and Kállay assigned important roles to prominent opposition figures including, for example, Károly Peyer, Zoltán Tildy and Károly Rassay. It was hoped that if Hungary succeeded in pulling out of the war it would be able to retain the territories annexed since the beginning of 1938. Horthy, Kállay, Bethlen, and others wanted to see this change of sides accomplished independently of the Soviet Union. Only one person, Nobel Prize winner Albert Szent-Györgyi, conducted talks on behalf of the section of the Hungarian opposition which wished to see a change of regime. He met British representatives and was accorded the respect due to the head of a possible provisional administration. However, it was not the Hungarian opposition but the government itself which possessed the means to undermine the German war effort by ending the German alliance and by cutting off valuable deliveries to Germany.

Initially Hungarian hopes had been raised by the Allied landing in Sicily and the arrest of Mussolini on instructions from the Italian monarch, King Victor Emanuel III. However, the advance of the Anglo–American forces in Italy ground to a halt and German troops occupied Rome. Mussolini was freed from captivity by the Germans and formed his own government in the north of the country.

On September 9, 1943 the Kállay government's representative received from the British conditions for an armistice, to come into force when British and American troops reached the Hungarian frontier. Until then convincing signs of a break with Berlin were requested. This echoed the demands of the anti-German opposition in Hungary which was trying to force the government to act. Believing that the end of the war was at hand, convinced that Germany's defeat was certain, and fearing the consequences of a German occupation, Kállay tried to play for time. Hungary was to await the outcome of events on the battlefield.

The Nazi intelligence service discovered Hungary's negotiations with the West: Hitler repeatedly demanded Kállay's dismissal—and the deportation of the Jews. The Arrow-Cross stood in the wings, ready to take over power. Fearing that an imminent Anglo–American military move in Hungary would enable the Kállay government to go over to the Allies, Hitler ordered implementation of "Operation Margarethe". A stormy meeting between Horthy and Hitler at Klessheim (near Munich) on March 18, 1944 ended in the regent agreeing to the German occupation of Hungary.

On March 19, 1944 the German army moved into Hungary and the German ambassador, Edmund Veesenmayer, now became Reich plenipotentiary in the country.

Although domestic political circles had feared that a German occupation might take place, they were surprised and unprepared when it actually happened. The supporters of a break with Germany were not united. None of their groups could boast armed fighters. The Hungarian army remained passive. No one issued orders to resist. Officially, the occupiers had to be received as friends.

No sooner had the occupation taken place than the arrest—on the basis of pre-compiled lists—began of opponents of the Nazis. Politicians representing the labour movement and the bourgeois opposition were taken into custody, together with leaders of the opposition to Germany within the governing circles. In the course of March and April, some 3,000 people were apprehended and most were deported to German concentration camps.

The Kállay government now resigned. The former prime minister took refuge in the Turkish embassy, but in the autumn he, too, was arrested by the Germans. Key posts in the government and in other bodies were filled by pro-German politicians. Every political party and organization that was not of the extreme right was dissolved, and every non-Nazi newspaper was banned. In May Jews living in the countryside began to be confined to ghettos, and in the course of the summer they were deported to the death camps. Although Budapest's Jewry escaped this fate, some 50 per cent of Hungary's Jews died in Auschwitz and in other concentration camps.

All this took place while Horthy remained regent and while the machinery of the Hungarian state continued to function. The arrests and deportations were not carried out exclusively by the Germans, but mainly by the gendarmerie and certain extreme right-wing public administration officials. In many places the population, the Churches, and the democratic opposition organizations protected and sheltered the persecuted. The Swedish diplomat Raoul Wallenberg played an outstanding part in this.

After the German occupation of Hungary—and in line with an earlier announcement—Anglo–American aircraft began to bomb the country. Budapest experienced its first big air-raid on April 3, 1944. The horrors of the war had finally reached the hinterland.

As everywhere in Europe, the resistance movement only emerged in Hungary after the country had been occupied by the Germans. In this the Communists played a significant role: unlike the Social Democrats and anti-German bourgeois forces they could draw on twenty-five years' experience in underground organzation. The anti-Nazi forces set up various groups which carried out military operations and undertook acts of sabotage. Bearing such names as "Szir", "Marót", "Laci", and "Szent-György", they issued pamphlets urging armed opposition and prepared forged papers for the persecuted. The impact of the resistance was, however, greatly reduced by the fact that the majority of its potential leaders and organizers were arrested in March. On July 27, Endre Ságvári, a prominent member of the Communist movement, was shot dead in an armed clash with the Hungarian police. In spite of this, the Hungarian Front's executive committee was formed with Árpád Szakasits as its president. Its membership was broadly based and included Communists,

Smallholders and legitimist politicians alike. György Pálffy presided over the Communist Party's military committee.

On August 23, 1944, after the Soviet army crossed the Romanian frontier, the government of pro-Nazi Marshal Antonescu was overthrown and Romania changed sides. These developments, in addition to the Soviet advance into Hungary in September, had a decisive impact on Horthy and his entourage. Having finally accepted that they could not count on the appearance in the country of British or American troops, they now discarded their anti-Soviet stance. On September 28 a delegation was dispatched to Moscow to negotiate an armistice.

On October 11, 1944 the Hungarian delegates signed the preliminary armistice agreement in the Soviet capital. Withdrawal from the war and a break with the Germans now became a distinct possibility. On October 15, Radio Budapest broadcast Horthy's announcement of the armistice. For a moment a wave of joy swept through the country.

However, the implementation of the agreement and the neutralization of the probable German opposition to it were inadequately prepared, both politically and militarily. Horthy had even informed Hitler about the armistice plan, and the Germans were able to respond accordingly. Hungary's ruling circles dismally failed this test of history; the price of their irresponsibility and dilettante approach was paid by the nation.

Encountering no serious resistance, the German army occupied the capital's strategic points and installations, including Buda Castle. Using Horthy's son, whom they now held, the Germans blackmailed the regent into appointing Ferenc Szálasi "Leader of the Nation", thereby creating the semblance of legal continuity. Szálasi, an ex-major and the leader of the Arrow-Cross Party, became the symbol of Nazi power in Hungary. With Horthy and his family transported to Germany, power therefore passed into the hands of the Arrow-Cross movement, which was prepared to serve Hitler's Germany to the last.

On the Socialist Road

The liberation of Hungary

In the autumn of 1944 Soviet troops crossed the Hungarian border, entering Békés and Csongrád counties. In ferocious battles the troops of the Second and Third Ukrainian Fronts pushed the German and Hungarian forces westwards. In October 1944, the Debrecen area was the scene of a devastating tank battle, as was the Székesfehérvár area in March 1945, when the German army launched the last major counter-offensive of the Second World War to the north of Lake Balaton. By Christmas 1944 the Soviet army had surrounded Budapest, and, prepared to spare the city the horrors of a siege, sent two officers (under a flag of truce) to propose the town's surrender. The Soviet offer was, however, rejected by the German commander of the city—thus precipitating the two-month battle which devastated the Hungarian capital. The country was now divided into two parts—one liberated by the Soviet army and the other in the hands of the Arrow-Cross.

In the constantly diminishing area of their rule, the Arrow-Cross instituted a reign of terror, which primarily affected Budapest. The accession to power of the Arrow-Cross was accompanied by another wave of arrests, and the Jews of Budapest were confined to ghettos. Thousands were executed or died as a result of ill-treatment. The inmates of the labour service camps were moved westward, and mostly on foot. The majority were eventually murdered.

In October 1944 the Communists and the Social Democrats agreed to establish a united front. This was a decisive development which not only strengthened resistance to the Germans, but also laid the foundations for Hungary's postwar life. The agreement was valid not only for the struggle against the Nazis and their fellow-travellers, but also for the building of a democratic Hungary. In November the liberation committee of the Hungarian National Uprising was formed with Endre Bajcsy-Zsilinszky as president. Lieutenant-General János Kiss was responsible for its military operations. The Hungarian Front sent representatives to Moscow. The "Szir", "Marót", and other communist-led partisan groups, as well as the partisans working in the auxiliary law-enforcement units, carried out successful operations. They blew up the statue of Gyula Gömbös in Buda and also bombed the "House of Loyalty", an Arrow-Cross centre. In many places partisans prevented the transportation of industrial and medical equipment to Germany. Hospitals, Church organizations, and monastic orders offered refuge to the persecuted. The population of Csepel refused to carry out evacuation orders.

The Gestapo and the Arrow-Cross dealt ruthlessly with Hungarian patriots. Lieutenant-General János Kiss, Colonel Jenő Nagy, and Captain Vilmos Tarcsay were all captured and executed. At Christmas 1944 Endre Bajcsy-Zsilinszky was also executed, along with István Pataki, Barnabás Pesti, and other Communists.

In their flight from the oncoming Soviet army, the Germans and the Arrow-Cross took with them much which was of value to the country. Machinery, hospital supplies, art treasures, and foodstuffs were all moved by rail. The Hungarian Crown, the royal insignia, and such national relics as King Stephen I's Holy Dexter were taken out of Hungary. Most of the leading figures in the state and in the public administration fled abroad, as did many ordinary people who feared the fighting.

Hostilities in Hungary lasted 194 days and the last German military units were expelled from the country only on April 13, 1945. After fierce street fighting, the Pest side of the capital was liberated on January 18, 1945, but Buda had to wait until February 13. The Buda Volunteer Regiment, under Oszkár Variházy's command, made its own modest contribution to the liberation of Budapest. Partisan groups, such as those led by Pál Maléter, gave support to the Soviet army.

In those parts of Hungary which had been liberated, the organization of democratic groups began. As far as was possible, life returned to normal. On December 2, 1944 the Hungarian Independence Front was established in Szeged and was supported by Communists returning from Moscow, by the Social Democratic Party, the Independent Smallholders' Party, the National Peasant Party, and by the Civic Democratic Party. By December 20, 230 members of a Provisional National Assembly had been elected in forty-five localities.

On December 21, 1944 the Provisional National Assembly convened in the oratory of the Calvinist College in Debrecen. The following day the Provisional National Government was elected with Béla Dálnoki Miklós, a general who went over to the Soviet army, as its chairman. Seen constitutionally, the democratic transformation of Hungary began with the formation of this goverment, which was recognized by the Allies as the *de facto* representative authority of the nation.

One of the earliest and most important actions of the new government was to declare war on Germany—on December 28, 1944. It also began to organize an army, wishing to send a division to assist the Soviet troops. However, as it turned out, this division never saw action.

The new power

After the liberaton of the whole of Hungary and the elections of November 1945, Hungary was governed by a coalition government based on the four major parties of the Independence Front. However, from the very beginning the Hungarian Communist Party, now led by Mátyás Rákosi, played a decisive role.

Although the pre-liberation programmes of the four coalition parties had much in common, on fundamental issues they differed profoundly. As to the form Hungary's government should take, convictions ranged from parliamentary democracy to dictatorship of the proletariat. This divergence of opinion inside the coalition inevitably resulted in efforts to alter its internal balance of power, as well as in disagreements over policy and methods. These political struggles were influenced not only by domestic considerations; developments external to the country played an important part in what was happening. The wartime alliance of Britain, the United States, and the Soviet Union was breaking up and giving way to East-West confrontation. The start of the Cold War, along with Stalinist policy and its assertion in Eastern Europe, had considerable influence on events.

In March 1945 the government issued its land reform decree. This was a step of historical significance in doing away with the shackles of the past. For the first time in Hungary's history, land was distributed to the peasants across the whole country. The process began with great ceremony on March 29, 1945 at Pusztaszer, in Csongrád county, and 35 per cent of the country's land—nearly 3.2 million hectares —was distributed. Sixty per cent of this land went to a total of 642,000 peasant families, while state and model farms were established over the rest. Ninety per cent of those receiving land were farm servants, dwarfholders, or peasants with no land originally. The land reform carried out in Hungary was one of the most radical of the post-1945 period, and in itself pointed beyond the final elimination of feudalism.

The coalition government settled the country's constitutional form, an issue unresolved ever since 1918. Law I of 1946 abolished the monarchy and proclaimed Hungary a republic.

The coalition was now obliged to sign the Peace Treaty concluding the Second World War and to face the consequences of the Horthy regime's policy and the bargaining between the Allied Powers. The document signed in Paris on February 10, 1947 restored Hungary's 1937 frontiers, restricted the strength of its army, and ordered it to pay 300 million U.S. dollars in reparations. The treaty did not include articles safeguarding the rights of the ethnic minorities. The Allies accepted the principle of "collective responsibility", which was unjust from both a legal and a human viewpoint, and asserted this against the Hungarians and Germans in the Danube Basin. As a result, for example in Czechoslovakia, inhabitants of Hungarian nationality were stripped of all civic rights. Some were deported to take the place of Germans expelled from the Sudetenland, while others—more than 100,000 people —were forcibly resettled in Hungary. At the same time the Hungarian government, complying with the decision of the Allies but also with considerable domestic approval, expelled the majority of ethnic Germans living in Hungary, and not merely those who had belonged to the *Volksbund*. All this constituted a serious burden on government policy and the whole of society. One major reason was that for decades the old regime had made nationality grievances a taboo subject, and a rift between reality and ideology predominated from 1948 onwards.

Despite circumstances which were rather unfavourable in many regards, the liberation paved the way for popular creativity and talent. Throughout the country, committees were spontaneously formed. Made up of local democratic and socialist elements and free from any central control, these were able to assume political power; the total collapse of the public administration apparatus meant that the new committees could fulfil functions previously reserved to national and local government. With the re-establishment of central power, however, and with the growth of central control, these promising democratic forums were eliminated.

Popular democratic social and political transformation began with the approval and active participation of the overwhelming majority of Hungarians—a fact borne out by the turnout and results at the general election of autumn 1945. But the variety in political life, as well as its openness, lasted only a very short time. The *Magyar Kommunista Párt* (Hungarian Communist Party), in the leadership of which Mátyás Rákosi (just back from Moscow), Ernő Gerő, József Révai, and Mihály Farkas all played a leading role, forcibly imposed the Stalinist political model on Hungary. The presence of the Soviet army, Soviet interests in the region, and Soviet political influence (all of which were acknowledged by the Allies) gave backing to this. The transition from democracy to dictatorship was enhanced by the international climate emerging in the wake of the deterioration in relations between the Soviet Union and the Western Allies, generating a war atmosphere on both sides.

The Communist Party systematically excluded from the political scene all parties and groupings that did not fit in with the Stalinist model. To this end it not only employed the usual political means, but also resorted to trials on trumped-up charges, arrests, forced exile, and deportations—thereby paving the way for the popular revolution that came in 1956. A number of Social Democrat leaders agreed with the Communist aims in many respects and, not wishing to be excluded from power, backed the Communists against the bourgeois and democratic parties and groups. The "merger" of the Social Democrats and the Communist in June 1948—which occurred in an atmosphere of mounting suspicion and mistrust—actually spelled the end of the Social Democratic Party. The new formation took the name *Magyar Dolgozók Pártja* (Hungarian Workers' Party).

As a result of a similar process, Communist-dominated united workers' parties came to monopolize power not only in Hungary, but also in the neighbouring countries. Everywhere at around this time Social Democrats were soon removed from the leaderships of these parties. Coalition-based democracy was replaced in Hungary by a monolithic, centralized, and bureaucratic Soviet-type system, one which introduced alien institutions and methods. Between 1947 and 1953, bourgeois politicians, intellectuals, peasants, workers, and clergymen were arrested and imprisoned in vast numbers. Most of the population of "liberated" Hungary did not in fact become free.

The character and timing of the change were geared to the power and security interests of the Soviet Union: the Stalinist leadership aimed at the establishment of a homogeneous and rigid bloc in Eastern Europe. Consequently, the identification of the Soviet system with socialism precluded any chance of asserting any national interest or characteristic trait. All this hit Hungary particularly hard, as the country could not even compensate itself with the kind of achievements boasted of by Czechoslovakia and Romania—both of which had "assimilated" their ethnic minorities.

The introduction of the Stalinist system led, on the international level, to the break with Yugoslavia and, at home, to the use of coercive and unlawful methods— all under the pretext of the "constant sharpening of the class struggle". This policy also hit the Communists themselves, including a number of their leaders.

Following the execution of certain directors of firms with foreign links, highly-publicized show trials were organized in 1949. These resulted in the execution of László Rajk, György Pálffy, László Sólyom, and András Szalai, János Kádár, Gyula Kállai, Árpád Szakasits; and others (including Cardinal-Primate József Mindszenty and József Grósz, archbishop of Kalocsa) were imprisoned.

In 1953 a new opportunity presented itself for the amelioration of the regime's political and governmental methods. Stalin's death, on March 5, 1953, led to a thaw in the Soviet Union which triggered off developments in Hungary. As a result of these, Imre Nagy, who represented the Reform Communist wing, became the country's prime minister. However, the bastions of Stalinist dogmatism were still strong, and in 1955 Nagy was not only removed from his post, but also expelled from the Hungarian Workers' Party. The Rákosi-led dictatorship which was now restored refused to address itself to mounting tensions even after the 20th Congress of the Soviet Communist Party (at which Khrushchev denounced Stalin's crimes) and neither was it willing to acknowledge the need for reforms. This was in spite of the unmistakeable discontent manifest among the radical intelligentsia, in the Petőfi Circle, at rallies demanding Rákosi's removal, and at the funerals of Rajk and his associates (after their rehabilitation).

The inevitable explosion came in 1956. Discontent that had built up over many years and which had permeated every layer of society burst forth in a revolutionary uprising that swept away a system characterized by Rákosi and Gerő, dictatorial methods, and the tyranny of the security police. The driving force behind the 1956 uprising was the desire to create democracy, along with political and national liberty. People wished to restore Hungary's national sovereignty, and to prevent the country and its inhabitants from being confined in an alien and unviable political mould. Imre Nagy once more became prime minister and, returning to his programme of 1953, wished to establish political democracy by creating a multi-party system, by putting an end to the forced collectivization of agriculture, and by allowing grassroots workers' councils. The Nagy government subsequently formulated other demands (for example, neutrality for Hungary) which would have been quite impossible to achieve, even amidst consolidated conditions. The Hungarian Workers' Party, now a shambles, was replaced by the *Magyar Szocialista Munkáspárt* (Hungarian Socialist Workers' Party)—founded by Imre Nagy, János Kádár, and their associates.

The events in Hungary in the autumn of 1956 were, as far as international public opinion was concerned, somewhat overshadowed by the Suez crisis. None of the Western Powers wished to intervene in the country. The revolution which began on October 23 was defeated and suppressed by Soviet military and political intervention, which became decisive on November 4. The crushing of the revolution was fully supported by the leaders of China and some neighbouring states. János Kádár left the Nagy government and, on November 4, announced the creation of a new one in the town of Szolnok. This new government requested Soviet assistance. In the eyes of some, Kádár's actions legitimized the ousting of the Nagy administration.

It was only very slowly and gradually that the Kádár regime, which lasted from 1956 until 1988, could gain acceptance. During this time several hundred thousand

Hungarians left the country, whilst the new regime severely punished those who had played an active part in the revolution—regardless of whether they were politicians, workers, or members of the intelligentsia. In 1958 Imre Nagy, Miklós Gimes, Pál Maleter, and József Szilágyi were executed, while Géza Losonczy died in jail. Other members of the Nagy government were given long prison sentences, as were thousands of lesser-known individuals. The trials, imprisonments, and executions continued into the 1960s. Subsequently, too, political critics of the regime were also persecuted.

The new order thereby managed to consolidate its rule comparatively quickly. Also, by exploiting the favourable opportunities offered by the world economy in the 1960s, the Kádár regime was able to improve living standards substantially. Moving away from its earlier dogmatic intransigence, it created a more relaxed political climate. Kádár proclaimed that "Those who are not against us are with us", thus broadening the social base of the system. A consensus began to emerge, a consensus based partly on the easing of the "class struggle", and partly on the material prosperity of the depoliticized masses. Within the so-called socialist bloc, the Hungarian political leadership was seldom criticized, and was regarded as representing reform.

The Kádár regime was very active in developing Hungary's international ties and also in promoting co-operation between East and West. To this end, it pursued a foreign policy that pressed for the alleviation of tensions. It participated actively in formulating the principles enshrined in the Helsinki Agreement. Hungary's prestige, along with that of the regime, improved considerably in the 1960s and 1970s—with prominent Western politicians expressing opinions of a most complimentary nature.

However, the democratization process, which at the outset was encouraging compared to the 1950s, now ground to a halt. The regime lost its flexibility, and political life continued to be characterized by the hegemony of the Hungarian Socialist Workers' Party. Despite the experiments in reform, the system of plan directives was continued in the economy, and corruption became rife. Heavy borrowing served to prop up the old structure together with the bureaucracy, instead of facilitating modernization and the development of the infrastructure. Hungary became entangled in ventures which were detrimental to its interests within the framework of the Council for Mutual Economic Assistance (COMECON).

Because of all this, by the 1980s the Kádár regime had lost an appreciable part of its social base. A combination of changes in the world economy and mistaken economic policy decisions in Hungary wiped out earlier achievements. For reasons both political and economic, discontent became widespread throughout the population. Ultimately, it became questionable whether socialism had been built in Hungary, indeed whether the system developed in the country after the Second World War was workable at all. In the 1980s these doubts were expressed, with growing force, by the various opposition groups and semi-legal (samizdat) publications. So, too, was the need for radical economic and political change.

The economy

The reconstruction of the economy, along with its transformation, commenced in 1945—a time when conditions were extremely difficult.

War damage was estimated at 22,000 million *pengős*, the equivalent of 5,000 million US dollars, or five times the country's 1938 national income. Approximately 40 per cent of Hungary's national assets had been destroyed in the war, 74 per cent of the buildings in Budapest had been damaged in the course of the hostilities, and the retreating Germans had blown up all the Danube bridges. The Trianon area of Hungary together lost over half a million soldiers and civilians during the war. This number includes the dead, the wounded, prisoners of war, those who disappeared, and Jews who were exterminated.

Reconstruction together with the restarting of production and supply began with tremendous zeal. From the very beginning renewed economic activity was coupled with restrictions on capitalist enterprise—for instance, banks and industry. Indicative of the speed of reconstruction is the fact that the annual growth rate of the economy was 76 per cent in the year 1946–47. Between 1947 and 1948 it was still 30 per cent.

By August 1, 1946 inflation had been halted and the *pengő* replaced by a new, stable currency, the forint. The coal mines were nationalized and the major banks placed under supervision. A Three Year Plan was launched on August 1, 1947 which further extended state intervention in the economy and introduced new methods of business operation. In 1948 the factories and banks were nationalized. In addition, privately-owned workshops and retail outlets were almost completely eradicated.

This burgeoning economic policy did not, however, take properly into account the conditions and possibilities existing in the country. It aspired to autarchy and was very much influenced by military considerations in the wake of the Cold War. It dictated a pace of development beyond the capabilities of the economy and society. In economic development, priority was given to industry in general and to heavy industry in particular. In 1948 industrial production actually reached its 1938 level, but the output of light industry and the food industry remained considerably below this. Things were even worse in agriculture where various factors had conspired to depress the level of production still further. On the land output was 10–20 per cent lower than in 1937–38. Even in 1949 the production of commodities reached only 75 per cent of its prewar level.

The launching of the first Five Year Plan on January 1, 1950 marked the beginning of a new system in the management of the national economy based on compulsory "plan targets" and centralized production and management. The plan did not permit independent initiative and it distorted incentives. Economic management under this system necessitated the complete restructuring of agriculture and the abolition of small-scale peasant farming: from December 1948 onwards compulsory collectivization began on the land.

During the interwar period, Hungary's economy was of an agrarian-industrial character, with industry playing a relatively minor role. The new economic strategy, however, aimed to transform the country into an industrial state in which farming would be of secondary importance. Accordingly, 48 per cent of investment went into industry, while agriculture only received 13 per cent. On the land, motivation among the peasants declined, causing a fall in output. Production targets for food were not met and this resulted in serious disruption of supplies. The agricultural co-operatives and peasant farms were obliged to make compulsory deliveries to the state and these were stringently enforced. The consequence was that fierce animosity was aroused in the rural population and, at the same time, the people generally were not supplied with food at the required level. By the mid-1950s wages had dropped by over 20 per cent in real terms instead of rising by 50 per cent, as planned.

Tensions which accumulated in the economic spheres constituted a decisive cause of the political revolution of 1956.

After the consolidation of the post-1956 system, economic policy was reviewed and the method of planning modernized. However, the drawing up of a comprehensive and radical reform extending to the entire system of economic management commenced only in 1965. This gave rise to the New Economic Mechanism, which was put into effect in January 1968. The new economic policy assessed economic opportunities more realistically, reduced the enforced pace of investment, and provided better incentives. More resources were now made available for the production of consumer goods, and steps were taken to raise the population's standard of living. The development of industry was made less of a priority, and agriculture along with the infrastructure generally were to receive more attention than earlier. In addition, the new policy allocated considerable investment capital for the modernization of farming and abandoned the idea that Hungary should aim at economic self-sufficiency.

As methods of management were corrected so co-operatives along with industrial and agricultural firms attained greater independence. Under the new system of regulation, they made greater efforts than previously to adjust to market conditions and consumer demand. Economic links with other countries became more important and were established not only with states in the socialist bloc. In addition to production under licence, there occurred new developments in the Hungarian economy, including co-operation with foreign firms in production, trade, and the utilization of foreign labour and capital to develop the services sector. (The results of this policy can be seen in the improvement of the hotel network.) Radical changes have taken place in the overall character of Hungarian industry—changes which have reflected international trends. (For example, the telecommunications and chemical industry sectors have both grown.) Natural gas and crude oil have become important as sources of energy, and to offset shortages of electricity Hungary has built its first nuclear power-station. In foreign trade, the export of industrial commodities, instruments, and entire factory units has increased. The same is true of raw material and agricultural exports. In addition to the state and co-operative sectors, which dominate the economy, various forms of private enterprise have been given considerable scope. Private enterprise fills the gaps left by the state and co-operative sectors, and operates in the fields of retailing, repairs, catering, and other services.

Between 1958 and 1961 agriculture was re-collectivized (the earlier collectives had disintegrated at the time of the 1956 revolution). The shock of this development was alleviated by the two decades of prosperity which followed. This time the main consideration was production. Rapid development was not attempted and less force was used. Over 77 per cent of Hungary's agricultural land was now collectivized, with state farms being established on 16 per cent. Yields increased substantially, as did the pace of mechanization. By 1965 the number of tractors per unit of arable land exceeded the figure for Greece or Spain. By the same year, harvesting had been completely mechanized, as had the major operations in soil cultivation. Between 1931 and 1940 an average of five kilos of artificial fertilizer was used annually per *hold* but by the early seventies this figure had more than trebled. Substantial growth of the livestock population from the sixties onwards resulted in a better relationship between animal husbandry and the raising of crops. Household plots, as well as specialized agricultural co-operatives whose members are only part-time, became important in the supply of food for the population. The general growth of worker motivation and the much greater independence of the co-operatives decisively and favourably affected not only economic performance and the supply situation, but also the public mood. The decline of prosperity at the end of the 1970s and beginning of the 1980s affected the whole of society, and its consequences were not just confined to agriculture and the peasantry.

The concepts and methods characterizing economic reform in Hungary had a smaller impact on industry than on agriculture. No major renewal occurred in the structure, management, regulation, and development of industry. The improvement of the infrastructure lagged behind the requirements of the time and was neglected. The same was true of health and social welfare, which, according to the declared principles of the regime, should have been given more attention. Under strong internal and external pressure, the economic reforms ground to a halt in the early 1970s, and even after the world recession at that time failed to move ahead consistently. Hungary's foreign debts mounted, while more and more capital was diverted from agriculture. By the 1980s the entire national economy was in a state of serious crisis. All this was due not only to the lack of governmental consistency, but also to the suspicion and hostility Hungarian reform attempts aroused in neighbouring countries.

Changes in society and living conditions

The whole face of Hungarian society changed after the Second World War, and none of the social classes or strata from the interwar years survived in its old form or position. The two classes at the opposite extremes of pre-1945 Hungarian society vanished altogether. Having lost the bases of their livelihoods, the big landowners and capitalists who had formerly held power ceased to exist in their old capacities. Many left the country; the rest, especially their children, adjusted to the new conditions. The huge class made up of farm servants and other landless peasants also disappeared, since the land distribution raised them to the ranks of the smallholders. In 1949, 90 per cent of earners in agricultures were private farmers.

The gentry middle class, which had played such an important role in prewar Hungary, also disappeared. Top posts in the government, the public administration, and the economy were now filled from the ranks of the workers and peasants. It became a general tendency to promote manual workers from the shopfloor to leading white-

221

collar positions. By the early sixties, 40 per cent of earners in managerial and intellectual occupations came from a working-class background and 26 per cent from peasant families.

In education, too, the former proletariat enjoyed greatly improved opportunities. Before 1945 about 4 per cent of secondary school pupils and 4 per cent of university students came from working-class backgrounds. These figures increased to 44 and 33 per cent respectively during the period 1945–60. The numerical strength of the working class grew rapidly over a short period, and the number of workers in state industry and in the building industry doubled in the years 1950–70. This large growth inevitably changed the internal composition of the working class as well. Now integrated into it were the various *déclassé* elements and, most importantly, agricultural workers who were no longer needed on the land. In the sixties, half of the workers in Hungary came from peasant backgrounds. The policy of locating industry in particular areas substantially contributed to the emergence of a group of workers more than 300,000 strong who commuted considerable distances to their places of employment. With greater decentralization of industry and with the increasing prosperity of agricultural co-operatives, the number of such workers afterwards dropped to quite an extent.

Private farming in the traditional sense of the term disappeared almost entirely. The private farmer either joined a producers' co-operative or left agriculture altogether. The proportion of private farmers among agricultural earners has fallen to 5 per cent since the completion of collectivization. However, the former smallholder who joined a co-operative has witnessed considerable changes. Former differences in social status within the village gradually disappeared as the work itself altered. The growth of mechanization produced new types of work and shaped a new set of values with regard to employment on the land. Lowest in prestige are the various types of crop raising which still require manual work and which almost exclusively employ women. Most agricultural activity has become skilled work requiring special qualifications. The fact that the co-operative farms also carry on supplementary activities, mostly of an industrial character, has meant that members no longer perform agricultural work only.

As a result of nationalization in the 1950s, the employment position of self-employed tradesmen and shopkeepers, who numbered about 350,000 between the two world wars, underwent transformation. These people became members of industrial co-operatives, factory workers, or white-collar workers in the public sector. Only a few were able to preserve their self-employed status and only then in a few branches of the service sector. Since the launching of the New Economic Mechanism self-employed tradesmen and shopkeepers have set up businesses in growing numbers. These operate mainly in the fields of services, catering, and the retail of clothing and foodstuffs.

Nevertheless, the number of those who are self-employed has dropped to a negligible proportion among earners generally. Only 2–3 per cent of earners work for themselves.

Since the First World War, Hungarian women have been entering paid employment in growing numbers. This process has speeded up so much over the past forty years that, in 1981, women accounted for almost 45 per cent of all earners. Certain occupations (for example, teaching, the judiciary, and certain medical occupations) have become almost entirely dominated by women. The fact that women have entered paid employment in such a big way has affected not only the economy and public life, but also the traditional pattern of family life.

Clearly indicative of the structural changes which have occurred in Hungarian society are the developments which have taken place in the pattern of employment. In 1981 over 40 per cent of earners worked in industry. Slightly over 20 per cent worked in agriculture, and not exclusively in "peasant" occupations. Almost 10 per cent worked in commerce. All this represented a great and many-sided change. In 1941 almost half of Hungary's active earners still worked in agriculture, with industry and construction work providing a livelihood for just over 23 per cent. Nowadays it is the services sector, and not industry, which shows a rise in the numbers it employs. These developments have led to a transformation of the Hungarian way of life, a transformation also influenced by modernization generally, government measures, trends in fashion, and new customs.

The insecurity of livelihood and threat of unemployment which earlier affected so many disappeared for a long time, only to return again in the second half of the 1980s. For the most part, those hit have been workers in overdeveloped and unprofitable heavy industry plants. After a required number of years in employment, men may retire at sixty and women at fifty-five. While in the 1930s social security provisions covered 31 per cent of the population, today free medical care is the constitutional right of every Hungarian citizen. However, in recent years the quality of this service has deteriorated significantly.

The introduction of the forty-eight hour working week was followed in the 1980s by the switch to a five-day working week. Mechanization, together with health and safety regulations, have made work considerably easier. At the same time heavy manual work has been reduced appreciably.

Under a special scheme greatly affecting the whole of society, a working mother is entitled to three years leave of absence from her workplace for each of her children. During this period she receives a regular monthly allowance from the state. This scheme has recently been extended to fathers, who may now stay at home with children more than twelve months old.

There has been growing movement of population into the towns and, in the countryside itself, a simultaneous drift from outlying areas into the villages. Urbanization, formerly centred on Budapest, has become more general throughout the country. Between 1931 and 1980 the proportion of those living in the capital has risen far more slowly than the urban population as a whole. Nevertheless, about one-fifth of Hungary's population lives in Budapest, and more than half in towns and urban settlements. This process was connected with a settlement policy on the basis of which smaller villages were deliberately left underdeveloped on instructions from the central authorities. These villages were then merged with neighbouring ones, and their old names abolished. Similarly, the majority of the characteristic homesteads on the Great Plain were also forcibly done away with. In 1949, 17 per cent of the people lived in remote homesteads, isolated from larger communities. By the mid-1970s this figure had dropped to about 7 per cent. The benefits and comforts made possible by modern technology have become accessible to all. In 1980 there was electricity in almost every home in the country and 65 per cent of homes had running water. Almost half the country settlements also had running water. Traditional cooking stoves burning wood or coal have been replaced by electric and gas cookers. The use of washing machines has become widespread and the same is true for electric refrigerators, radios, and television sets. In 1960 there were only 104,000 television sets in the country, but twenty years later the figure was almost three million.

The improvement in living conditons has also affected nutrition. It seems that Hungarians still wish to eat more, and eating habits are still very much bound up with tradition. Between 1934 and 1938 average annual per capita consumption of meat was slightly below thirty-four kilos but in 1980 the annual figure was seventy-three kilos. Over the same period consumption of sugar increased from an annual per capita figure of ten and a half kilos to thirty-five kilos. Carbohydrates and fats yield the overwhelming majority of the 3,054 calories the average person consumes each day. As a result of medical advice and trends in fashion, healthier eating habits have struck root. However, progress towards a more healthy diet has been slow.

Taking holidays and the pursuit of recreational activities was part of the middle-class way of life between the world wars. They were subsequently extended to the workers through the holiday homes of trade unions, companies, and co-operatives. The spread of motoring has made people more mobile and has helped the expansion of both domestic and foreign tourism. In 1930 there were slightly over 13,000 cars on Hungary's roads, a number which had risen to 1.2 million by 1983. Sport (mainly soccer), which in the 1950s served as an outlet for enthusiasm and as an opportunity for social advancement, has become the main way for people to refresh their spirits. Even the so-called "white" sports (fencing, tennis and sailing), which were formerly the preserve of the upper classes, are now pursued on a mass scale.

It is a fact that the standard of living of millions has reached a level unimaginable during the interwar period. However, the changes that enabled this to occur also created difficulties. Changes in social position and way of life had a dramatic effect both on those who descended on the social ladder and on the people who rose. The consolidation of society was accompanied by a reduction of social mobility, as well as the beginnings of petrification in certain strata. The party and state apparatus mushroomed, and the leaders in state, political, and economic life came to constitute an entirely new grouping. They and their entourage enjoyed privileges in every area at the expense of the majority of citizens. Inequalities multiplied in an alarming manner, and by the end of the 1980s poverty had again become the dominant factor in the lives of an ever-expanding section of the population.

Cultural and intellectual life

The Second World War, as well as bringing great material destruction, caused serious losses to literary and intellectual life as well. The painter Imre Ámos and writers György Bálint, Gábor Halász, Miklós Radnóti, and Antal Szerb all perished as members of labour service battalions. Those who survived the Holocaust drew upon their appalling experiences even decades afterwards. In the spring of 1945, however, prominent figures of Hungarian intellectual life enthusiastically joined forces to create an entirely new culture, one accessible to the whole people.

To make education open to all and to raise the level of culture, the government issued a decree in August 1945. This made the introduction of the eight-grade elementary school system compulsory. In 1948 the schools were nationalized, including those run by the Churches. With education taken out of the Church hands, religious instruction at school became optional. Various agreements were concluded to normalize relations between the state and the Churches. The first of these was the agreement with the Calvinist Church and the last with the Roman Catholics. Sects which had previously been tolerated now became officially-acknowledged denominations. The Churches received certain financial assistance from the state and were allowed to run nine of their own theological colleges, as well as thirteen secondary schools. In 1951 the State Office for Church Affairs was set up. All this generated tensions between believers and the regime, and between the Churches and the state.

With the reform of the educational system, education became free at every level. The old four-class secondary school (which followed four years of primary school education) was replaced by various types of vocational secondary school. Although the grammar school, which had been designed to provide an all-round general education, continued in existence, it lost much of its appeal. New textbooks and curricula were prepared for every educational institution and level. In 1945 all the university faculties opened their doors to women. The network of people's colleges, which was established in the forties, together with the new university admission system, made it possible mainly for young peasants and workers to pursue further education studies. Later, by means of evening and correspondence courses, those who already started work could also acquire a degree. In 1949 the autonomy of the universities was restricted, and the old teaching staff replaced. At the same time the network of people's colleges was dismantled—out of political considerations.

Initially, the schooling of the population underwent spectacular improvement, with the number of secondary-school pupils, for example, trebling in comparison with 1938. But as economic difficulties mounted the regime reduced the funds available for education. This, along with other factors, had a detrimental effect on both the impact of education and on the conditions under which it was provided.

The earlier duality and division of culture disappeared. To begin with, the new cultural policy acknowledged those artists and values officially shunned during the interwar period. Culture became a public affair, the concern of the people in general. As early as summer 1945, a time when conditions were far from easy, the traditional book day was held. In 1948 the Kossuth Prize was established, followed in 1950 by the creation of the titles "Outstanding Artist" and "Artist of Merit" given in recognition of excellence. The whole of Hungarian cultural and scientific life was affected by the approach, methods, and themes preferred by Marxism, which by now was much studied. In Hungary Marxist philosophy already greatly influenced the representation and evaluation of the phenomenal world.

The cultural life of the second half of the 1940s was extremely rich and colourful. Side by side in the literary life of the day were writers of considerable diversity. These included Communist authors, advocates of socialism, populists, members of the *Nyugat* generation, and those belonging to the "urban" wing of liberal democracy. Among these writers were Lajos Kassák, Lajos Nagy, Gyula Illyés, László Németh, Pál Szabó, Péter Veres, Lőrinc Szabó, Milán Füst, Tibor Déry, István Vas, László Cs. Szabó, Sándor Márai, and Lajos Zilahy. In fine art the Szentendre School, the European School, the former Group of Socialist Artists, and others all represented different styles and forms of expression. In 1947 Hungary became a member of UNESCO and this broadened its cultural and scientific links internationally.

From the late 1940s onwards the distortions apparent in Hungarian political life also affected every area of culture and science. Here, too, central control became stronger. Political and ideological struggle, lack of artistic confidence, the mistaken interpretation of socialist realism, and easy understanding all had their effect. The result was the spread of stereotyped work, empty formalism and monotony. The depiction of genuine social and individual conflicts became impossible. This was not, however, a state of affairs exclusively confined to Hungary, but merely a part of a general development that took place in Eastern Europe at this time. In the 1950s Hungarian cultural policy was directed by József Révai.

In 1949 the publication of a whole host of journals ceased, and various groups of artists disbanded. Centralized organizations were established for writers, painters, sculptors, architects, etc. Artistic debate acquired political significance and could have serious consequences for the livelihoods of those taking part. Writers and artists were denied opportunities to publish and exhibit their works. Considering their situation hopeless, many left the country—including László Cs. Szabó, Sándor Márai, and Lajos Zilahy. Precisely for this reason, creative artists and the intelligentsia played an outstanding role in the mid-1950s for political and intellectual renewal embracing the whole of society.

After 1956 the settling of the relationship between the regime and the arts progressed slowly and with difficulty. On the one hand the regime applied stringent measures against intellectuals and writers and, on the other, it eased the pressure of dogmatism and schematicism to an appreciable extent. The three elements of cultural policy—support, toleration, and prohibition—were well suited for the demoralization and suppression of a counter-culture. In spite of all this though, the regime did allow conditions which enabled Hungarian intellectual life to join once again the main stream of world culture. Its relative liberalism was manifest in an expansion of the freedom to create, in book publication, and in the policy of theatres and exhibitions.

In this new atmosphere the lifework of Gyula Illyés and the Lőrinc Szabó generation reached their zenith. At the same time the writings of István Örkény, Zoltán Zelk and Sándor Weöres also struck root. Writers whose careers took off after the liberation in 1945 include László Nagy, János Pilinszky, Sándor Csoóri and Ferenc Juhász. Behind them a new generation is already clamouring for similar renown —for example, Péter Esterházy, Péter Dobai, and György Spiró.

Hungarian novelists and playwrights have turned with passionate interest to those issues of the national past which are topical today (cf. the historical plays of Illyés and Németh). Some works search for the responsibility of the Hungarian people for what happened between the two world wars, for example *Hideg napok* (Cold Days) by Tibor Cseres. Others uncover the dramatic experiences of the 1950s, for instance *Ménesgazda* (The Stud Manager) by István Gáll, and the writings of Erzsébet Galgóczi. The volumes of the "Discovering Hungary" series reflect an interest in both literary sociography and the present.

Excellent new Hungarian plays have been performed in the theatres. Long-forgotten or deliberately ignored authors and works (for example, Milán Füst and *Moses* by Imre Madách) have been rediscovered. István Örkény's *Macskajáték* (Cat's Play) and *Tóték* (The Tóth Family) have enjoyed great success highly inside and outside Hungary, winning recognition even in the United States. Outstanding actors and actresses of the postwar period include Margit Dayka, Mária Sulyok, Margit Lukács, Klári Tolnay, Elma Bulla. Ferenc Bessenyei, Ferenc Kállai, György Kálmán, Lajos Öze, Sándor Pécsi, and Lajos Básti.

The painters Endre Bálint, Ignác Kokas, Béla Kondor, Dezső Korniss, Ferenc Martyn, and Jenő Barcsay, together with sculptors Miklós Borsos, József Somogyi, Erzsébet Schaár, Imre Varga, and Tibor Vilt have made substantial contributions to Hungarian art. The recognition and acceptance of artists such as Tivadar Csontváry Kosztka have brought enrichment to the fine arts in Hungary. The Hungarian National Gallery, established in 1957, along with the galleries and museums of a number of provincial towns, make art accessible to a far broader section of the population.

One of the great achievements of musical life is that the works of Béla Bartók have now won in Hungary not just acceptance but also appreciation. Hungarian concert audiences are likely to contain very many whose musical education at school was based on the Kodály Method. This method of teaching music has been introduced in many countries, from Canada to Australia. The Kodály Seminar in Kecskemét is regularly attended by foreign teachers of music. In addition to the composition of many new pieces of music (for example, by Pál Kadosa, András Mihály, Zsolt Durkó, and György Kurtág), Hungarian opera (with Sándor Szokolay and Emil Petrovics) has recently experienced a revival. A number of Hungarian opera singers have become famous abroad (Éva Marton and Sylvia Sass), as have some instrumentalists (Zoltán Kocsis and Dezső Ránki). Every year concerts are organized at the former Esterházy palace at Fertőd, where Haydn himself worked. These are intended to give young musicians the opportunity of an impressive international debut. Musical life in Hungary has been further enriched by the reconstruction not long ago of the Vigadó concert hall in Budapest. Another achievement has been the restoration, in all its splendour, of the Budapest Opera House to mark the centenary of its foundation.

As well as operetta, which has always enjoyed followers, new genres such as the musical and the rock opera have become widely liked. The popularity of the first Hungarian rock opera, which dealt with Stephen, the first king of Hungary, surpassed all expectations.

The cinema, the art form of the twentieth century, acquired a special role in Hungary after 1945. Directors emerged who were capable of presenting Hungarian problems of the past and present but yet at the same time making them relevant to everyone. While primarily serving the cause of national self-knowledge, they brought happenings and conflicts of general interest onto the screen. The new wave

227

in film commenced with Géza Radványi's *Valahol Európában* (Somewhere in Europe) and was followed by the works of Zoltán Fábri, Miklós Jancsó, András Kovács, Márta Mészáros, István Szabó, and others. Over the years Hungarian films have achieved great success abroad; Miklós Jancsó was the first Hungarian film director to win international renown. The greatest success of all has been achieved by István Szabó, whose *Mephisto* was given an Oscar award for the best foreign picture.

During the past few decades, cartoons and animated films have emerged as an independent branch of cinematographic art. A special contribution has been made to this by the works of Otto Foky, Gyula Macskássy, and József Nepp. Ferenc Rófusz's *The Fly* (A légy) won an Oscar for short animated productions.

After the war, architecture in Hungary was confronted by an enormous task. In addition to all the rebuilding that had to be done, architecture was burdened by fixed ideas concerning design. Another problem was the unfamiliarity of such things as prefabricated building sections and the technology which went with them. Together, these factors paralyzed the imagination of Hungarian architects and, in the face of large-scale homebuilding and limited financial resources, the aesthetic side of architecture became overshadowed. A monotonous uniformity was produced in Hungarian towns and villages. Recently, however, there have been favourable changes—aesthetic criteria have again become important in architecture and urban development generally. The new hotels in Budapest and Keszthely together with the centre for music in Kecskemét bear witness to this new approach.

Regular and fruitful contacts have been established with Hungarian writers and artists who, for many years, have lived outside Hungary. Among these are György Cziffra, Amerigo Tot, Victor Vasarely, László Cs. Szabó and Győző Határ. Hungarian intellectual life also preserves its links with the cultural development of Hungarians living just beyond the country's borders, as well as in other parts of the world.

As we have seen, in earlier centuries the history of Hungary abounded in dramatic turns and vicissitudes. But the twentieth century created a radically new situation. After the First World War, Hungary—which had for so long dominated the Carpathian Basin—entered the ranks of the small European states. Historic Hungary disintegrated. Some three million Hungarians became separated from their mother country and began a minority existence—amidst increasingly difficult circumstances.

As a result of the new conditions, the fate of the country became largely subordinated to the international balance of power and influence between larger states. Hungary's sovereignty became limited, and even the preservation of this limited sovereignty demanded constant effort. Society was oppressed not only as a result of mistakes by politicians and by economic and other woes, but also by concern for the survival of ethnic Hungarians beyond the borders. The postwar programme, described as socialist, of social and political renewal served to cast doubt on its declared principles not only from the social angle, but also from the national viewpoint. The nation has been forced to wage a constant struggle not merely for sheer survival, but also against the danger of isolation and of losing touch with Europe.

This struggle is by no means over. The story does not end here, only the telling of it—at a time when, it is hoped, a whole new chapter is in the making.

Glossary

alispán: A deputy to a *főispán*

Bácska: A flat, agricultural region of Yugoslavia just south of present-day Hungary. It is bounded by the Danube to the west and the Tisza to the east.

Csallóköz: A region north of the westernmost section of the present Hungarian–Czechoslovak border. It is bounded by the Danube to the south, and by the Little Danube and the river Vág (Váh) to the north.

Etelköz: The "Land Between Rivers" was the last homeland of the Magyar tribes before their conquest of the Carpathian Basin. It embraces the territory between the Dnieper and the Lower Danube rivers.

főispán: The royal official who headed the administration of a county.

ispán: A royal official, first appointed under King Stephen I, who directed the administration of a county. Later on, the term *ispán* was used to denote officials employed by landowners to supervise the agricultural labourers, or "farm servants", on their estates.

Jászkunság: An area in central Hungary where the Hungarians allowed nomadic Jazygians and Cumans to settle during the Middle Ages.

Muraköz: The region of Yugoslavia between the Drava (Drave) and Mura rivers.

Muravidék: The small piece of Yugoslav territory between the river Mura and the Hungarian border.

Székelyföld: The "Land of the Szeklers", a mountainous Hungarian-populated region in eastern Transylvania.

Nyírség: A flat grassy steppe region east and southeast of the town of Nyíregyháza, in northeast Hungary.

Temesköz: The region between the Temes and the Maros rivers and bordering on southeastern Hungary. It contains the town of Temesvár (*today* Timişoara, Romania).

Tiszahát: The area around the upper reaches of the river Tisza.

Tiszántúl: The region of present-day Hungary east of the river Tisza.

Contributors

Péter Hanák was born on August 9, 1921. After graduating from Budapest's Péter Pázmány University (now the Loránd Eötvös University), he joined the staff of the Hungarian Academy of Sciences' Institute of History. In 1980 Péter Hanák was appointed to the chair of cultural history at the Loránd Eötvös University; he has also been visiting professor at a number of foreign universities—among them Columbia, Yale and Rutgers.

Professor Hanák's publications are many and varied. They include *A magyar pamutipar története* (A History of the Hungarian Cotton Industry), 1964; *Ungarn in der Donaumonarchie*, 1984; *Jászi Oszkár dunai patriotizmusa* (The Danube Patriotism of Oszkár Jászi), 1985; and *A kert és a műhely* (The Garden and the Workshop), a study of *fin-de-siècle* Vienna and Budapest, 1988.

The other contributors to this volume—Kálmán Benda, Zsuzsa L. Nagy, László Makkai, Emil Niederhauser, György Spira and Károly Vörös—are all accomplished historians at the Hungarian Academy of Sciences' Institute of History.

Index of Persons

238

Index of Place-names

As a result of the post–1918 redrawings of Hungary's borders, many Hungarian towns and villages passed into the possession of neighbouring states. In the case of a Hungarian-named settlement now outside the country, the present official name and the country of location are given in brackets.

Printed in Hungary, 1991
Kner Printing House, Gyomaendrőd